The Sabbath in Puritan New England

by

Alice Morse Earle

Double 9
BOOKS

The Sabbath in Puritan New England
by Alice Morse Earle

ISBN: 978-93-59325-53-8

Published by

DOUBLE 9 BOOKS

2/13-B, Ansari Road
Daryaganj, New Delhi – 110002
info@double9books.com
www.double9books.com
Tel. 011-40042856

This book is under public domain

ABOUT THE AUTHOR

Alice Morse Earle (April 27, 1851 – February 16, 1911) was a Worcester, Massachusetts-born American historian and author. Her parents, Edwin Morse and Abby Mason Clary, named her Mary Alice. She married Henry Earle of New York City on April 15, 1874, and they had four children, including the botanical illustrator Alice Clary Earle Hyde. Her name was altered from Mary Alice Morse to Alice Morse Earle. Beginning in 1890, her publications focused on little sociological aspects rather than large issues, making them essential to current social historians. She published several novels about colonial America (particularly the New England region), including Curious Punishments of Bygone Days.

CONTENTS

I
The New England Meeting-House

When the Pilgrim Fathers landed at Plymouth they at once assigned a Lord's Day meeting-place for the Separatist church,--"a timber fort both strong and comely, with flat roof and battlements;" and to this fort, every Sunday, the men and women walked reverently, three in a row, and in it they worshipped until they built for themselves a meeting-house in 1648.

As soon as each successive outlying settlement was located and established, the new community built a house for the purpose of assembling therein for the public worship of God; this house was called a meeting-house. Cotton Mather said distinctly that he "found no just ground in Scripture to apply such a trope as church to a house for public assembly." The church, in the Puritan's way of thinking, worshipped in the meeting-house, and he was as bitterly opposed to calling this edifice a church as he was to calling the Sabbath Sunday. His favorite term for that day was the Lord's Day.

The settlers were eager and glad to build their meeting-houses; for these houses of God were to them the visible sign of the establishment of that theocracy which they had left their fair homes and had come to New England to create and perpetuate. But lest some future settlements should be slow or indifferent about doing their duty promptly, it was enacted in 1675 that a meeting-house should be erected in every town in the colony; and if the people failed to do so at once, the magistrates were empowered to build it, and to charge the cost of its erection to the town. The number of members necessary to establish a separate church was very distinctly given in the Platform of Church Discipline: "A church ought not to be of greater number than can ordinarilie meet convenientlie in one place, nor ordinarilie fewer than may convenientlie carry on church-work." Each church was quite independent in its work and government, and had absolute power to admit, expel, control, and censure its members.

These first meeting-houses were simple buildings enough,--square log-houses with clay-filled chinks, surmounted by steep roofs thatched with long straw or grass, and often with only the beaten earth for a floor. It was considered a great advance and a matter of proper pride when the settlers had the meeting-house "lathed on the inside, and so daubed and whitened over workmanlike." The dimensions of many of these first essays at church architecture are known to us, and lowly little structures they were. One, indeed, is preserved for us under cover at Salem. The first meeting-house in Dedham was thirty-six feet long, twenty feet wide, and twelve feet high "in the stud;" the one in Medford was smaller still; and the Haverhill edifice was only twenty-six feet long and twenty wide, yet "none other than the house of God."

As the colonists grew in wealth and numbers, they desired and built better sanctuaries, "good roomthy meeting-houses" they were called by Judge Sewall, the most valued and most interesting journal-keeper of the times. The rude early buildings were then converted into granaries or storehouses, or, as was the Pentucket meeting-house, into a "house of shelter or a house to sett horses in." As these meeting-houses had not been consecrated, and as they were town-halls, forts, or court-houses as well as meeting-houses, the humbler uses to which they were finally put were not regarded as profanations of holy places.

The second form or type of American church architecture was a square wooden building, usually unpainted, crowned with a truncated pyramidal roof, which was surmounted (if the church could afford such luxury) with a belfry or turret containing a bell. The old church at Hingham, the "Old Ship" which was built in 1681, is still standing, a well-preserved example of this second style of architecture. These square meeting-houses, so much alike, soon abounded in New England; for a new church, in its contract for building, would often specify that the structure should be "like in every detaile to the Lynn meeting-house," or like the Hadley, Milford, Boston, Danvers, or New Haven meeting-house. This form of edifice was the prototype of the fine great First Church of Boston, a large square brick building, with three rows of windows and two galleries, which stood from the year 1713 to 1808, and of which many pictures exist.

The third form of the Puritan meeting-house, of which the Old South Church of Boston is a typical model, has too many representatives throughout New England to need any description, as have also the succeeding forms of New England church architecture.

The first meeting-houses were often built in the valleys, in the meadow lands; for the dwelling-houses must be clustered around them, since the colonists were ordered by law to build their new homes within half a mile of the meeting-house. Soon, however, the houses became too closely crowded for the most convenient uses of a farming community; pasturage for the cattle had to be obtained at too great a distance from the farmhouse;

firewood had to be brought from too distant woods; nearness to water also had to be considered. Thus the law became a dead letter, and each new-coming settler built on outlying and remote land, since the Indians were no longer so deeply to be dreaded. Then the meeting-houses, having usually to accommodate a whole township of scattered farms, were placed on remote and often highly elevated locations; sometimes at the very top of a long, steep hill,--so long and so steep in some cases, especially in one Connecticut parish, that church attendants could not ride down on horseback from the pinnacled meeting-house, but were forced to scramble down, leading their horses, and mount from a horse-block at the foot of the hill. The second Roxbury church was set on a high hill, and the story is fairly pathetic of the aged and feeble John Eliot, the glory of New England Puritanism, that once, as he toiled patiently up the long ascent to his dearly loved meeting, he said to the person on whose supporting arm he leaned (in the Puritan fashion of teaching a lesson from any event and surrounding): "This is very like the way to heaven; 'tis uphill. The Lord by His grace fetch us up."

The location on a hilltop was chosen and favored for various reasons. The meeting-house was at first a watch-house, from which to keep vigilant lookout for any possible approach of hostile or sneaking Indians; it was also a landmark, whose high bell-turret, or steeple, though pointing to heaven, was likewise a guide on earth, for, thus stationed on a high elevation, it could be seen for miles around by travellers journeying through the woods, or in the narrow, tree-obscured bridle-paths which were then almost the only roads. In seaside towns it could be a mark for for sailors at sea; such was the Truro meeting-house. Then, too, our Puritan ancestors dearly loved a "sightly location," and were willing to climb uphill cheerfully, even through bleak New England winters, for the sake of having a meeting-house which showed off well, and was a proper source of envy to the neighboring villages and the country around. The studiously remote and painfully inaccessible locations chosen for the site of many fine, roomy churches must astonish any observing traveller on the byroads of New England. Too often, alas! these churches are deserted, falling down, unopened from year to year, destitute alike of minister and congregation. Sometimes, too, on high hilltops, or on lonesome roads leading through a tall second growth of woods, deserted and neglected old graveyards--the most lonely and forlorn of all sad places--by their broken and fallen headstones, which surround a half-filled-in and uncovered cellar, show that once a meeting-house for New England Christians had stood there. Tall grass, and a tangle of blackberry brambles cover the forgotten graves, and perhaps a spire of orange tiger-lilies, a shrub of southernwood or of winter-killed and dying box, may struggle feebly for life under the shadow of the "plumed ranks of tall wild cherry," and prove that once these lonely graves were cared for and loved for the sake of those who lie buried in this now waste spot. No traces remain of the old meeting-house save the cellar and the narrow stone steps, sadly leading nowhere, which once were pressed by the feet of the children of the Pilgrims, but now are trodden only by the curious and infrequent passer-by, or the epitaph-seeking antiquary.

It is difficult often to understand the details in the descriptions of these early meeting-houses, the colonial spelling is so widely varied, and so cleverly ingenious. Uniformity of spelling is a strictly modern accomplishment, a hampering innovation. "A square roofe without Dormans, with two Lucoms on each side," means, I think, without dormer windows, and with luthern windows. Another church paid a bill for the meeting-house roof and the "Suppolidge." They had "turritts" and "turetts" and "turits" and "turyts" and "feriats" and "tyrryts" and "toryttes" and "turiotts" and "chyrits," which were one and the same thing; and one church had orders for "juyces and rayles and nayles and bymes and tymber and gaybels and a pulpyt, and three payr of stayrs," in its meeting-house,--a liberal supply of the now fashionable y's. We read of "pinakles" and "pyks" and "shuthers" and "scaffills" and "bimes" and "lynters" and "bathyns" and "chymbers" and "bellfers;" and often in one entry the same word will be spelt in three or four different ways. Here is a portion of a contract in the records of the Roxbury church: "Sayd John is to fence in the Buring Plas with a Fesy ston wall, sefighiattly don for Strenk and workmanship as also to mark a Doball gatt 6 or 8 fote wid and to hing it." *Sefighiattly* is "sufficiently;" but who can translate "Fesy"? can it mean "facy" or faced smoothly?

The church-raising was always a great event in the town. Each citizen was forced by law to take part in or contribute to "raring the Meeting hows." In early days nails were scarce,--so scarce that unprincipled persons set fire to any buildings which chanced to be temporarily empty, for the sake of obtaining the nails from the ruins; so each male inhabitant supplied to the new church a certain "amount of nayles." Not only were logs, and lumber, and the use of horses' and men's labor given, but a contribution was also levied for the inevitable barrel of rum and its unintoxicating accompaniments. "Rhum and Cacks" are frequent entries in the account books of early churches. No wonder that accidents were frequent, and that men fell from the scaffolding and were killed, as at the raising of the Dunstable meeting-house. When the Medford people built their second meeting-house, they provided for the workmen and bystanders, five barrels of rum, one barrel of good brown sugar, a box of fine lemons, and two loaves of sugar. As a natural consequence, two thirds of the frame fell, and many were injured. In Northampton, in 1738, ten gallons of rum were bought for

£8 "to raise the meeting-house"--and the village doctor got "£3 for setting his bone Jonathan Strong, and £3 10s. for setting Ebenezer Burt's thy" which had somehow through the rum or the raising, both gotten broken. Sometimes, as in Pittsfield in 1671, the sum of four shillings was raised on every acre of land in the town, and three shillings a day were paid to every man who came early to work, while one shilling a day was apportioned to each worker for his rum and sugar. At last no liquor was allowed to the workmen until after the day's work was over, and thus fatal accidents were prevented.

The earliest meeting-houses had oiled paper in the windows to admit the light. A Pilgrim colonist wrote to an English friend about to emigrate, "Bring oiled paper for your windows." Higginson, however, writing in 1629, asks for "glasse for windowes." When glass was used it was not set in the windows as now. We find frequent entries of "glasse and nayles for it," and in Newbury, in 1665, the church ordered that the "Glasse in the windows be ... look't to if any should happen to be loosed with winde to be nailed close again." The glass was in lozenge-shaped panes, set in lead in the form of two long narrow sashes opening in the middle from top to bottom, and it was many years before oblong or square panes came into common use.

These early churches were destitute of shade, for the trees in the immediate vicinity were always cut down on account of dread of the fierce fires which swept often through the forests and overwhelmed and destroyed the towns. The heat and blazing light in summer were as hard to bear in these unscreened meeting-houses as was the cold in winter.

> "Old house of Puritanic wood,
> Through whose unpainted windows streamed,
> On seats as primitive and rude
> As Jacob's pillow when he dreamed,
> The white and undiluted day."

We have all heard the theory advanced that it is impossible there should be any true religious feeling, any sense of sanctity, in a garish and bright light,--"the white and undiluted day,"--but I think no one can doubt that to the Puritans these seething, glaring, pine-smelling hothouses were truly God's dwelling-place, though there was no "dim, religious light" within.

Curtains and window-blinds were unknown, and the sunlight streamed in with unobstructed and unbroken rays. Heavy shutters for protection were often used, but to close them at time of service would have been to plunge the church into utter darkness. Permission was sometimes given, as in Haverhill, to "sett up a shed outside of the window to keep out the heat of the sun there,"--a very roundabout way to accomplish a very simple end. As years passed on, trees sprang up and grew apace, and too often the churches became overhung and heavily shadowed by dense, sombre spruce, cedar, and fir trees. A New England parson was preaching in a neighboring church which was thus gloomily surrounded. He gave out as his text, "Why do the wicked live?" and as he peered in the dim light at his manuscript, he exclaimed abruptly, "I hope they will live long enough to cut down this great hemlock-tree back of the pulpit window." Another minister, Dr. Storrs, having struggled to read his sermon in an ill-lighted, gloomy church, said he would never speak in that building again while it was so overshadowed with trees. A few years later he was invited to preach to the same congregation; but when he approached the church, and saw the great umbrageous tree still standing, he rode away, and left the people sermonless in their darkness. The chill of these sunless, unheated buildings in winter can well be imagined.

Strange and grotesque decorations did the outside of the earliest meeting-houses bear,--grinning wolves' heads nailed under the windows and by the side of the door, while splashes of blood, which had dripped from the severed neck, reddened the logs beneath. The wolf, for his destructiveness, was much more dreaded by the settlers than the bear, which did not so frequently attack the flocks. Bears were plentiful enough. The history of Roxbury states that in 1725, in one week in September, twenty bears were killed within two miles of Boston. This bear story requires unlimited faith in Puritan probity, and confidence in Puritan records to credit it, but believe it, ye who can, as I do! In Salem and in Ipswich, in 1640, any man who brought a living wolf to the meeting-house was paid fifteen shillings by the town; if the wolf were dead, ten shillings. In 1664, if the wolf-killer wished to obtain the reward, he was ordered to bring the wolf's head and "nayle it to the meeting-house and give notis thereof." In Hampton, the inhabitants were ordered to "nayle the same to a little red oake tree at northeast end of the meeting-house." One man in Newbury, in 1665, killed seven wolves, and was paid the reward for so doing. This was a great number, for the wary wolf was not easily destroyed either by musket or wolf-hook. In 1723 wolves were so abundant in Ipswich that parents would not suffer their children to go to and from church and school without the attendance of some grown person. As late as 1746 wolves made sad havoc in Woodbury, Connecticut; and a reward of five dollars for each wolf's head was offered by law in that township in 1853.

In 1718 the last public reward was paid in Salem for a wolf's head, but so late as the year 1779 the howls of wolves were heard every night in Newbury, though trophies of shrivelled wolves' heads no longer graced the walls of the meeting-house.

All kinds of notices and orders and regulations and "bills" were posted on the meeting-house, often on the door, where they would greet the eye of all who entered: prohibitions from selling guns and powder to the Indians, notices of town meetings, intentions of marriage, copies of the laws against Sabbath-breaking, messages from the Quakers, warnings of "vandoos" and sales, lists of the town officers, and sometimes scandalous and insulting libels, and libels in verse, which is worse, for our forefathers dearly loved to rhyme on all occasions. On the meeting-house green stood those Puritanical instruments of punishment, the stocks, whipping-post, pillory, and cage; and on lecture days the stocks and pillory were often occupied by wicked or careless colonists, or those everlasting pillory-replenishers, the Quakers. It is one of the unintentionally comic features of absurd colonial laws and punishments in which the early legal records so delightfully abound, that the first man who was sentenced to and occupied the stocks in Boston was the carpenter who made them. He was thus fitly punished for his extortionate charge to the town for the lumber he used in their manufacture. This was rather better than "making the punishment fit the crime," since the Boston magistrates managed to force the criminal to furnish his own punishment. In Shrewsbury, also, the unhappy man who first tested the wearisome capacity and endured the public mortication of the town's stocks was the man who made them. He "builded better than he knew." Pillories were used as a means of punishment until a comparatively recent date,--in Salem until the year 1801, and in Boston till 1803.

Great horse-blocks, rows of stepping-stones, or hewn logs further graced the meeting-house green; and occasionally one fine horse-block, such as the Concord women proudly erected, and paid for by a contribution of a pound of butter from each house-wife.

The meeting-house not only was employed for the worship of God and for town meetings, but it was a storehouse as well. Until after the Revolutionary War it was universally used as a powder magazine; and indeed, as no fire in stove or fireplace was ever allowed within, it was a safe enough place for the explosive material. In Hanover, the powder room was in the steeple, while in Quincy the "powder-closite" was in the beams of the roof. Whenever there chanced to be a thunderstorm during the time of public worship, the people of Beverly ran out under the trees, and in other towns they left the meeting-house if the storm seemed severe or near; still they built no powder houses. Grain, too, was stored in the loft of the meeting-house for safety; hatches were built, and often the corn paid to the minister was placed there. "Leantos," or "linters," were sometimes built by the side of the building for use for storage. In Springfield, Mr. Pyncheon was allowed to place his corn in the roof chamber of the meeting-house;

but as the people were afraid that the great weight might burst the floor, he was forbidden to store more than four hundred bushels at a time, unless he "underpropped the floor."

In one church in the Connecticut valley, in a township where it was forbidden that tobacco be smoked upon the public streets, the church loft was used to dry and store the freshly cut tobacco-leaves which the inhabitants sold to the "ungodly Dutch." Thus did greed for gain lead even blue Connecticut Christians to profane the house of God.

The early meeting-houses in country parishes were seldom painted, such outward show being thought vain and extravagant. In the middle of the eighteenth century paint became cheaper and more plentiful, and a gay rivalry in church-decoration sprang up. One meeting-house had to be as fine as its neighbor. Votes were taken, "rates were levied," gifts were asked in every town to buy "colour" for the meeting-house. For instance, the new meeting-house in Pomfret, Connecticut, was painted bright yellow; it proved a veritable golden apple of discord throughout the county. Windham town quickly voted that its meeting-house be "coloured something like the Pomfret meeting-house." Killingly soon ordered that the "cullering of the body of our meeting-house should be like the Pomfret meeting-house, and the Roff shal be cullered Read." Brooklyn church then, in 1762, ordered that the outside of its meeting-house be "culered" in the approved fashion. The body of the house was painted a bright orange; the doors and "bottom boards" a warm chocolate color; the "window-jets," corner-boards, and weather-boards white. What a bright nosegay of color! As a crowning glory Brooklyn people put up an "Eleclarick Rod" on the gorgeous edifice, and proudly boasted that--Brooklyn meeting-house was the "newest biggest and yallowest" in the county. One old writer, however, spoke scornfully of the spirit of envious emulation, extravagance, and bad taste that spread and prevailed from the example of the foolish and useless "colouring" of the Pomfret meeting-house.

Within the meeting-house all was simple enough: raftered walls, sanded floors, rows of benches, a few pews, and the pulpit, or the "scaffold," as John Cotton called it. The bare rafters were often profusely hung with dusty spiders' webs, and were the home also of countless swallows, that flew in and out of the open bell-turret. Sometimes, too, mischievous squirrels, attracted by the corn in the meeting-house loft, made their homes in the sanctuary; and they were so prolific and so omnivorous that the Bible and the pulpit cushions were not safe from their nibbling attacks. On every Sunday afternoon the Word of God and its sustaining cushion had to be removed to the safe shelter of a neighboring farmhouse or tavern, to prevent total annihilation by these Puritanical, Bible-loving squirrels.

The pulpits were often pretentious, even in the plain and undecorated meeting-houses, and were usually high desks, to which a narrow flight of stairs led. In the churches of the third stage of architecture, these stairs were often inclosed in a towering hexagonal mahogany structure, which was ornamented with pillars and panels. Into this the minister walked, closed the door behind him, and invisibly ascended the stairs; while the children counted the seconds from the time he closed the door until his head appeared through the trap-door at the top of the pulpit. The form known as a tub-pulpit was very popular in the larger churches. The pulpit of one old, unpainted church retained until the middle of this century, as its sole decoration, an enormous, carefully painted, staring eye, a terrible and suggestive illustration to youthful wrong-doers of the great, all-seeing eye of God.

As the ceiling and rafters were so open and reverberating, it was generally thought imperative to hang above the pulpit a great sounding-board, which threatened the minister like a giant extinguisher, and was really as devoid of utility as it was curious in ornamentation, "reflecting most part an empty ineffectual sound." This great sound-killer was decorated with carved and painted rosettes, as in the Shrewsbury meeting-house; with carved ivy leaves, as in Farmington; with a carved bunch of grapes or pomegranates, as in the Leicester church; with letters indicating a date, as, "M. R. H." for March, in the Hadley church; with appropriate mottoes and texts, such as the words, "Holiness is the Lords," in the Windham church; with cords and tassels, with hanging fringes, with panels and balls; and thus formed a great ornament to the church, and a source of honest pride to the church members. The clumsy sounding-board was usually hung by a slight iron rod, which looked smaller still as it stretched up to the high, raftered roof, and always appeared to be entirely insufficient to sustain the great weight of the heavy machine. In Danvers, one of these useless though ornamental structures hung within eighteen inches of the preacher's nose, on a slender bar thirty feet in length; and every Sunday the children gazed with fascinated anticipation at the slight rod and the great hexagonal extinguisher, thinking and hoping that on this day the sounding-board would surely drop, and "put out" the minister. In fact, it was regarded by many a child, though this idea was hardly formulated in the little brain, as a visible means of possible punishment for any false doctrine that might issue from the mouth of the preacher.

Another pastime and source of interest to the children in many old churches was the study of the knots and veins in the unpainted wood of which the pews and galleries were made. Age had developed and darkened and rendered visible all the natural irregularities in the wood, just as it had brought out and strengthened the dry-woody, close, unaired, penetrating scent which permeated the meeting-house and gave it the distinctive "church smell." The children, and perhaps a few of the grown people, found in these clusters of knots queer similitudes of faces, strange figures and constellations, which, though conned Sunday after Sunday until known by heart, still seemed ever to show in their irregular groupings a puzzling possibility of the discovery of new configurations and monstrosities.

The dangling, dusty spiders' webs afforded, too, an interesting sight and diversion for the sermon-hearing, but not sermon-listening, young Puritans, who watched the cobwebs swaying, trembling, forming strange maps of imaginary rivers with their many tributaries, or outlines of intersecting roads and lanes. And if little Yet-Once, Hate-Evil, or Shearjashub chanced, by good fortune, to be seated near a window where a crafty spider and a foolish buzzing fly could be watched through the dreary exposition and attempted reconciliation of predestination and free will, that indeed were a happy way of passing the weary hours.

II
The Church Militant

For many years after the settlement of New England the Puritans, even in outwardly tranquil times, went armed to meeting; and to sanctify the Sunday gun-loading they were expressly forbidden to fire off their charges at any object on that day save an Indian or a wolf, their two "greatest inconveniencies." Trumbull, in his "Mac Fingal," Avrites thus in jest of this custom of Sunday arm-bearing:--

> "So once, for fear of Indian beating,
> Our grandsires bore their guns to meeting,--
> Each man equipped on Sunday morn
> With psalm-book, shot, and powder-horn,
> And looked in form, as all must grant,
> Like the ancient true church militant."

In 1640 it was ordered in Massachusetts that in every township the attendants at church should carry a "competent number of peeces, fixed and compleat with powder and shot and swords every Lords-day to the meeting-house;" one armed man from each household was then thought advisable and necessary for public safety. In 1642 six men with muskets and powder and shot were thought sufficient for protection for each church. In Connecticut similar mandates were issued, and as the orders were neglected "by divers persones," a law was passed in 1643 that each offender should forfeit twelve pence for each offence. In 1644 a fourth part of the "trayned hand" was obliged to come armed each Sabbath, and the sentinels were ordered to keep their matches constantly lighted for use in their match-locks. They were also commanded to wear armor, which consisted of "coats basted with cotton-wool, and thus made defensive against Indian arrows." In 1650 so much dread and fear were felt of Sunday attacks from the red men that the Sabbath-Day guard was doubled in number. In 1692, the Connecticut Legislature ordered one fifth of the soldiers in each town to come armed to each meeting, and that nowhere should be present as a guard at time of public worship fewer than eight soldiers and a sergeant. In Hadley the guard was allowed annually from the public treasury a pound of lead and a pound of powder to each soldier.

No details that could add to safety on the Sabbath were forgotten or overlooked by the New Haven church; bullets were made common currency at the value of a farthing, in order that they might be plentiful and in every one's possession; the colonists were enjoined to determine in advance what to do with the women and children in case of attack, "that they do not hang about them and hinder them;" the men were ordered to bring at least six charges of powder and shot to meeting; the farmers were forbidden to "leave more arms at home than men to use them;" the half-pikes were to be headed and the whole ones mended, and the swords "and all piercing weapons furbished up and dressed;" wood was to be placed in the watch-house; it was ordered that the "door of the meeting-house next the soldiers' seat be kept clear from women and children sitting there, that if there be occasion for the soldiers to go suddenly forth, they may have free passage." The soldiers sat on either side of the main door, a sentinel was stationed in the meeting-house turret, and armed watchers paced the streets; three cannon were mounted by the side of this "church militant," which must strongly have resembled a garrison.

Military duty and military discipline and regard for the Sabbath, and for the House of God as well, did not always make the well-equipped occupants of these soldiers' seats in New Haven behave with the dignity and decorum befitting such guardians of the peace and protectors in war. Serious disorders and disturbances among the guard were reported at the General Court on June 16, 1662. One belligerent son of Mars, as he sat in the meeting-house, threw lumps of lime--perhaps from the plastered chinks in the log wall--at a fellow-warrior, who in turn, very naturally, kicked his tormentor with much agility and force. There must have ensued quite a free fight all around in the meeting-house, for "Mrs. Goodyear's boy had his head broke that day in meeting, on account of which a woman said she doubted not the wrath of God was upon us." And well might she think so, for divers other unseemly incidents which occurred in the meeting-house at the same time were narrated in Court, examined into, and punished.

In spite of these events in the New Haven church (which were certainly exceptional), the seemingly incongruous union of church and army was suitable enough in a community that always began and ended the military exercises on "training day" with solemn prayer and psalm-singing; and that used the army and encouraged a true soldier-like spirit not chiefly as aids in war, but to help to conquer and destroy the adversaries of truth, and to "achieve greater matters by this little handful of men than the world is aware of."

The Salem sentinels wore doubtless some of the good English armor owned by the town,--corselets to cover the body; gorgets to guard the throat; tasses to protect the thighs; all varnished black, and costing each suit "twenty-four shillings a peece." The sentry also wore a bandileer, a large "neat's leather" belt thrown over the right shoulder, and hanging down under the left arm. This bandileer sustained twelve boxes of cartridges, and a well-filled bullet-bag. Each man bore either a "bastard musket with a snaphance," a "long fowling-piece with musket bore," a "full musket," a "barrell with a match-cock," or perhaps (for they were purchased by the town) a leather gun (though these leather guns may have been cannon). Other weapons there were to choose from, mysterious in name, "sakers, minions, ffaulcons, rabinets, murthers (or murderers, as they were sometimes appropriately called) chambers, harque-busses, carbins,"--all these and many other death-dealing machines did our forefathers bring and import from their war-loving fatherland to assist them in establishing God's Word, and exterminating the Indians, but not always, alas! to aid them in converting those poor heathen.

The armed Salem watcher, besides his firearms and ammunition, had attached to his wrist by a cord a gun-rest, or gun-fork, which he placed upon the ground when he wished to fire his musket, and upon which that constitutional kicker rested when touched off. He also carried a sword and sometimes a pike, and thus heavily burdened with multitudinous arms and cumbersome armor, could never have run after or from an Indian with much agility or celerity; though he could stand at the church-door with his leather gun,--an awe-inspiring figure,--and he could shoot with his "harquebuss," or "carbin," as we well know.

These armed "sentinells" are always regarded as a most picturesque accompaniment of Puritan religious worship, and the Salem and Plymouth armed men were imposing, though clumsy. But the New Haven soldiers, with their bulky garments wadded and stuffed out with thick layers of cotton wool, must have been more safety-assuring and comforting than they were romantic or heroic; but perhaps they too wore painted tin armor, "corselets and gorgets and tasses."

In Concord, New Hampshire, the men, who all came armed to meeting, stacked their muskets around a post in the middle of the church, while the honored pastor, who was a good shot and owned the best gun in the settlement, preached with his treasured weapon in the pulpit by his side, ready from his post of vantage to blaze away at any red man whom he saw sneaking without, or to lead, if necessary, his congregation to battle. The church in York, Maine, until the year 1746, felt it necessary to retain the custom of carrying arms to the meeting-house, so plentiful and so aggressive were Maine Indians.

Not only in the time of Indian wars were armed men seen in the meeting-house, but on June 17, 1775, the Provincial Congress recommended that the men "within twenty miles of the sea-coast carry their arms and ammunition with them to meeting on the Sabbath and other days when they meet for public worship." And on many a Sabbath and Lecture Day, during the years of war that followed, were proved the wisdom and foresight of that suggestion.

The men in those old days of the seventeenth century, when in constant dread of attacks by Indians, always rose when the services were ended and left the house before the women and children, thus making sure the safe exit of the latter. This custom prevailed from habit until a late date in many churches in New England, all the men, after the benediction and the exit of the parson, walking out in advance of the women. So also the custom of the men always sitting at the "head" or door of the pew arose from the early necessity of their always being ready to seize their arms and rush unobstructed to fight. In some New England village churches to this day, the man who would move down from his end of the pew and let a woman sit at the door, even if it were a more desirable seat from which to see the clergyman, would be thought a poor sort of a creature.

III
By Drum and Horn and Shell

At about nine o'clock on the Sabbath morning the Puritan colonists assembled for the first public service of the holy day; they were gathered together by various warning sounds. The Haverhill settlers listened for the ringing toot of Abraham Tyler's horn. The Montague and South Hadley people were notified that the hour of assembling had arrived by the loud blowing of a conch-shell. John Lane, a resident of the latter town, was engaged in 1750 to "blow the Cunk" on the Sabbath as "a sign for meeting." In Stockbridge a strong-lunged "praying" Indian blew the enormous shell, which was safely preserved until modern times, and which, when relieved from Sunday use, was for many years sounded as a week-day signal in the hay-field. Even a conch-shell was enough of an expense to the poor colonial churches. The Montague people in 1759 paid £1 10s. for their "conk," and also on the purchase year gave Joseph Root 20 shillings for blowing the new shell. In 1785 the Whately church voted that "we will not improve anybody to blow the conch," and so the church-attendants straggled to Whately meeting each at his own time and pleasure.

In East Hadley the inhabitant who "blew the kunk" (as phonetic East Hadleyites spelt it) and swept out the meeting-house was paid annually the munificent sum of three dollars for his services. Conch-blowing was not so difficult and consequently not so highly-paid an accomplishment as drum-beating. A verse of a simple old-fashioned hymn tells thus of the gathering of the Puritan saints:--

"New England's Sabbath day
Is heaven-like still and pure,
When Israel walks the way
Up to the temple's door.
The time we tell
When there to come
By beat of drum
Or sounding shell."

The drum, as highly suitable for such a military people, was often used as a signal for gathering for public worship, and was plainly the favorite means of notification. In 1678 Robert Stuard, of Norwalk, "ingages yt his son James shall beate the Drumb, on the Sabbath and other ocations," and in Norwalk the "drumb," the "drumne," the "drumme," and at last the drum was beaten until 1704, when the Church got a bell. And the "Drumber" was paid, and well paid too for his "Cervices," fourteen shillings a year of the town's money, and he was furnished a "new strong drumme;" and the town supplied to him also the flax for the drum-cords which he wore out in the service of God. Johnson, in his "Wonder Working Providence," tells of the Cambridge Church: "Hearing the sound of a drum he was directed toward it by a broade beaten way; following this rode he demands of the next man he met what the signall of the drum ment; the reply was made they had as yet no Bell to call men to meeting and therefore made use of the drum." In 1638 a platform was made upon the top of the Windsor meeting-house "from the Lanthornc to the ridge to walk conveniently to sound a trumpet or a drum to give warning to meeting."

Sometimes three guns were fired as a signal for "church-time." The signal for religious gathering, and the signal for battle were always markedly different, in order to avoid unnecessary fright.

In 1647 Robert Basset was appointed in New Haven to drum "twice upon Lordes Dayes and Lecture Dayes upon the meeting house that soe those who live farr off may heare the more distinkly." Robert may have been a good drummer, but he proved to be a most reprehensible and disreputable citizen; in the local Court Records of August 1, 1648, we find a full report of an astounding occurrence in which he played an important part. Ten men, who Avere nearly all sea-faring men,--gay, rollicking sailors,--went to Bassctt's house and asked for strong drink. The magistrates had endeavored zealously, and in the main successfully, to prevent all intoxication in the community, and had forbidden the sale of liquor save in very small quantities. The church-drummer, however, wickedly unmindful of his honored calling, furnished to the sailors six quarts of strong liquor, with which they all, host and visitors, got prodigiously drunk and correspondingly noisy. The Court Record says: "The miscarriage continued till betwixt tenn and eleven of the clock, to the great provocation of God, disturbance of the peace, and to such a height of disorder that strangers wondered at it." In the midst of the carousal the master of the pinnace called the boatswain "Brother Loggerheads." This must have been a particularly insulting epithet, which no respectable boatswain could have been expected quietly to endure, for "at once the two men fell fast to wrestling, then to blowes and theirin grew to that feircnes that the master of the pinnace thought the boatswain would have puled out his eies; and they toumbled on the ground down the hill into the creeke and mire shamefully wallowing theirin." In his pain and terror the master called out, "Hoe, the Watch! Hoe, the Watch!" "The Watch made hast and for the present stopped the disorder, but in his rage and distemper the boatswaine fell a-swearinge Wounds and Hart as if he were not only angry with men but would provoke the high and blessed God." The master of the pinnace, being freed from his fellow-combatant, returned to Basset's house--perhaps to tell his tale of woe, perhaps to get more liquor--and was assailed by the drummer with amazing words of "anger and distemper used by drunken companions;" in short, he was "verey offensive, his noyes and oathes being hearde to the other side of the creeke." For aiding and abetting this noisy and disgraceful spree, and also for partaking in it, Drummer Basset was fined £5, which must have been more than his yearly salary, and in disgrace, and possibly in disgust, quitted drumming the New Haven good people to meeting and moved his residence to Stamford, doubtless to the relief and delight of both magistrates and people of the former town.

Another means of notification of the hour for religious service was by the use of a flag, often in addition to the sound of the drum or bell. Thus in Plymouth, in 1697, the selectmen were ordered to "procure a flagg to be put out at the ringing of the first bell, and taken in when the last bell was rung." In Sutherland also a flag was used as a means of announcement of "meeting-time," and an old goody was paid ten shillings a year for "tending the flagg."

Mr. Gosse, in his "Early Bells of Massachusetts," gives a full and interesting account of the church-bells of the first colonial towns in that State. Lechford, in his "Plaine Dealing," wrote in 1641 that they came together in Boston on the Lord's Day by "the wringing of a bell," and it is thought that that bell was a hand-bell. The first bells, for the lack of bell-towers, were sometimes hung on trees by the side of the meeting-houses, to the great amazement and distress of the Indians, who regarded them with superstitious dread, thinking--to paraphrase Herbert's beautiful line--"when the bell did chime 't was devils' music;" but more frequently the bells were hung in a belfry or bell-turret or "bellcony," and from this belfry depended a long bell-rope quite to the floor; and thus in the very centre of the church the sexton stood when he rung the summons for lire or for meeting. This rope was of course directly in front of the pulpit; and Jonathan Edwards, who was devoid of gestures and looked always straight before him when preaching, was jokingly said to have "looked-off" the bell-rope, when it fell with a crash in the middle of his church.

At the first sound of the drum or horn or bell the town inhabitants issued from their houses in "desent order," man and wife walking first, and the children in quiet procession after them. Often a man-servant and a maid walked on either side of the heads of the family. In some communities the congregation waited outside the church door until the minister and his wife arrived and passed into the house; then the church-attendants followed, the loitering boys always contriving to scuffle noisily in from the horse-sheds at the last moment, making much scraping and clatter with their heavy boots on the sanded floor, and tumbling clumsily up the uucarpeted, creaking stairs.

In other churches the members of the congregation seated themselves in their pews upon their arrival, but rose reverently when the parson, dressed in black skull-cap and Geneva cloak, entered the door; and they stood, in token of respect, until after he entered the pulpit and was seated.

It was also the honor-giving and deferential custom in many New England churches, in the eighteenth century, for the entire congregation to remain respectfully standing within the pews at the end of the serice until the minister had descended from his lofty pulpit, opened the door of his wife's pew, and led her with stately dignity to the church-porch, where, were he and she genial and neighborly minded souls, they in turn stood and greeted with carefully adjusted degrees of warmth, interest, respect, or patronage, the different members of the congregation as they slowly passed out.

IV
The Old-Fashioned Pews

In the early New England meeting-houses the seats were long, narrow, uncomfortable benches, which were made of simple, rough, hand-riven planks placed on legs like milking-stools. They were without any support or rest for the back; and perhaps the stiff-backed Pilgrims and Puritans required or wished no support. Quickly, as the colonies grew in wealth and the colonists in ambition and importance, "Spots for Pues" were sold (or "pitts" as they were sometimes called), at first to some few rich or influential men who wished to sit in a group together, and finally each family of dignity or wealth sat in its own family-pew. Often it was stipulated in the permission to build a pew that a separate entrance-door should be cut into it through the outside wall of the meeting-house, thus detracting grievously from the external symmetry of the edifice, but obviating the necessity of a space-occupying entrance aisle within the church, where there was little enough sitting-room for the quickly increasing and universally church-going population. As these pews were either oblong or square, were both large and small, painted and unpainted, and as each pewholder could exercise his own "tast or disresing" in the kind of wood he used in the formation of his pew, as well as in the style of finish, much diversity and incongruity of course resulted. A man who had a wainscoted pew was naturally and properly much respected and envied by the entire community. These pews, erected by individual members, were individual and not communal property. A widow in Cape Cod had her house destroyed by fire. She was given from the old meeting-house, which was being razed, the old building materials to use in the construction of her new home. She was not allowed, however, to remove the wood which formed the pews, as they were adjudged to be the property of the members who had built them, and those owners only could sell or remove the materials of which they were built.

Many of the pews in the old meeting-houses had towering partition walls, which extended up so high that only the tops of the tallest heads could be seen when the occupants were seated. Permissions to build were often given with modifying restrictions to the aspiring pew-builders, as for instance is recorded of the Haverhill church, "provided they would not build so high as to damnify and hinder the light of them windows," or of the Waterbury church, "if the pues will not progodish the hous." Often the floor of the pews was several inches and occasionally a foot higher than the floor of the "alleys," thus forming at the entrance-door of the pew one or two steps, which were great stumbling-blocks to clumsy and to childish feet, that tripped again when within the pew over the "crickets" and foot-benches which were, if the family were large, the accepted and lowly church-seats of the little children. Occasionally one long, low foot-rest stretched quite across one side of the pew-floor. I have seen these long benches with a tier of three shelves; the lower and broader shelf was used as a foot-rest, the second one was to hold the hats of the men, and the third and narrower shelf was for the hymn-books and Bibles. Such comfortable and luxurious pew-furnishings could never have been found in many churches.

An old New Englander relates a funny story of his youth, in which one of these triple-tiered foot-benches played an important part. When he was a boy a travelling show visited his native town, and though he was not permitted to go within the mystic and alluring tent, he stood longingly at the gate, and was prodigiously diverted and astonished by an exhibition of tight-rope walking, which was given outside the tent-door as a bait to lure pleasure-loving and frivolous townspeople within, and also as a tantalization to the children of the saints who were not allowed to enter the tent of the wicked. Fired by that bewildering and amazing performance, he daily, after the wonderful sight, practised walking on rails, on fences, on fallen trees, and on every narrow foothold which he could find, as a careful preparation for a final feat and triumph of skill on his mother's clothes-line. In an evil hour, as he sat one Sunday in the corner of his father's pew, his eyes rested on the narrow ledge which formed the top of the long foot-bench. Satan can find mischief for idle boys within church as well as without, and the desire grew stronger to try to walk on that narrow foothold. He looked at his father and mother, they were peacefully sleeping; so also were the grown-up occupants of the neighboring pews; the pew walls were high, the minister seldom glanced to right or left; a thousand good reasons were whispered in his ear by the mischief-finder, and at last he willingly yielded, pulled off his heavy shoes, and softly mounted the foot-bench. He walked forward and back with great success twice, thrice, but when turning for a fourth tour he suddenly lost his balance, and over he went with a resounding crash--hats, psalm-books, heavy bench, and all. He crushed into hopeless shapelessness his father's gray beaver meeting-hat, a long-treasured and much-loved antique; he nearly smashed his mother's kid-slippered foot to jelly, and the fall elicited from her, in the surprise of the sudden awakening and intense pain, an ear-piercing shriek, which, with the noisy crash, electrified the entire meeting. All the grown people stood up to investigate, the children climbed on the seats to look at the guilty offender and his deeply mortified parents; while the minister paused in his sermon and said with cutting severity, "I have always regretted that the office of tithingman has been abolished in this community, as his presence and his watchful care are sadly needed by both the grown persons and the children in this congregation." The wretched boy who had caused all the commotion and disgrace was of course uninjured by his fall, but a final settlement at home between father and son on account of this sacrilegious piece of church disturbance made the unhappy would-be tight-rope walker wish that he had at least broken his arm instead of his father's hat and his mother's pride and the peace of the congregation.

The seats were sometimes on four sides of these pews, but oftener on three sides only, thus at least two thirds of the pew occupants did not face the minister. The pew-seats were as narrow and uncomfortable as the plebeian benches, though more exclusive, and, with the high partition walls, quite justified the comment of a little girl when she first attended a service in one of these old-fashioned, square-pewed churches. She exclaimed in dismay, "What! must I be shut up in a closet and sit on a shelf?" Often elderly people petitioned to build separate small pens of pews with a single wider seat as "through the seats being so very narrow" they could not sit in comfort.

The seats were, until well into this century, almost universally hung on hinges, and could be turned up against the walls of the pew, thus enabling the standing congregation to lean for support against the sides of the pews during the psalm-singing and the long, long prayers.

> "And when at last the loud Amen
> Fell from aloft, how quickly then
> The seats came down with heavy rattle,
> Like musketry in fiercest battle."

This noise of slamming pew-seats could easily be heard over half a mile away from the meeting-house in the summer time, for the perverse boys contrived always in their salute of welcome to the Amen to give vent in a most tremendous bang to a little of their pent up and ill-repressed energies. In old church-orders such entries as this (of the Haverhill church) are frequently seen: "The people are to Let their Seats down without Such Nois." "The boyes are not to wickedly noise down there pew-seats." A gentleman attending the old church in Leicester heard at the beginning of the prayer, for the first time in his life, the noise of slamming pew-seats, as the seats were thrust up against the pew-walls. He jumped into the aisle at the first clatter, thinking instinctively that the gallery was cracking and falling. Another stranger, a Southerner, entering rather late at a morning service in an old church in New England, was greeted with the rattle of falling seats, and exclaimed in amazement, "Do you Northern people applaud in church?"

In many meeting-houses the tops of the pews and of the high gallery railings were ornamented with little balustrades of turned wood, which were often worn quite bare of paint by childish fingers that had tried them all "to find which ones would turn," and which, alas! would also squeak. This fascinating occupation whiled away many a tedious hour in the dreary church, and in spite of weekly forbidding frowns and whispered reproofs for the shrill, ear-piercing squeaks elicited by turning the spindle-shaped balusters, was entirely too alluring a time-killer to be abandoned, and consequently descended, an hereditary church pastime, from generation to generation of the children of the Puritans; and indeed it remained so strong an instinct that many a grown person, visiting in after life a church whose pews bore balustrades like the ones of his childhood, could scarce keep his itching fingers from trying them each in succession "to see which ones would turn."

These open balustrades also afforded fine peep-holes through which, by standing or kneeling upon "the shelf," a child might gaze at his neighbor; and also through which sly missiles--little balls of twisted paper--could be snapped, to the annoyance of some meek girl or retaliating boy, until the young marksman was ignominiously pulled down by his mother from his post of attack. And through these balustrades the same boy a few years later could thrust sly missives, also of twisted paper, to the girl whom he had once assailed and bombarded with his annoying paper bullets.

Through the pillared top-rail a restless child in olden days often received, on a hot summer Sabbath from a farmer's wife or daughter in an adjoining pew, friendly and quieting gifts of sprigs of dill, or fennel, or caraway, famous anti-soporifics; and on this herbivorous food he would contentedly browse as long as it lasted. An uneasy, sermon-tired little girl was once given through the pew-rail several stalks of caraway, and with them a large bunch of aromatic southernwood, or "lad's-love" which had been brought to meeting by the matron in the next pew, with a crudely and unconsciously aesthetic sense that where eye and ear found so little to delight them, there the pungent and spicy fragrance of the southernwood would be doubly grateful to the nostrils. Little Missy sat down delightedly to nibble the caraway-seed, and her mother seeing her so quietly and absorbingly occupied, at once fell contentedly and placidly asleep in her corner of the pew. But five heads of caraway, though each contain many score of seeds, and the whole number be slowly nibbled and eaten one seed at a time, will not last through the child's eternity of a long doctrinal sermon; and when the umbels were all devoured, the young experimentalist began upon the stalks and stems, and they, too, slowly disappeared. She then attacked the sprays of southernwood, and in spite of its bitter, wormwoody flavor, having nothing else to do, she finished it, all but the tough stems, just as the long sermon was brought to a close. Her waking mother, discovering no signs of green verdure in the pew, quickly drew forth a whispered confession of the time-killing Nebuchadnezzar-like feast, and frightened and horrified, at once bore the leaf-gorged child from the church, signalling in her retreat to the village doctor, who quickly followed and administered to the omnivorous young New Englander a bolus which made her loathe to her dying day, through a sympathetic association and memory, the taste of caraway, and the scent of southernwood.

An old gentleman, lamenting the razing of the church of his childhood, told the story of his youthful Sabbaths in rhyme, and thus refers with affectionate enthusiasm to the old custom of bringing bunches of esculent "sallet" herbs to meeting:--

"And when I tired and restless grew,
Our next pew neighbor, Mrs. True,
Reached her kind hand the top rail through
To hand me dill, and fennel too,
And sprigs of caraway.

"And as I munched the spicy seeds,
I dimly felt that kindly deeds
That thus supply our present needs,
Though only gifts of pungent weeds,
Show true religion.

"And often now through sermon trite
And operatic singer's flight,
I long for that old friendly sight,
The hand with herbs of value light,
To help to pass the time."

Were the dill and "sweetest fennel" chosen Sabbath favorites for their old-time virtues and powers?

"Vervain and dill
Hinder witches of their ill."

And of the charmed fennel Longfellow wrote:--

"The fennel with its yellow flowers
That, in an earlier age than ours,
Was gifted with the wondrous powers,
    Lost vision to restore."

And traditions of mysterious powers, dream-influencing, spirit-exorcising, virtue-awakening, health-giving properties, hung vaguely around the southernwood and made it specially fit to be a Sabbath-day posy. These traditions are softened by the influence of years into simply idealizing, in the mind of every country-bred New Englander, the peculiar refreshing scent of the southernwood as a typical Sabbath-day fragrance. Half a century ago, the pretty feathery pale-green shrub grew in every country door-yard, humble or great, throughout New England; and every church-going woman picked a branch or spray of it when she left her home on Sabbath morn. To this day, on hot summer Sundays, many a staid old daughter of the Puritans may be seen entering the village meeting-house, clad in a lilac-sprigged lawn or a green-striped barège,--a scanty-skirted, surplice-waisted relic of past summers,--with a lace-bordered silk cape or a delicate, time-yellowed, purple and white cashmere scarf on her bent shoulders, wearing on her gray head a shirred-silk or leghorn bonnet, and carrying in her lace-mitted hand a fresh handkerchief, her spectacle-case and well-worn Bible, and a great sprig of the sweet, old-fashioned "lad's-love." A rose, a bunch of mignonette would be to her too gay a posy for the Lord's House and the Lord's Day. And balmier breath than was ever borne by blossom is the pure fragrance of green growing things,--southernwood, mint, sweet fern, bayberry, sweetbrier. No rose is half so fresh, so countrified, so memory-sweet.

The benches and the pew-seats in the old churches were never cushioned. Occasionally very old or feeble women brought cushions to meeting to sit upon. It is a matter of recent tradition that Colonel Greenleaf caused a nine days' talk in Newbury town at the beginning of this century when he cushioned his pew. The widow of Sir William Pepperell, who lived in imposing style, had her pew cushioned and lined and curtained with worsted stuff, and carpeted with a heavy bear-skin. This worn, faded, and moth-eaten furniture remained in the Kittery church until the year 1840, just as when Lady Pepperell furnished and occupied the pew. Nor were even the seats of the pulpit cushioned. The "cooshoons" of velvet or leather, which were given by will to the church, and which were kept in the pulpit, and were nibbled by the squirrels, were for the Bible, not the minister, to rest upon.

In many churches--in Durham, Concord and Sandwich--the pews had swing-shelves, "leaning shelves," upon which a church attendant could rest his paper and his arm when taking notes from the sermon, as was at one time the universal custom, and in which even school-boys of a century ago had to take part. Funny stories are told of the ostentatious notes taken by pompous parishioners who could neither write nor read, but who could scribble, and thus cut a learned figure.

The doors of the pews were usually cut down somewhat lower than the pew-walls, and frequently had no top-rails. They sometimes bore the name of the pew-owner painted in large white letters. They were secured when closed by clumsy wooden buttons. In many country congregations the elderly men--stiff old farmers--had a fashion of standing up in the middle of the sermon to stretch their cramped limbs, and they would lean against and hang over the pew door and stare up and down the aisle. In Andover, Vermont, old Deacon Puffer never let a summer Sunday pass without thus resting and diverting himself. One day, having ill-secured the wooden button at the door of his pew, the leaning-place gave way under his weight, and out he sprawled on all-fours, with a loud clatter, into the middle of the aisle, to the amusement of the children, and the mortification of his wife.

Thus it may be seen, as an old autobiography phrases it, "diversions was frequent in meeting, and the more duller the sermon, the more likely it was that some accident or mischief would be done to help to pass the time."

V
Seating the Meeting

Perhaps no duty was more important and more difficult of satisfactory performance in the church work in early New England than "seating the meeting-house." Our Puritan forefathers, though bitterly denouncing all forms and ceremonies, were great respecters of persons; and in nothing was the regard for wealth and position more fully shown than in designating the seat in which each person should sit during public worship. A committee of dignified and influential men was appointed to assign irrevocably to each person his or her place, according to rank and importance. Whittier wrote of this custom:--

> "In the goodly house of worship, where in order due and fit,
> As by public vote directed, classed and ranked the people sit;
> Mistress first and goodwife after, clerkly squire before the
> clown,
> From the brave coat, lace embroidered: to the gray frock
> shading down."

In many cases the members of the committee were changed each year or at each fresh seating, in order to obviate any of the effects of partiality through kinship, friendship, personal esteem, or debt. A second committee was also appointed to seat the members of committee number one, in order that, as Haverhill people phrased it, "there may be no Grumbling at them for picking and placing themselves."

This seating committee sent to the church the list of all the attendants and the seats assigned to them, and when the list had been twice or thrice read to the congregation, and nailed on the meeting-house door, it became a law. Then some such order as this of the church at Watertown, Connecticut, was passed: "It is ordered that the next Sabbath Day every person shall take his or her seat appointed to them, and not go to any other seat where others are placed: And if any one of the inhabitants shall act contrary, he shall for the first offence be reproved by the deacons, and for a second pay a fine of two shillings, and a like fine for each offence ever after." Or this of the Stratham church: "When the comety have Seatid the meeting-house every person that is Seatid shall set in those Seats or pay Five Shillings Pir Day for every day they set out of There seats in a Disorderly Manner to advance themselves Higher in the meeting-house." These two church-laws were very lenient. In many towns the punishments and fines were much more severe. Two men of Newbury were in 1669 fined £27 4s. each for "disorderly going and setting in seats belonging to others." They were dissatisfied with the seats assigned to them by the seating committee, and openly and defiantly rebelled. Other and more peaceable citizens "entred their Decents" to the first decision of the committee and asked for reconsideration of their special cases and for promotion to a higher pew before the final orders were "Jsued."

In all the Puritan meetings, as then and now in Quaker meetings, the men sat on one side of the meeting-house and the women on the other; and they entered by separate doors. It was a great and much-contested change when men and women were ordered to sit together "promiscuoslie." In front, on either side of the pulpit (or very rarely in the foremost row in the gallery), was a seat of highest dignity, known as the "foreseat," in which only the persons of greatest importance in the community sat.

Sometimes a row of square pews was built on three sides of the ground floor, and each pew occupied by separate families, while the pulpit was on the fourth side. If any man wished such a private pew for himself and family, he obtained permission from the church and town, and built it at his own expense. Immediately in front of the pulpit was either a long seat or a square inclosed pew for the deacons, who sat facing the congregation. This was usually a foot or two above the level of the other pews, and was reached by two or three steep, narrow steps. On a still higher plane was a pew for the ruling elders, when ruling elders there were. The magistrates also had a pew for their special use. What we now deem the best seats, those in the middle of the church, were in olden times the free seats.

Usually, on one side of the pulpit was a square pew for the minister's family. When there were twenty-six children in the family, as at least one New England parson could boast, and when ministers' families of twelve or fourteen children were far from unusual, it is no wonder that we find frequent votes to "inlarge the ministers wives pew the breadth of the alley," or to "take in the next pue to the ministers wives pue into her pue." The seats in the gallery were universally regarded in the early churches as the most exalted, in every sense, in the house, with the exception, of course, of the dignity-bearing foreseat and the few private pews.

It is easy to comprehend what a source of disappointed anticipation, heart-burning jealousy, offended dignity, unseemly pride, and bitter quarrelling this method of assigning seats, and ranking thereby, must have been in those little communities. How the goodwives must have hated the seating committee! Though it was expressly ordered, when the committee rendered their decision, that "the inhabitants are to rest silent and sett down satysfyed," who can still the tongue of an envious woman or an insulted man? Though they were Puritans, they were first of all men and women, and complaints and revolts were frequent. Judge Sewall records that one indignant dame "treated Captain Osgood very roughly on account of seating the meeting-house." To her the difference between a seat in the first and one in the second row was immeasurably great. It was not alone the Scribes and Pharisees who desired the highest seats in the synagogue.

It was found necessary at a very early date to "dignify the meeting," which was to make certain seats, though in different localities, equal in dignity; thus could peace and contented pride be partially restored. For instance, the seating committee in the Sutton church used their "best discresing," and voted that "the third seat below be equal in dignity with the foreseat in the front gallery, and the fourth seat below be equal in dignity with the foreseat in the side gallery," etc., thus making many seats of equal honor. Of course wives had to have seats of equal importance with those of their husbands, and each widow retained the dignity apportioned to her in her husband's lifetime. We can well believe that much "discresing" was necessary in dignifying as well as in seating. Often, after building a new meeting-house with all the painstaking and thoughtful judgment that could be shown, the dissensions over the seating lasted for years. The conciliatory fashion of "dignifying the seats" clung long in the Congregational churches of New England. In East Hartford and Windsor it was not abandoned until 1824.

Many men were unwilling to serve on these seating committees, and refused to "medle with the seating," protesting against it on account of the odium that was incurred, but they were seldom "let off." Even so influential and upright a man as Judge Sewall felt a dread of the responsibility and of the personal spleen he might arouse. He also feared in one case lest his seat-decisions might, if disliked, work against the ministerial peace of his son, who had been recently ordained as pastor of the church. Sometimes the difficulty was settled in this way: the entire church (or rather the male members) voted who should occupy the foreseat, or the highest pew, and the voted-in occupants of this seat of honor formed a committee, who in turn seated the others of the congregation.

In the town of Rowley, "age, office, and the amount paid toward building the meeting-house were considered when assigning seats." Other towns had very amusing and minute rules for seating. Each year of the age counted one degree. Military service counted eight degrees. The magistrate's office counted ten degrees. Every forty shillings paid in on the church rate counted one degree. We can imagine the ambitious Puritan adding up his degrees, and paying in forty shillings more in order to sit one seat above his neighbor who was a year or two older.

In Pittsfield, as early as the year 1765, the pews were sold by "vandoo" to the highest bidder, in order to stop the unceasing quarrels over the seating. In Windham, Connecticut, in 1762, the adoption of this pacificatory measure only increased the dissension when it was discovered that some miserable "bachelors who never paid for more than one head and a horse" had bid in several of the best pews in the meeting-house. In New London, two women, sisters-in-law, were seated side by side. Each claimed the upper or more dignified seat, and they quarrelled so fiercely over the occupation of it that they had to be brought before the town meeting.

In no way could honor and respect be shown more satisfactorily in the community than by the seat assigned in meeting. When Judge Sewall married his second wife, he writes with much pride: "Mr. Oliver in the names of the Overseers invites my Wife to sit in the foreseat. I thought to have brought her into my pue. I thankt him and the Overseers." His wife died in a few months, and he reproached himself for his pride in this honor, and left the seat which he had in the men's foreseat. "God in his holy Sovereignty put my wife out of the Fore Seat. I apprehended I had Cause to be ashamed of my Sin and loath myself for it, and retired into my Pue," which was of course less dignified than the foreseat.

Often, in thriving communities, the "pues" and benches did not afford seating room enough for the large number who wished to attend public worship, and complaints were frequent that many were "obliged to sit squeased on the stairs." Persons were allowed to bring chairs and stools into the meeting-house, and place them in the "alleys." These extra seats became often such encumbering nuisances that in many towns laws were passed abolishing and excluding them, or, as in Hadley, ordering them "back of the women's seats." In 1759 it was ordered in that town to "clear the Alleys of the meeting-house of chairs and other Incumbrances." Where the chairless people went is not told; perhaps they sat in the doorway, or, in the summer time, listened outside the windows. One forward citizen of Hardwicke had gradually moved his chair down the church alley, step by step, Sunday after Sunday, from one position of dignity to another still higher, until at last he boldly invaded the deacons' seat. When, in the year 1700, this honored position was forbidden him, in his chagrin and mortification he committed suicide by hanging.

The young men sat together in rows, and the young women in corresponding seats on the other side of the house. In 1677 the selectmen of Newbury gave permission to a few young women to build a pew in the gallery. It is impossible to understand why this should have roused the indignation of the bachelors of the town, but they were excited and angered to such a pitch that they broke a window, invaded the meeting-house, and "broke the pue in pessis." For this sacrilegious act they were fined £10 each, and sentenced to be whipped or pilloried. In consideration, however, of the fact that many of them had been brave soldiers, the punishment was omitted when they confessed and asked forgiveness. This episode is very comical; it exhibits the Puritan youth in such an ungallant and absurd light. When, ten years later, liberty was given to ten young men, who had sat in the "foure backer seats in the gallery," to build a pew in "the hindermost seat in the gallery behind the pulpit," it is not recorded that the Salem young women made any objection. In the Woburn church, the four daughters of one of the most respected families in the place received permission to build a pew in which to sit. Here also such indignant and violent protests were made by the young men that the selectmen were obliged to revoke the permission. It would be interesting to know the bachelors' discourteous objections to young women being allowed to own a pew, but no record of their reasons is given. Bachelors were so restricted and governed in the colonies that perhaps they resented the thought of any independence being allowed to single women. Single men could not live alone, but were forced to reside with some family to whom the court assigned them, and to do in all respects just what the court ordered. Thus, in olden times, a man had to marry to obtain his freedom. The only clue to a knowledge of the cause of the fierce and resentful objection of New England young men to permitting the young women of the various congregations to build and own a "maids pue" is contained in the record of the church of the town of Scotland, Connecticut. "An Hurlburt, Pashants and Mary Lazelle, Younes Bingham, prudenc Hurlburt and Jerusha meachem" were empowered to build a pew "provided they build within a year and raise ye pue no higher than the seat is on the Mens side." "Never ye Less," saith the chronicle, "ye above said have built said pue much higher than ye order, and if they do not lower the same within one month from this time the society comitte shall take said pue away." Do you wonder that the bachelors resented this towering "maids pue?" that they would not be scornfully looked down upon every Sabbath by women-folk, especially by a girl named "meachem"? Pashants and Younes and prudenc had to quickly come down from their unlawfully high church-perch and take a more humble seat, as befitted them; thus did their "vaulting ambition o'erleap itself and fall on the other side." Perhaps the Salem maids also built too high and imposing a pew. In Haverhill, in 1708, young women were permitted to build pews, provided they did not "damnify the Stairway." This somewhat profane-sounding restriction they heeded, and the Haverhill maids occupied their undamnifying "pue" unmolested. Medford young women, however, in 1701, when allowed only one side gallery for seats, while the young men were assigned one side and all the front gallery, made such an uproar that the town had to call a meeting, and restore to them their "woman's rights" in half the front gallery.

Infants were brought to church in their mothers' arms, and on summer days the young mothers often sat at the meeting-house door or in the porch,--if porch there were,--where, listening to the word of God, they could attend also to the wants of their babes. I have heard, too, of a little cage, or frame, which was to be seen in the early meeting-houses, for the purpose of holding children who were too young to sit alone,--poor Puritan babies! Little girls sat with their mothers or elder sisters on "crickets" within the pews; or if the family were over-numerous, the children and crickets exundated into "the alley without the pues." Often a row of little daughters of Zion sat on three-legged stools and low seats the entire length of the aisle,--weary, sleepy, young sentinels "without the gates."

The boys, the Puritan boys, those wild animals who were regarded with such suspicion, such intense disfavor, by all elderly Puritan eyes, and who were publicly stigmatized by the Duxbury elders as "ye wretched boys on ye Lords Day," were herded by themselves. They usually sat on the pulpit and gallery stairs, and constables or tithingmen were appointed to watch over them and control them. In Salem, in 1676, it was ordered that "all ye boyes of ye towne are and shall be appointed to sitt upon ye three pair of stairs in ye meeting-house on ye Lords Day, and Wm. Lord is appointed to look after ye boyes yt sitte upon ye pulpit stairs. Reuben Guppy is to look and order soe many of ye boyes as may be convenient, and if any are unruly, to present their names, as the law directs." Nowadays we should hardly seat boys in a group if we wished them to be orderly and decorous, and I fear the man "by the name of Guppy" found it no easy task to preserve order and due gravity among the Puritan boys in Salem meeting. In fact, the rampant boys behaved thus badly for the very reason that they were seated together instead of with their respective families; and not until the fashion was universal of each family sitting in a pew or group by itself did the boys in meeting behave like human beings rather than like mischievous and unruly monkeys.

In Stratford, in 1668, a tithingman was "appointed to watch over the youths of disorderly carriage, and see that they behave themselves comelie, and use such raps and blows as in his discretion meet."

I like to think of those rows of sober-faced Puritan boys seated on the narrow, steep pulpit stairs, clad in knee-breeches and homespun flapped coats, and with round, cropped heads, miniature likenesses in dress and countenance (if not in deportment) of their grave, stern, God-fearing fathers. Though they were of the sedate Puritan blood, they were boys, and they wriggled and twisted, and scraped their feet noisily on the sanded floor; and I know full well that the square-toed shoes of one in whom "original sin" waxed powerful, thrust many a sly dig in the ribs and back of the luckless wight who chanced to sit in front of and below him on the pulpit stairs. Many a dried kernel of Indian corn was surreptitiously snapped at the head of an unwary neighbor, and many a sly word was whispered and many a furtive but audible "snicker" elicited when the dread tithingman was "having an eye-out" and administering "discreet raps and blows" elsewhere.

One of these wicked youths in Andover was brought before the magistrate, and it was charged that he "Sported and played and by Indecent Gestures and Wry Faces caused laughter and misbehavior in the Beholders." The girls were not one whit better behaved. One of "ye tything men chosen of ye town of Norwich" reported that "Tabatha Morgus of s'd Norwich Did on ye 24th day February it being Sabbath on ye Lordes Day, prophane ye Lordes Day in ye meeting house of ye west society in ye time of ye forenoone service on s'd Day by her rude and Indecent Behaviour in Laughing and Playing in ye time of ye s'd Service which Doinges of ye s'd Tabatha is against ye peace of our Sovereign Lord ye King, his Crown and Dignity." Wanton Tabatha had to pay three shilings sixpence for her ill-timed mid-winter frolic. Perhaps she laughed to try to keep warm. Those who laughed at the misdemeanors of others were fined as well. Deborah Bangs, a young girl, in 1755 paid a fine of five shillings for "Larfing in the Wareham Meeting House in time of Public Worship," and a boy at the same time, for the same offence, paid a fine of ten shillings. He may have laughed louder and longer. In a law-book in which Jonathan Trumbull recorded the minor cases which he tried as justice of the peace, was found this entry: "His Majesties Tithing man entered complaint against Jona. and Susan Smith, that on the Lords Day during Divine Service, they did *smile*." They were found guilty, and each was fined five shillings and costs,--poor smiling Susan and Jonathan.

Those wretched Puritan boys, those "sons of Belial," whittled, too, and cut the woodwork and benches of the meeting-house in those early days, just as their descendants have ever since hacked and cut the benches and desks in country schoolhouses,--though how they ever eluded the vigilant eye and ear of the ubiquitous tithingman long enough to whittle will ever remain an unsolved mystery of the past. This early forerunning evidence of what has become a characteristic Yankee trait and habit was so annoyingly and extensively exhibited in Medford, in 1729, that an order was passed to prosecute and punish "all who cut the seats in the meeting-house."

Few towns were content to have one tithingman and one staff, but ordered that there should be a guardian set over the boys in every corner of the meeting-house. In Hanover it was ordered "That there be some sticks set up in various places in the meeting-house, and fit persons by them and *to use them.*" I doubt not that the sticks were well used, and Hanover boys were well rapped in meeting.

The Norwalk people come down through history shining with a halo of gentle lenity, for their tithingman was ordered to bear a short, small stick only, and he was "Desired to use it with clemency." However, if any boy proved "incoridgable," he could be "presented" before the elders; and perhaps he would rather have been treated as were Hartford boys by cruel Hartford church folk, who ordered that if "any boye shall be taken playing or misbehaving himself in the time of publick worship whether in the meeting-house or about the walls he shall be examined and punished at the present publickly before the assembly depart." Parson Chauncey, of Durham, when a boy misbehaved in meeting, and was "punched up" by the tithingman, often stopped in his sermon, called the godless young offender by name, and asked him to come to the parsonage the next day. Some very tender and beautiful lessons were taught to these Durham boys at these Monday morning interviews, and have descended to us in tradition; and the good Mr. Chauncey stands out a shining light of Christian patience and forbearance at a time when every other New England minister, from John Cotton down, preached and practised the stern repression and sharp correction of all children, and chanted together in solemn chorus, "Foolishness is bound up in the heart of a child."

One vicious tithingman invented, and was allowed to exercise on the boys, a punishment which was the refinement of cruelty. He walked up to the laughing, sporting, or whittling boy, took him by the collar or the arm, led him ostentatiously across the meeting-house, and seated him by his shamefaced mother on the women's side. It was as if one grandly proud in kneebreeches should be forced to walk abroad in petticoats. Far rather would the disgraced boy have been whacked soundly with the heavy knob of the tithingman's staff; for bodily pain is soon forgotten, while mortifying abasement lingers long.

The tithingman could also take any older youth who misbehaved or "acted unsivill" in meeting from his manly seat with the grown men, and force him to sit again with the boys; "if any over sixteen are disorderly, they shall be ordered to said seats." Not only could these men of authority keep the boys in order during meeting, but they also had full control during the nooning, and repressed and restrained and vigorously corrected the luckless boys during the midday hours. When seats in the galleries grew to be regarded as inferior to seats and pews on the ground floor, the boys, who of course must have the worst place in the house, were relegated from the pulpit stairs to pews in the gallery, and these square, shut-off pews grew to be what Dr. Porter called "the Devil's play-houses," and turbulent outbursts were frequent enough.

The little boys still sat downstairs under their parents' watchful eyes. "No child under 10 alowed to go up Gailary." In the Sutherland church, if the big boys (who ought to have known better) "behaved unseemly," one of the tithing-men who "took turns to set in the Galary" was ordered "to bring Such Bois out of the Galary & set them before the Deacon's Seat" with the small boys. In Plainfield, Connecticut, the "pestigeous" boys managed to invent a new form of annoyance,--they "damnified the glass;" and a church regulation had to be passed to prevent, or rather to try to prevent them from "opening the windows or in any way damnifying the glass." It was doubtless hot work scuffling and wrestling in the close, shut-in pews high up under the roof, and they naturally wished to cool down by opening or breaking the windows. Grown persons could not inconsiderately open the church windows either. "The Constables are desired to *take notic* of the persons that open the windows in the tyme of publick worship." No rheumatic-y draughts, no bronchitis-y damps, no pure air was allowed to enter the New England meeting-house. The church doubtless took a vote before it allowed a single window to be opened.

In Westfield, Massachusetts, the boys became so abominably rampant that the church formally decided "that if there is not a Reformation Respecting the Disorders in the Pews built on the Great Beam in the time of Publick Worship the comite can pul it down."

The fashion of seating the boys in pews by themselves was slow of abolishment in many of the churches. In Windsor, Connecticut, "boys' pews" were a feature of the church until 1845. As years rolled on, the tithingmen became restricted in their authority: they could no longer administer "raps and blows;" they were forced to content themselves with loud rappings on the floor, and pointing with a staff or with a condemning finger at the misdemeanant. At last the deacons usurped these functions, and if rapping and pointing did not answer the purpose of establishing order (if the boy "psisted"), led the stubborn offender out of meeting; and they had full authority soundly to thrash the "wretched boy" on the horse-block. Rev.

Dr. Dakin tells the story that, hearing a terrible noise and disturbance while he was praying in a church in Quincy, he felt constrained to open his eyes to ascertain the cause thereof; and he beheld a red-haired boy firmly clutching the railing on the front edge of the gallery, while a venerable deacon as firmly clutched the boy. The young rebel held fast, and the correcting deacon held fast also, until at last the balustrade gave way, and boy, deacon, and railing fell together with a resounding crash. Then, rising from the wooden debris, the thoroughly subdued boy and the triumphant deacon left the meeting-house to finish their little affair; and unmistakable swishing sounds, accompanied by loud wails and whining protestations, were soon heard from the region of the horse-sheds. Parents never resented such chastisings; it was expected, and even desired, that boys should be whipped freely by every school-master and person of authority who chose so to do.

In some old church-orders for seating, boys were classed with negroes, and seated with them; but in nearly all towns the negroes had seats by themselves. The black women were all seated on a long bench or in an inclosed pew labelled "B.W.," and the negro men in one labelled "B.M." One William Mills, a jesting soul, being asked by a pompous stranger where he could sit in meeting, told the visitor that he was welcome to sit in Bill Mills's pew, and that it was marked "B.M." The man, who chanced to be ignorant of the local custom of marking the negro seats, accepted the kind invitation, and seated himself in the black men's pew, to the delight of Bill Mills, the amusement of the boys, the scandal of the elders, and his own disgust.

Sometimes a little pew or short gallery was built high up among the beams and joists over the staircase which led to the first gallery, and was called the "swallows' nest," or the "roof pue," or the "second gallery." It was reached by a steep, ladder-like staircase, and was often assigned to the negroes and Indians of the congregation.

Often "ye seat between ye Deacons seat and ye pulpit is for persons hard of hearing to sett in." In nearly every meeting a bench or pew full of aged men might be seen near the pulpit, and this seat was called, with Puritan plainness of speech, the "Deaf Pew." Some very deaf church members (when the boys were herded elsewhere) sat on the pulpit stairs, and even in the pulpit, alongside the preacher, where they disconcertingly upturned their great tin ear-trumpets directly in his face. The persistent joining in the psalm-singing by these deaf old soldiers and farmers was one of the bitter trials which the leader of the choir had to endure.

The singers' seats were usually in the galleries; sometimes upon the ground floor, in the "hind-row on either side." Occasionally the choir sat in two rows of seats that extended quite across the floor of the house, in front of the deacons' seat and the pulpit. The men singers then sat facing the congregation, while the women singers faced the pulpit. Between them ran a long rack for the psalm-books. When they sang they stood up, and bawled and fugued in each other's faces. Often a square pew was built for the singers, and in the centre of this enclosure was a table, on which were laid, when at rest, the psalm-books. When they sang, the choir thus formed a hollow square, as does any determined band, for strength.

One other seat in the old Puritan meeting-house, a seat of gloom, still throws its darksome shadow down through the years,--the stool of repentance. "Barbarous and cruel punishments" were forbidden by the statutes of the new colony, but on this terrible soul-rack the shrinking, sullen, or defiant form of some painfully humiliated man or woman sat, crushed, stunned, stupefied by overwhelming disgrace, through the long Christian sermon; cowering before the hard, pitiless gaze of the assembled and godly congregation, and the cold rebuke of the pious minister's averted face; bearing on the poor sinful head a deep-branding paper inscribed in "Capitall Letters" with the name of some dark or mysterious crime, or wearing on the sleeve some strange and dread symbol, or on the breast a scarlet letter.

Let us thank God that these soul-blasting and hope-killing exposures-- so degrading to the criminal, so demoralizing to the community,--these foul, in-human blots on our fair and dearly loved Puritan Lord's Day, were never frequent, nor did the form of punishment obtain for a long time. In 1681 two women were sentenced to sit during service on a high stool in the middle alley of the Salem meeting-house, having on their heads a paper bearing the name of their crime; and a woman in Agamenticus at about the same date was ordered "to stand in a white sheet publicly two several Sabbath-Days with the mark of her offence on her forehead." These are the latest records of this punishment that I have chanced to see.

Thus, from old church and town records, we plainly discover that each laic, deacon, elder, criminal, singer, and even the ungodly boy had his alloted place as absolutely assigned to him in the old meeting-house as was the pulpit to the parson. Much has been said in semi-ridicule of this old custom of "seating" and "dignifying," yet it did not in reality differ much from our modern way of selling the best pews to whoever will pay the most. Perhaps the old way was the better, since, in the early churches, age, education, dignity, and reputation were considered as well as wealth.

VI
The Tithingman and the Sleepers

The most grotesque, the most extraordinary, the most highly colored figure in the dull New England church-life was the tithingman. This fairly burlesque creature impresses me always with a sense of unreality, of incongruity, of strange happening, like a jesting clown in a procession of monks, like a strain of low comedy in the sober religious drama of early New England Puritan life; so out of place, so unreal is this fussy, pompous, restless tithingman, with his fantastic wand of office fringed with dangling foxtails,--creaking, bustling, strutting, peering around the quiet meeting-house, prodding and rapping the restless boys, waking the drowsy sleepers; for they slept in country churches in the seventeenth century, notwithstanding dread of fierce correction, just as they nod and doze and softly puff, unawakened and unrebuked, in village churches throughout New England in the nineteenth century.

This absurd and distorted type of the English church beadle, this colonial sleep banisher, was equipped with a long staff, heavily knobbed at one end, with which he severely and pitilessly rapped the heads of the too sleepy men, and the too wide-awake boys. From the other end of this wand of office depended a long foxtail, or a hare's-foot, which he softly thrust in the faces of the sleeping Priscillas, Charitys, and Hopestills, and which gently brushed and tickled them into reverent but startled wakefulness.

One zealous but too impetuous tithingman in his pious ardor of office inadvertently applied the wrong end, the end with the heavy knob, the masculine end, to a drowsy matron's head; and for this severely ungallant mistake he was cautioned by the ruling elders to thereafter use "more discresing and less heist."

Another over-watchful Newbury "awakener" rapped on the head a nodding man who protested indignantly that he was wide-awake, and was only bowing in solemn assent and approval of the minister's arguments. Roger Scott, of Lynn, in 1643 struck the tithingman who thus roughly and suddenly wakened him; and poor sleepy and bewildered Roger, who is branded through all time as "a common sleeper at the publick exercise," was, for this most naturally resentful act, but also most shockingly grave offence, soundly whipped, as a warning both to keep awake and not to strike back in meeting.

Obadiah Turner, of Lynn, gives in his Journal a sad, sad disclosure of total depravity which was exposed by one of these sudden church-awakenings, and the story is best told in the journalist's own vivid words:--

"June 3, 1616.--Allen Bridges hath bin chose to wake ye sleepers in meeting. And being much proude of his place, must needs have a fox taile fixed to ye ende of a long staff wherewith he may brush ye faces of them yt will have napps in time of discourse, likewise a sharpe thorne whereby he may pricke such as be most sound. On ye last Lord his day, as hee strutted about ye meeting-house, he did spy Mr. Tomlins sleeping with much comfort, hys head kept steadie by being in ye corner, and his hand grasping ye rail. And soe spying, Allen did quickly thrust his staff behind Dame Ballard and give him a grievous prick upon ye hand. Whereupon Mr. Tomlins did spring vpp mch above ye floore, and with terrible force strike hys hand against ye wall; and also, to ye great wonder of all, prophanlie exclaim in a loud voice, curse ye wood-chuck, he dreaming so it seemed yt a wood-chuck had seized and bit his hand. But on coming to know where he was, and ye greate scandall he had committed, he seemed much abashed, but did not speak. And I think he will not soon again goe to sleepe in meeting."

How clear the picture! Can you not see it?--the warm June sunlight streaming in through the narrow, dusty windows of the old meeting-house; the armed watcher at the door; the Puritan men and women in their sad-colored mantles seated sternly upright on the hard narrow benches; the black-gowned minister, the droning murmur of whose sleepy voice mingles with the out-door sounds of the rustle of leafy branches, the song of summer birds, the hum of buzzing insects, and the muffled stamping of horses' feet; the restless boys on the pulpit-stairs; the tired, sleeping Puritan with his head thrown back in the corner of the pew; the vain, strutting, tithingman with his fantastic and thornéd staff of office; and then--the sudden, electric wakening, and the consternation of the whole staid and pious congregation at such terrible profanity in the house of God. Ah!--it was not two hundred and forty years ago; when I read the quaint words my Puritan blood stirs my drowsy brain, and I remember it all well, just as I saw it last summer in June.

Another catastrophe from too fierce zeal on the part of the tithingman is recorded. An old farmer, worn out with a hard Saturday's work at sheep-washing, fell asleep ere the hour-glass had once been turned. Though he was a man of dignity, for he sat in his own pew, he could not escape the rod of the pragmatical tithingman. Being rudely disturbed, but not wholly wakened, the bewildered sheep-farmer sprung to his feet, seized his astonished and mortified wife by the shoulders and shook her violently, shouting at the top of his voice, "Haw back! haw back! Stand still, will ye?" Poor goodman and goodwife! many years elapsed ere they recovered from that keen disgrace.

The ministers encouraged and urged the tithingmen to faithfully perform their allotted work. One early minister "did not love sleepers in ye meeting-house, and would stop short in ye exercise and call pleasantlie to wake ye sleepers, and once of a warm Summer afternoon he did take hys hat off from ye pegg in ye beam, and put it on, saying he would go home and feed his fowles and come back again, and maybe their sleepe would be ended, and they readie to hear ye remainder of hys discourse." Another time he suggested that they might like better the Church of England service of sitting down and standing up, and we can be sure that this "was competent to keepe their eyes open for a twelvemonth."

All this was in the church of Mr. Whiting, of Lynn, a somewhat jocose Puritan,--if jocularity in a Puritan is not too anomalous an attribute to have ever existed. We can be sure that there was neither sleeping nor jesting allusion to such an irreverence in Mr. Mather's, Mr. Welde's, or Mr. Cotton's meetings. In many rigidly severe towns, as in Portsmouth in 1662 and in Boston in 1667, it was ordered by the selectmen as a proper means of punishment that a "cage be made or some other means invented for such as sleepe on the Lord's Daie." Perhaps they woke the offender up and rudely and summarily dragged him out and caged him at once and kept him thus prisoned throughout the nooning,--a veritable jail-bird.

A rather unconventional and eccentric preacher in Newbury awoke one sleeper in a most novel manner. The first name of the sleeping man was Mark, and the preacher in his sermon made use of these Biblical words: "I say unto you, mark the perfect man and behold the upright." But in the midst of his low, monotonous sermon-voice he roared out the word "mark" in a loud shout that brought the dozing Mark to his feet, bewildered but wide awake.

Mr. Moody, of York, Maine, employed a similar device to awaken and mortify the sleepers in meeting. He shouted "Fire, fire, fire!" and when the startled and blinking men jumped up, calling out "Where?" he roared back in turn, "In hell, for sleeping sinners." Rev. Mr. Phillips, of Andover, in 1755, openly rebuked his congregation for "sleeping away a great part of the sermon;" and on the Sunday following an earthquake shock which was felt throughout New England, he said he hoped the "Glorious Lord of the Sabbath had given them such a shaking as would keep them awake through one sermon-time." Other and more autocratic parsons did not hesitate to call out their sleeping parishioners plainly by name, sternly telling them also to "Wake up!" A minister in Brunswick, Maine, thus pointedly wakened one of his sweet-sleeping church-attendants, a man of some dignity and standing in the community, and received the shocking and tautological answer, "Mind your own business, and go on with your sermon."

The women would sometimes nap a little without being discovered. "Ye women may sometimes sleepe and none know by reason of their enormous bonnets. Mr. Whiting doth pleasantlie say from ye pulpit hee doth seeme to be preaching to stacks of straw with men among them."

From this seventeenth-century comment upon the size of the women's bonnets, it may be seen that objections to women's overwhelming and obscuring headgear in public assemblies are not entirely complaining protests of modern growth. Other records refer to the annoyance from the exaggerated size of bonnets. In 1769 the church in Andover openly "put to vote whether the parish Disapprove of the Female sex sitting with their Hats on in the Meeting-house in time of Divine Service as being Indecent." The parish did Disapprove, with a capital D, for the vote passed in the affirmative. There is no record, however, to tell whether the Indecent fashion was abandoned, but I warrant no tithingman was powerful enough to make Andover women take off their proudly worn Sunday bonnets if they did not want to. Another town voted that it was the "Town's Mind" that the women should take off their bonnets and "hang them on the peggs," as did the men their headgear. But the Town's Mind was not a Woman's Mind; and the big-bonnet wearers, vain though they were Puritans, did as they pleased with their own bonnets. And indeed, in spite of votes and in spite of expostulations, the female descendants of the Puritans, through constantly recurring waves of fashion, have ever since been indecently wearing great obscuring hats and bonnets in public assemblies, even up to the present day.

The tithingman had other duties than awakening the sleepers and looking after "the boyes that playes and rapping those boyes,"--in short, seeing that every one was attentive in meeting except himself,--and the duties and powers of the office varied in different communities. Several of these officers were appointed in each parish. In Newbury, in 1688, there were twenty tithingmen, and in Salem twenty-five. They were men of authority, not only on Sunday, but throughout the entire week. Each had several neighboring families (usually ten, as the word "tithing" would signify) under his charge to watch during the week, to enforce the learning of the catechism at home, especially by the children, and sometimes he heard them "Say their Chatachize." These families he also watched specially on the Sabbath, and reported whether all the members thereof attended public worship. Not content with mounting guard over the boys on Sundays, he also watched on weekdays to keep boys and "all persons from swimming in the water." Do you think his duties were light in July and August, when school was out, to watch the boys of ten families? One man watching one family cannot prevent such "violations of the peace" in country towns now-a-days. He sometimes inspected the "ordinaries" and made complaint of any disorders which he there discovered, and gave in the names of "idle tiplers and gamers," and he could warn the tavern-keeper to sell no more liquor to any toper whom he knew or fancied was drinking too heavily. Josselyn complained bitterly that during his visit to New England in 1663 at "houses of entertainment called ordinaries into which a stranger went, he was presently followed by one appointed to that office who would thrust himself into his company uninvited, and if he called for more drink than the officer thought in his judgment he could soberly bear away, he would presently countermand it, and appoint the proportion beyond which he could not get one drop." The tithingman had a "spetial eye-out" on all bachelors, who were also carefully spied upon by the constables, deacons, elders, and heads of families in general. He might, perhaps, help to collect the ministerial rate, though his principal duty was by no means the collecting of tithes. He "worned peple out of ye towne." This warning was not at all because the new-comers were objectionable or undesired, but was simply a legal form of precaution, so that the parish would never be liable for the keeping of the "worned" ones in case they thereafter became paupers. He administered the "oath of fidelity" to new inhabitants. The tithingman also watched to see that "no young people walked abroad on the eve of the Sabbath,"--that is, on a Saturday night. He also marked and reported all those "who lye at home," and others who "prophanely behaved, lingered without dores at meeting time on the Lordes Daie," all the "sons of Belial strutting about, setting on fences, and otherwise desecrating the day." These last two classes of offenders were first admonished by the tithingman, then "Sett in stocks," and then cited before the Court. They were also confined in the cage on the meeting-house green, with the Lord's Day sleepers. The tithingman could arrest any who walked or rode at too fast a pace to and from meeting, and he could arrest any who "walked or rode unnecessarily on the Sabath." Great and small alike were under his control, as this notice from the "Columbian Centinel" of December, 1789, abundantly proves. It is entitled "The President and the Tything man:"--

> "The President, on his return to New York from his
> late tour through Connecticut, having missed his way
> on Saturday, was obliged to ride a few miles on Sunday

morning in order to gain the town at which he had
previously proposed to have attended divine service.
Before he arrived however he was met by a Tything man,
who commanding him to stop, demanded the occasion of
his riding; and it was not until the President had informed
him of every circumstance and promised to go no further
than the town intended that the Tything man would permit
him to proceed on his journey."

Various were the subterfuges to outwit the tithingman and elude his vigilance on the Sabbath. We all remember the amusing incident in "Oldtown Folks." A similar one really happened. Two gay young sparks driving through the town on the Sabbath were stopped by the tithingman; one offender said mournfully in excuse of his Sabbath travel, "My grandmother is lying dead in the next town." Being allowed to drive on, he stood up in his wagon when at a safe distance and impudently shouted back, "And she's been lying dead in the graveyard there for thirty years."

Thus it may be seen that the ancient tithingman was pre-eminently a general *snook*, to use an old and expressive word,--an informer, both in and out of meeting,--a very necessary, but somewhat odious, and certainly at times very absurd officer. He was in a degree a constable, a selectman, a teacher, a tax-collector, an inspector, a sexton, a home-watcher, and above all, a Puritan Bumble, whose motto was *Hie et ubique*. He was, in fact, a general law-enforcer and order-keeper, whose various duties, wherever still necessary and still performed, are now apportioned to several individuals. The ecclesiastical functions and authority of the tithingman lingered long after the civil powers had been removed or had gradually passed away from his office. Persons are now living who in their early and unruly youth were rapped at and pointed at by a New England tithingman when they laughed or were noisy in meeting.

VII
The Length of the Service

Watches were unknown in the early colonial days of New England, and for a long time after their introduction both watches and clocks were costly and rare. John Davenport of New Haven, who died in 1670, left a clock to his heirs; and E. Needham, who died in 1677, left a "Striking clock, a watch, and a Larum that dus not Strike," worth £5; these are perhaps the first records of the ownership of clocks and watches in New England. The time of the day was indicated to our forefathers in their homes by "noon marks" on the floor or window-seats, and by picturesque sundials; and in the civil and religious meetings the passage of time was marked by a strong brass-bound hour-glass, which stood on a desk below or beside the pulpit, or which was raised on a slender iron rod and standard, so that all the members of the congregation could easily watch "the sands that ran i' the clock's behalf." By the side of the desk sat, on the Sabbath, a sexton, clerk, or tithingman, whose duty it was to turn the hour-glass as often as the sands ran out. This was a very ostentatious way of reminding the clergyman how long he had preached; but if it were a hint to bring the discourse to an end, it was never heeded; for contemporary historical registers tell of most painfully long sermons, reaching up through long sub-divisions and heads to "twenty-seventhly" and "twenty-eighthly."

At the planting of the first church in Woburn, Massachusetts, the Rev. Mr. Symmes showed his godliness and endurance (and proved that of his parishioners also) by preaching between four and five hours. Sermons which occupied two or three hours were customary enough. One old Scotch clergyman in Vermont, in the early years of this century, bitterly and fiercely resented the "popish innovation and Sabbath profanation" of a Sunday-school for the children, which some daring and progressive parishioners proposed to hold at the "nooning." This canny Parson Whiteinch very craftily and somewhat maliciously prolonged his morning sermons until they each occupied three hours; thus he shortened the time between the two services to about half an hour, and victoriously crowded out the Sunday-school innovators, who had barely time to eat their cold lunch and care for their waiting horses, ere it was time for the afternoon service to begin. But one man cannot stop the tide, though he may keep it for a short time from one guarded and sheltered spot; and the rebellious Vermont congregation, after two or three years of tedious three-hour sermons, arose in a body and crowded out the purposely prolix preacher, and established the wished-for Sunday-school. The vanquished parson thereafter sullenly spent the noonings in the horse-shed, to which he ostentatiously carried the big church-Bible in order that it might not be at the service of the profaning teachers.

An irreverent caricature of the colonial days represents a phenomenally long-preaching clergyman as turning the hour-glass by the side of his pulpit and addressing his congregation thus, "Come! you are all good fellows, we'll take another glass together!" It is recorded of Rev. Urian Oakes that often the hour-glass was turned four times during one of his sermons. The warning legend, "Be Short," which Cotton Mather inscribed over his study door was not written over his pulpit; for he wrote in his diary that at his own ordination he prayed for an hour and a quarter, and preached for an hour and three quarters. Added to the other ordination exercises these long Mather addresses must have been tiresome enough. Nathaniel Ward deplored at that time, "Wee have a strong weakness in New England that when wee are speaking, wee know not how to conclude: wee make many ends before wee make an end."

Dr. Lord of Norwich always made a prayer which was one hour long; and an early Dutch traveller who visited New England asserted that he had heard there on Fast Day a prayer which was two hours long. These long prayers were universal and most highly esteemed,--a "poor gift in prayer" being a most deplored and even despised clerical short-coming. Had not the Puritans left the Church of England to escape "stinted prayers"? Whitefield prayed openly for Parson Barrett of Hopkinton, who could pray neither freely, nor well, that "God would open this dumb dog's mouth;" and everywhere in the Puritan Church, precatory eloquence as evinced in long prayers was felt to be the greatest glory of the minister, and the highest tribute to God.

In nearly all the churches the assembled people stood during prayer-time (since kneeling and bowing the head savored of Romish idolatry) and in the middle of his petition the minister usually made a long pause in order that any who were infirm or ill might let down their slamming pew-seats and sit down; those who were merely weary stood patiently to the long and painfully deferred end. This custom of standing during prayer-time prevailed in the Congregational churches in New England until quite a recent date, and is not yet obsolete in isolated communities and in solitary cases. I have seen within a few years, in a country church, a feeble, white-haired old deacon rise tremblingly at the preacher's solemn words "Let us unite in prayer," and stand with bowed head throughout the long prayer; thus pathetically clinging to the reverent custom of the olden time, he rendered tender tribute to vanished youth, gave equal tribute to eternal hope and faith, and formed a beautiful emblem of patient readiness for the last solemn summons.

Sometimes tedious expounding of the Scriptures and long "prophesying" lengthened out the already too long service. Judge Sewall recorded that once when he addressed or expounded at the Plymouth Church, "being afraid to look at the glass, ignorantly and unwittingly I stood two hours and a half," which was doing pretty well for a layman.

The members of the early churches did not dislike these long preachings and prophesyings; they would have regarded a short sermon as irreligious, and lacking in reverence, and besides, would have felt that they had not received in it their full due, their full money's worth. They often fell asleep and were fiercely awakened by the tithingman, and often they could not have understood the verbose and grandiose language of the preacher. They were in an icy-cold atmosphere in winter, and in glaring, unshaded heat in summer, and upon most uncomfortable, narrow, uncushioned seats at all seasons; but in every record and journal which I have read, throughout which ministers and laymen recorded all the annoyances and opposition which the preachers encountered, I have never seen one entry of any complaint or ill-criticism of too long praying or preaching. Indeed, when Rev. Samuel Torrey, of Weymouth, Massachusetts, prayed two hours without stopping, upon a public Fast Day in 1696, it is recorded that his audience only wished that the prayer had been much longer.

When we consider the training and exercise in prayer that the New England parsons had in their pulpits on Sundays, in their own homes on Saturday nights, on Lecture Days and Fast Days and Training Days, and indeed upon all times and occasions, can we wonder at Parson Boardman's prowess in New Milford in 1735? He visited a "praying" Indian's home wherein lay a sick papoose over whom a "pow-wow" was being held by a medicine-man at the request of the squaw-mother, who was still a heathen. The Christian warrior determined to fight the Indian witch-doctor on his own grounds, and while the medicine-man was screaming and yelling and dancing in order to cast the devil out of the child, the parson began to pray with equal vigor and power of lungs to cast out the devil of a medicine-man. As the prayer and pow-wow proceeded the neighboring Indians gathered around, and soon became seriously alarmed for the success of their prophet. The battle raged for three hours, when the pow-wow ended, and the disgusted and exhausted Indian ran out of the wigwam and jumped into the Housatonic River to cool his heated blood, leaving the Puritan minister triumphant in the belief, and indeed with positive proof, that he could pray down any man or devil.

The colonists could not leave the meeting-house before the long sen ices were ended, even had they wished, for the tithingman allowed no deserters. In Salem, in 1676, it was "ordered by ye Selectmen yt the three Constables doe attend att ye three greate doores of ye meeting-house every Lordes Day att ye end of ye sermon, both forenoone and afternoone, and to keep ye doores fast and suffer none to goe out before ye whole exercises bee ended." Thus Salem people had to listen to no end of praying and prophesying from their ministers and elders for they "couldn't get out."

As the years passed on, the church attendants became less referential and much more impatient and fearless, and soon after the Revolutionary War one man in Medford made a bargain with his minister--Rev. Dr. Osgood--that he would attend regularly the church services every Sunday morning, provided he could always leave at twelve o'clock. On each Sabbath thereafter, as the obstinate preacher would not end his sermon one minute sooner than his habitual time, which was long after twelve, the equally stubborn limited-time worshipper arose at noon, as he had stipulated, and stalked noisily out of meeting.

A minister about to preach in a neighboring parish was told of a custom which prevailed there of persons who lived at a distance rising and leaving the house ere the sermon was ended. He determined to teach them a lesson, and announced that he would preach the first part of his sermon to the sinners, and the latter part to the saints, and that the sinners would of course all leave as soon as their portion had been delivered. Every soul remained until the end of the service.

At last, when other means of entertainment and recreation than church-going became common, and other forms of public addresses than sermons were frequently given, New England church-goers became so restless and rebellious under the regime of hour-long prayers and indefinitely protracted sermons that the long services were gradually condensed and curtailed, to the relief of both preacher and hearers.

VIII
The Icy Temperature of the Meeting-House

In colonial days in New England the long and tedious services must have been hard to endure in the unheated churches in bitter winter weather, so bitter that, as Judge Sewall pathetically recorded, "The communion bread was frozen pretty hard and rattled sadly into the plates." Sadly down through the centuries is ringing in our ears the gloomy rattle of that frozen sacramental bread on the Church plate, telling to us the solemn story of the austere and comfortless church-life of our ancestors. Would that the sound could bring to our chilled hearts the same steadfast and pure Christian faith that made their gloomy, freezing services warm with God's loving presence!

Again Judge Sewall wrote: "Extraordinary Cold Storm of Wind and Snow. Blows much more as coming home at Noon, and so holds on. Bread was frozen at Lord's Table. Though 't was so cold John Tuckerman was baptized. At six o'clock my ink freezes, so that I can hardly write by a good fire in my Wives chamber. Yet was very Comfortable at Meeting." In the penultimate sentence of this quotation may be found the clue and explanation of the seemingly incredible assertion in the last sentence. The reason why he was comfortable in church was that he was accustomed to sit in cold rooms; even with the great open-mouthed and open-chimneyed fireplaces full of blazing logs, so little heat entered the rooms of colonial dwelling-houses that one could not be warm unless fairly within the chimney-place; and thus, even while sitting by the fire, his ink froze. Another entry of Judge Sewall's tells of an exceeding cold day when there was "Great Coughing" in meeting, and yet a new-born baby was brought into the icy church to be baptized. Children were always carried to the meeting-house for baptism the first Sunday after birth, even in the most bitter weather. There are no entries in Judge Sewall's diary which exhibit him in so lovable and gentle a light as the records of the baptism of his fourteen children,--his pride when the child did not cry out or shrink from the water in the freezing winter weather, thus early showing true Puritan fortitude; and also his noble resolves and hopes for their future. On this especially cold day when a baby was baptized, the minister prayed for a mitigation of the weather, and on the same day in another town "Rev. Mr. Wigglesworth preached on the text,

Who can stand before His Cold? Then by his own and people's sickness three Sabbaths passed without public Worship." February 20 he preached from these words: "He sends forth his word and thaws them." And the very next day a thaw set in which was regarded as a direct answer to his prayer and sermon. Sceptics now-a-days would suggest that he chose well the time to pray for milder weather.

Many persons now living can remember the universal and noisy turning up of great-coat collars, the swinging of arms, and knocking together of the heavy-booted feet of the listeners towards the end of a long winter sermon. Dr. Hopkins used to say, when the noisy tintamarre began, "My hearers, have a little patience, and I will soon close."

Another clergyman was irritated beyond endurance by the stamping, clattering feet, a *supplosio pedis* that he regarded as an irreverent protest and complaint against the severity of the weather, rather than as a hint to him to conclude his long sermon. He suddenly and noisily closed his sermon-book, leaned forward out of his high pulpit, and thundered out these Biblical words of rebuke at his freezing congregation, whose startled faces stared up at him through dense clouds of vapor. "Out of whose womb came the ice? And the hoary frost of heaven, who hath gendered it? The waters are hid as with a stone, and the face of the deep is frozen. Knowest thou the ordinance of heaven? Canst thou set the dominion thereof on the earth? Great things doth God which we cannot comprehend. He saith to the snow, Be thou on the earth. By the breath of God frost is given. He causeth it to come, whether for correction, or for his land, or for mercy. Hearken unto this. *Stand still*, and consider the wondrous works of God." We can believe that he roared out the words "stand still," and that there was no more noise in that meeting-house on cold Sundays during the remainder of that winter.

The ministers might well argue that no one suffered more from the freezing atmosphere than they did. In many records I find that they were forced to preach and pray with their hands cased in woollen or fur mittens or heavy knit gloves; and they wore long camlet cloaks in the pulpit and covered their heads with skull caps--as did Judge Sewall--and possibly wore, as he did also, a *hood*. Many a wig-hating minister must, in the Arctic meeting-house, have longed secretly for the grateful warmth to his head and neck of one of those "horrid Bushes of Vanity," a full-bottomed flowing wig.

On bitter winter days Dr. Stevens of Kittery used to send a servant to the meeting-house to find out how many of his flock had braved the piercing blasts. If only seven persons were present, the servant asked them to return with him to the parsonage to listen to the sermon; but if there were eight members in the meeting-house he so reported to the Doctor, who then donned his long worsted cloak, tied it around his waist with a great handkerchief, and attired thus, with a fur cap pulled down over his ears, and with heavy mittens on his hands, ploughed through the deep snow to the church, and in the same dress preached his long, knotty sermon in his pulpit, while fierce wintry blasts rattled the windows and shook the turret, and the eight godly, shivering souls wished profoundly that one of their number had "lain at home in a slothfull, lazey, prophane way," and thus permitted the seven others and the minister to have the sermon in comfort in the parsonage kitchen before the great blazing logs in the open fireplace.

Ah, it makes one shiver even to think of those gloomy churches, growing colder, and more congealed through weeks of heavy frost and fierce northwesters until they bore the chill of death itself. One can but wonder whether that fell scourge of New England, that hereditary curse--consumption--did not have its first germs evolved and nourished in our Puritan ancestors by the Spartan custom of sitting through the long winter services in the icy, death-like meeting-houses.

Of the insufficient clothing of the church attendants of olden times it is unnecessary to speak with much detail. The goodmen with their heavy top-boots or jack-boots, their milled or frieze stockings, their warm periwigs surmounted by fur caps or beaver hats or hoods; and with their many-caped great-coats or full round cloaks were dressed with a sufficient degree of comfort, though they did not possess the warm woollen and silken underclothing which now make a man's winter attire so comfortable. They carried muffs too, as the advertisements of the times show. The "Boston News Letter" of 1716 offers a reward for a man's muff lost on the Sabbath day in the street. In 1725 Dr. Prince lost his black bearskin muff, and in 1740 a "sableskin man's muff" was advertised as having been lost.

But the Puritan goodwives and maidens were dressed in a meagre and scanty fashion that when now considered seems fairly appalling. As soon as the colonies grew in wealth and fashion, thin silk or cotton hose were frequently worn in midwinter by the wives and daughters of well-to-do colonists; and correspondingly thin cloth or kid or silk slippers, high-channelled pumps, or low shoes with paper soles and "cross-cut" or wooden heels were the holiday and Sabbath-day covering for the feet. In wet weather clogs and pattens formed an extra and much needed protection when the fair colonists walked. Linen underclothing formed the first superstructure of the feminine costume and threw its penetrating chill to the very marrow of the bones. Often in mid-winter the scant-skirted French calico gowns were made with short elbow sleeves and round, low necks, and the throat and shoulders were lightly covered with thin lawn neckerchiefs or dimity tuckers. The flaunting hooped-petticoat of another decade was worn with a silk or brocade sacque. A thin cloth cape or mantle or spencer, lined with sarcenet silk, was frequently the only covering for the shoulders. In examining the treasured contents of old wardrobes, trunks, and high-chests, and in reading the descriptions of women's winter attire worn throughout the eighteenth and half through the nineteenth century, I am convinced that the only portions of Puritan female anatomy that were clothed with anything approaching respectable regard for health in the inclement New England climate were the head and the hands. The hands of "New English dames" were carefully protected with embroidered kid or leather gloves (for the early New Englanders were great glove wearers) or with warm knit woollen mittens, though mittens for women's wear were always fingerless. The well-gloved hands were moreover warmly ensconced in enormous stuffed muffs of bearskin which were almost as large as a flour barrel, or in smaller muffs of rabbit-skin or mink or beaver. The goodwives' heads bore, besides the close caps so universally worn, mufflers and veils and hoods,-- hoods of all kinds and descriptions, from the hoods of serge and camlet and gauze and black silk that Mistress Estabrook, wife of the Windham parson, proudly owned and wore, from the prohibited "silk and tiffany hoods" of the earliest planters down through the centuries' inflorescence of "hoods of crimson colored persian," "wild bore and hum-hum long hoods," "pointed velvet capuchins," "scarlet gipsys," "pinnered and tasselled hoods," "shirred lustring hoods," "hoods of rich pptuna," "muskmelon hoods," to the warm quilted "punkin hoods" worn within this century in country churches. These "punkin-hoods" were quilted with great rolls of woollen wadding and drawn tight between the rolls with strong cords. They formed a deafening and heating head-covering which always had to be loosened and thrust back when the wearer was within doors. It was only equalled in shapeless clumsiness and unique ugliness by its summer-sister of the same date, the green silk calash,--that funniest and quaintest of all New England feminine headgear,--a great sunshade that could not be called a bonnet, always made of bright green silk shirred on strong lengths of rattan or whalebone, and extendible after the fashion of a chaise top. It could be drawn out over the face by a little green ribbon or "bridle" that was fastened to the extreme front at the top; or it could be pushed in a close-gathered mass on the back of the head These calashes were frequently a foot and a half in diameter, and thus stood well up from the head and did not disarrange the hair nor crush the headdress or cap. They formed a perfect and easily-adjusted shade from the sun. Masks, too, the fair Puritans wore to further protect their heads and faces,--masks of green silk or black vehet, with silver mouthpieces to place within the lips and thus enable the wearer to keep the mask firmly in place. Sometimes two little strings with a silver bead at one end were fastened to the mask, and seined as mouthpieces. With a string and bead at either corner of the mouth the mask-wearer could talk quite freely while still retaining her face-covering in its protecting position. These masks were never worn within doors. In the list of goods ordered by George Washington from Europe for his fair bride Martha were several of these riding-masks, and the kind step-father even ordered a supply of small masks for "Miss Custis," his little step-daughter.

In bitter winter weather women carried to meeting little foot-stoves,-- metal boxes which stood on legs and were filled with hot coals at home, and a second time during the morning from the hearthstone of a neighboring farm-house or a noon-house. These foot-warmers helped to make endurable to the goodwives the icy chill of the meeting-house; and round their mother's foot-stove the shivering little children sat on their low crickets, warming their half-frozen fingers.

Some of these foot-stoves were really pretentious church-furnishings. I have seen one "brassen foot-stove" which had the owner's cipher cut out of the sheet metal, and from the side was hung a wrought brass chain. By this chain, a century ago, the shining polished brass stove was carried into church in the hands of a liveried black man, who held it ostentatiously at arms' length, that neither ash nor scorch might touch his scarlet velvet breeches. And after he had tucked it under my lady's tiny feet as she sat in her pew, he retired to his freezing loft high up among the beams,--the "Nigger Pew,"-- where, I am sorry to record, he more than once solaced and warmed himself with a bottle of "kill-devil" which he had smuggled into church, until he fell ignominiously asleep and his drunken snores so disturbed the minister and the congregation, that two tithingmen were forced to climb the ladder-like staircase and pull him down and out of the church and to the neighboring tavern to sleep off the effects of the liquor. For being "a man and a brother" and, above all, in spite of his petty idiosyncrasies, a very good and cherished servant, he could not be thrust out into the snow to freeze to death.

But with the extreme Puritan contempt of comfort even foot-stoves were not always allowed. The First Church of Roxbury, after having one church edifice destroyed by fire in 1747, prohibited the use of footstoves in meeting, and the Roxbury matrons sat with frozen toes in their fine new meeting-house. The Old South Church of Boston was not so rigid, though it felt the same dread of fire; for we find this entry on the records of the church under the date of January 10, 1771: "Whereas, danger is apprehended from the [foot] stoves that arc frequently left in the meeting-house after the publick worship is over; Voted, that the Saxton make diligent search on the Lord's Day evening and in the evening after a lecture, to see if any stoves are left in the house, and that if he find any there he take them to his own house; and it is expected that the owners of such stoves make reasonable satisfaction to the Saxton for his trouble before they take them away."

In Hardwicke, in 1792, it was ordered that "no stows be carried into our new meeting-house with fire in them." The Hardwicke women may have found comfort in a contrivance which is thus described in by an "old inhabitant:"

> "There to warm their feet
> Was seen an article now obsolete,
> A sort of basket tub of braided straw
> Or husks, in which is placed a heated stone,
> Which does half-frozen limbs superbly thaw.
> And warms the marrow of the oldest bone."

In some of the early, poorly built log meeting-houses, fur bags made of coarse skins, such as wolf-skin, were nailed or tied to the edges of the benches, and into these bags the worshippers thrust their feet for warmth. In some communities it was the custom for each family to bring on cold days its "dogg" to meeting; where, lying at or on his master's feet, he proved a source of grateful warmth. These animal stoves became such an abounding nuisance, however, that dog-whippers had to be appointed to serve on Sundays to drive out the dogs. All through the records of the early churches we find such entries as this: "Whatsoever doggs come into the meeting-house in time of public worship, their owners shall each pay sixpence." Sixpence seems little, but the thrifty and poor Puritans would rather freeze their toes than pay sixpence for their calorific dogs.

The church members made many rules and regulations to keep the cold out of the meeting-house during service-time, or perhaps we should say to keep the wind out. Thus in Woodstock, Connecticut, in 1725 it was ordered that the "several doors of the meeting-house be taken care of and kept shut in very cold and windy seasons according to the lying of the wind from time to time; and that people in such windy weather come in at the leeward doors only, and take care that they are easily shut both to prevent the breaking of the doors and the making of a noise." In other churches it was ordered that "no doors be opened to the windward and only one door to the leeward" during winter weather.

The first church of Salem built a "cattied chimney twelve feet long" in its meeting-house in 1662, but five years later it was removed, perhaps through the colonists' dread lest the building be destroyed by a conflagration caused by the combustible nature of the materials of which the chimney was composed. Felt, in his "Annals of Salem," asserts that the First Church of Boston was the first New England congregation to have a stove for heating the meeting-house at the time of public worship; this was in 1773. This statement is incorrect. Mr. Judd says the Hadley church had an iron stove in their meeting-house as early as 1734--the Hadley people were such sybarites and novelty-lovers in those early days! The Old South Church of Boston followed in the luxurious fashion in 1783, and the "Evening Post" of January 25, 1783, contained a poem of which these four lines show the criticising and deprecating spirit:--

> "Extinct the sacred fire of love,
>   Our zeal grown cold and dead,
> In the house of God we fix a stove
>   To warm us in their stead."

Other New England congregations piously froze during service-time well into this century. The Longmeadow church, early in the field, had a stove in 1810; the Salem people in 1815; and the Medford meeting in 1820. The church in Brimfield in 1819 refused to pay for a stove, but ordered as some sacrifice to the desire for comfort, two extra doors placed on the gallery-stairs to keep out draughts; but when in that town, a few years later, a subscription was made to buy a church stove, one old member refused to contribute, saying "good preaching kept him hot enough without stoves."

As all the church edifices were built without any thought of the possibility of such comfortable furniture, they had to be adapted as best they might to the ungainly and unsightly great stoves which were usually placed in the central aisle of the building. From these cast-iron monsters, there extended to the nearest windows and projected through them, hideous stove-pipes that too often spread, from every leaky and ill-fastened joint, smoke and sooty vapors, and sometimes pyroligneous drippings on the congregation. Often tin pails to catch the drippings were hung under the stove-pipes, forming a further chaste and elegant church-decoration. Many serious objections were made to the stoves besides the aesthetic ones. It was alleged that they would be the means of starting many destructive conflagrations; that they caused severe headaches in the church attendants; and worst of all, that the *heat warped the ladies' tortoise-shell back-combs*.

The church reformers contended, on the other hand, that no one could properly receive spiritual comfort while enduring such decided bodily discomfort. They hoped that with increased physical warmth, fervor in religion would be equally augmented,--that, as Cowper wrote,--

> "The churches warmed, they would no longer hold
> Such frozen figures, stiff as they are cold."

Many were the quarrels and discussions that arose in New England communities over the purchase and use of stoves, and many were the meetings held and votes taken upon the important subject.

"Peter Parley"--Mr. Samuel Goodrich--gave, in his "Recollections," a very amusing account of the sufferings endured by the wife of an anti-stove deacon. She came to church with a look of perfect resignation on the Sabbath of the stove's introduction, and swept past the unwelcome intruder with averted head, and into her pew. She sat there through the service, growing paler with the unaccustomed heat, until the minister's words about "heaping coals of fire" brought too keen a sense of the overwhelming and unhealthful stove-heat to her mind, and she fainted. She was carried out of church, and upon recovering said languidly that it "was the heat from the stove." A most complete and sudden resuscitation was effected, however, when she was informed of the fact that no fire had as yet been lighted in the new church-furnishing.

Similar chronicles exist about other New England churches, and bear a striking resemblance to each other. Rev. Henry Ward Beecher in an address delivered in New York on December 20, 1853, the anniversary of the Landing of the Pilgrims, referred to the opposition made to the introduction of stoves into the old meeting-house in Litchfield, Connecticut, during the ministry of his father, and gave an amusing account of the results of the introgression. This allusion called up many reminiscences of anti-stove wars, and a writer in the "New York Enquirer" told the same story of the fainting woman in Litchfield meeting, who began to fan herself and at length swooned, saying when she recovered "that the heat of the horrid stove had caused her to faint." A correspondent of the "Cleveland Herald" confirmed the fact that the fainting episode occurred in the Litchfield meeting-house. The editor of the "Hartford Daily Courant" thus added his testimony:--

> "Violent opposition had been made to the introduction of a stove in the old meeting-house, and an attempt made in vain to induce the soc to purchase one. The writer was one of seven young men who finally purchased a stove and requested permission to put it up in the meeting-house on trial. After much difficulty the committee consented. It was all arranged on Saturday afternoon, and on Sunday we took our seats in the Bass, rather earlier than usual, to see the fun. It was a warm November Sunday, in which the sun shone cheerfully and warmly on the old south steps and into the naked windows. The stove stood in the middle aisle, rather in front of the Tenor Gallery. People came in and stared. Good old Deacon Trowbridge, one of the most simple-

hearted and worthy men of that generation, had, as Mr. Beecher says, been induced to give up his opposition. He shook his head, however, as he felt the heat reflected from it, and gathered up the skirts of his great as he passed up the broad aisle to the deacon's seat. Old Uncle Noah Stone, a wealthy farmer of the West End, who sat near, scowled and muttered at the effects of the heat, but waited until noon to utter his maledictions over his nut-cakes and cheese at the intermission. There had in fact been *no fire in the stove*, the day being too warm. We were too much upon the broad grin to be very devotional, and smiled rather loudly at the funny things we saw. But when the editor of the village paper, Mr. Bunce, came in (who was a believer in stoves in churches) and with a most satisfactory air warmed his hands by the stove, keeping the skirts of his great-coat carefully between his knees, we could stand it no longer but dropped invisible behind the breastwork. But the climax of the whole was (as the Cleveland man says) when Mrs. Peck went out in the middle of the service. It was, however, the means of reconciling the whole society; for after that first day we heard no more opposition to the warm stove in the meeting-house."

With all this corroborative evidence I think it is fully proved that the event really happened in Litchfield, and that the honor was stolen for other towns by unveracious chroniclers; otherwise we must believe in an amazing unanimity of church-joking and sham-fainting all over New England.

The very nature, the stern, pleasure-hating and trial-glorying Puritan nature, which made our forefathers leave their English homes to come, for the love of God and the freedom of conscience, to these wild, barren, and unwelcoming shores, made them also endure with fortitude and almost with satisfaction all personal discomforts, and caused them to cling with persistent firmness to such outward symbols of austere contempt of luxury, and such narrow-minded signs of love of simplicity as the lack of comfortable warmth during the time of public worship. The religion which they had endured such bitter hardships to establish, did not, in their minds, need any shielding and coddling to keep it alive, but thrived far better on Spartan severity and simplicity; hence, it took two centuries of gradual and most tardy softening and modifying of character to prepare the Puritan mind for so advanced a reform and luxury as proper warmth in the meeting-houses in winter.

IX
The Noon-House

There might have been seen a hundred years ago, by the side of many an old meeting-house in New England, a long, low, mean, stable-like building, with a rough stone chimney at one end. This was the "noon-house," or "Sabba-day house," or "horse-hows," as it was variously called. It was a place of refuge in the winter time, at the noon interval between the two services, for the half-frozen members of the pious congregation, who found there the grateful warmth which the house of God denied. They built in the rude stone fireplace a great fire of logs, and in front of the blazing wood ate their noon-day meal of cold pie, of doughnuts, of pork and peas, or of brown bread with cheese, which they had brought safely packed in their capacious saddlebags. The dining-place smelt to heaven of horses, for often at the further end of the noon-house were stabled the patient steeds that, doubly burdened, had borne the Puritans and their wives to meeting; but this stable-odor did not hinder appetite, nor did the warm equine breaths that helped to temper the atmosphere of the noon-house offend the senses of the sturdy Puritans. From the blazing fire in this "life-saving station" the women replenished their little foot-stoves with fresh, hot coals, and thus helped to make endurable the icy rigor of the long afternoon service.

If the winter Sabbath Day were specially severe, a "hired-man," or one of the grown sons of the family, was sent at an early hour to the noon-house in advance of the other church-attendants, and he started in the rough fireplace a fire for their welcome after their long, cold, morning ride; and before its cheerful blaze they thoroughly warmed themselves before entering the icy meeting-house. The embers were carefully covered over and left to start a second blaze at the nooning, covered again during the afternoon service, and kindled up still a third time to warm the chilled worshippers ere they started for their cold ride home in the winter twilight. And when the horses were saddled, or were harnessed and hitched into the great box-sleighs or "pungs," and when the good Puritans were well wrapped up, the dying coals were raked out for safety and the noon-house was left as quiet and as cold as the deserted meeting-house until the following Sabbath or Lecture day.

If the meeting-house chanced to stand in the middle of the town (as was the universal custom in the earliest colonial days) of course a noon-house would be rarely built, for it would plainly not be needed. Nor was a "Sabba-day house" always seen in more lonely situations, if the sanctuary were placed near the substantial farm-house of a hospitable farmer; for to that friendly shelter the whole congregation would at noon-time repair and absorb to the fullest degree the welcome cider and warmth.

In Lexington for many years after the Revolutionary War, the winter church-goers who came from any distance spent the nooning at the Dudley Tavern, where a roaring fire was built in the inn-parlor, and there the women and children ate their midday lunch. The men gathered in the bar-room and drank flip, and ate the tavern gingerbread and cheese, and talked over the horrors and glories of the war. In Haverhill, Derby, and many other towns, the school-house, which was built on the village green beside the church, was used for a noon-house by the church members, though not by their horses. The house of learning was never chimneyless and fireless, as was the house of God.

As churches and towns multiplied, a meeting-house was often built to accommodate two little settlements or villages (and thus was convenient for neither), and was frequently placed in an isolated or inconvenient place, the top of a high hill being perhaps the most inconvenient and the most favored site. Thus a noon-house became an absolute necessity to Puritan health and existence, and often two or three were built near one meeting-house; while in some towns, as in Bristol, a whole row of disfiguring little "Sabba-day houses" stood on the meeting-house green, and in them the farmers (as they quaintly expressed in their petitions for permission to erect the buildings) "kept their duds and horses."

In Derby, after several petitions had been granted to build noon-houses, it was found necessary, in 1764, to place some restrictions as to the location of the buildings, which had hitherto evidently been placed with the characteristically Puritanical indifference to general convenience or appearance. While the town still permitted the little log-huts to be erected, and though they could be placed on either side of the highway, it was ordered that the builders must not so locate them as to "incommode any highways." As early as 1690 the thoughtful Stonington people built a house "14 foot square and seven foot posts" with a chimney at one side, for the express purpose of having a place where their minister, Rev. Mr. Noyes, could thaw out between services. The New Canaan Church built on the green beside their meeting-house a fine "Society House," twenty-one feet long and sixteen feet wide, with a big chimney and fireplace. The horses were plainly "not in society" in New Canaan, for they were excluded from the occupancy and privileges of the Society House.

"James June & all that lives at Larences" were allowed to build a "Sabbath-House" on the green near the New Britain meeting-house "as a Commodate for their conveniency of comeing to meeting on the Sabbath;" at the same time James Slason of the same village was given permission to "set yp a house for ye advantage of his having a place to go to" on the Sabbath. Frequently the petitions "to build a Sabbath Day House" or a "Housel for Shelter for Horss" were made in company by several farmers for their joint use and comfort, as shown by entries in the town and church records of Norwalk, New Milford, Durham, and Hartford.

Noon-houses were much more frequent in Connecticut than in Massachusetts, and in several small towns in the former State they were used weekly between Sunday services until within the memory of persons now living; and some of the buildings still exist, though changed into granaries or stables. There was one also in use for many years and until recent years in Topsfield, in Massachusetts. We chanced upon one still standing on a lonely Narragansett road. A little enclosed burial-place, with moss-grown and weather-smoothed head-stones and neglected graves, was by the side of a filled-in cellar, upon which a church evidently had once stood. At a short distance from the church-site was a long, low, gray, weather-beaten wooden building, with a coarse stone-and-mortar chimney at one end, and a great door at the other. Two small windows, destitute of glass, permitted us to peer into the interior of this dilapidated old structure, and we saw within, a floor of beaten earth, a rough stone fireplace, and a few rude horse-stalls. We felt sure that this tumble-down building had been neither a dwelling-house nor a stable, but a noon-house; and the occupants of a neighboring farm-house confirmed our decision. Too worthless to destroy, too out of the way to be of any use to any person, that old noon-house, through neglect and isolation, has remained standing until to-day.

It was not until the use of chaises and wagons became universal, and the new means of conveyance crowded out the old-fashioned saddle and pillion, and the trotting horse superseded the once fashionable but quickly despised pacer, that the great stretches of horse-sheds were built which now surround and disfigure all our country churches. These sheds protect, of course, both horse and carriage from wind and rain. Few churches had horse-sheds until after the War the Revolution, and some not until after the War of 1812. In 1796 the Longmeadow Church had "liberty to erect a Horse House in the Meeting House Lane." This horse house was a horse-shed.

The "wretched boys" were not permitted even in these noon-houses to talk, much less to "sporte and playe." In some parishes it was ordered by the minister and the deacons that the Bible should be read and expounded to them, or a sermon be read to keep them quiet during the nooning. Occasionally some old patriarch would explain to them the notes that he had taken during the morning sermon. More unbearable still, the boys were sometimes ordered to explain the notes which they had taken themselves. I would I had heard some of those explanations! Thus they literally, as was written in 1774, throve on the "Good Fare of Brown Bread and the Gospell."

In Andover, Judge Phillips left in his will a silver flagon to the church as an expression of interest and hope that the "laudable practice of reading between services may be continued so long as even a small number shall be disposed to attend the exercise." Mr. Abbott left another silver flagon to the Andover Church to encourage reading between services; though how this piece of plate encouraged personally, since neither the deacons nor the boys got it as a prize, cannot be precisely understood. The noon-house in Andover was a large building with a great chimney and open fireplace at either end. It has always seemed to me a piece of gratuitous posthumous cruelty in Judge Phillips and Mr. Abbott to try to cheat those Andover boys of their noon-time rest and relaxation, and to expect them, wriggling and twisting with repressed vitality, to listen to a long extra sermon, read perhaps by some unskilled reader, or explained by some incapable expounder. The Sabbath-school did not then exist, and was not in general favor until the noon-houses had begun to disappear. The Reverend Jedediah Morse, father of the inventor of the electric telegraph, was almost the first New England clergyman who approved of Sabbath-schools and established them in his parish. In Salem they were opened in 1808, and the scholars came at half-past six on Sunday mornings. Fancy the chill and gloom of the unheated, ill-lighted churches at that hour on winter mornings. The "Salem Gazette" openly characterized Sunday-schools, when first suggested, as profanations of the Sabbath, and for years they were not allowed in many Congregational churches. When the Sabbath-schools were universally established, and thus the attention and interest of the children was gained during the noon interval (the time the schools were usually held in country churches), and when each family sat in its own pew, and thus the boys were separated, and each under his parents' guardianship, the "wretched boys" of the Puritan Sabbath disappeared, and well-behaved, quiet, orderly boys were seen instead in the New England churches.

This fashion of sermon-reading at the nooning happily did not obtain in all parts of New England. In many villages the meetings in the society noon-houses were to the townspeople what a Sunday newspaper is to Sunday readers now-a-days, an advertisement and exposition of all the news of the past week, and also a suggestion of events to come. At noon they discussed and wondered at the announcements and publishings which were tacked on the door of the meeting-house or the notices that had been read from the pulpit. The men talked in loud voices of the points of the sermon, of the doctrines of predestination pedobaptism and antipedobaptism, of original sin, and that most fascinating mystery, the unpardonable sin, and in lower voices of wolf and bear killing, of the town-meeting, the taxes, the crops and cattle; and they examined with keen interest one another's horses, and many a sly bargain in horse-flesh or exchange of cows and pigs was suggested, bargained over, and clinched in the "Sabba'-day house." Many a piece of village electioneering was also discussed and "worked" between the services. The shivering women crowded around the blazing and welcome fire, and seated themselves on rude benches and log seats while they ate and exchanged doughnuts, slices of rusk, or pieces of "pumpkin and Indian mixt" pie, and also gave to each other receipts therefor; and they discoursed in low voices of their spinning and weaving, of their candle-dipping or candle-running, of their success or failure in that yearly trial of patience and skill--their soap-making, of their patterns in quilt-piecing, and sometimes they slyly exchanged quilt-patterns. A sentence in an old letter reads thus: "Anne Bradford gave to me last Sabbath in the Noon House a peecing of the Blazing Star; tis much Finer than the Irish Chain or the Twin Sisters. I want yelloe peeces for the first joins, small peeces will do. I will send some of my lilac flowered print for some peeces of Cicelys yelloe India bed vallants, new peeces not washed peeces." They gave one another medical advice and prescriptions of "roots and yarbs" for their "rheumatiz," "neuralgy," and "tissick;" and some took snuff together, while an ancient dame smoked a quiet pipe. And perhaps (since they were women as well as Puritans) they glanced with envy, admiration, or disapproval, or at any rate with close scrutiny, at one another's gowns and bonnets and cloaks, which the high-walled pews within the meeting-house had carefully concealed from any inquisitive, neighborly view.

The wood for these beneficent noon-house fires was given by the farmers of the congregation, a load by each well-to-do land-owner, if it were a "society-house," and occasionally an apple-growing farmer gave a barrel of "cyder" to supply internal instead of external warmth. Cider sold in 1782 for six shillings "Old Tenor" a barrel, so it was worth about the same as the wood both in money value and calorific qualities. A hundred years previously--in 1679--cider was worth ten shillings a barrel. In 1650, when first made in America, it was a costly luxury, selling for £4 4s. a barrel. That this thawed-out Sunday barrel of cider would prove invariably a source of much refreshment, inspiration, solace, tongue-loosing, and blood-warming to the chilled and shivering deacons, elders, and farmers who gathered in the noon-house, any one who has imbibed that all-potent and intoxicating beverage, oft-frozen "hard" cider, can fervently testify.

Sometimes a very opulent farmer having built a noon-house for his own and his family's exclusive use, would keep in it as part of his "duds" a few simple cooking utensils in which his wife or daughters would re-heat or partially cook his noon-day Sabbath meal, and mix for him a hot toddy or punch, or a mug of that "most insinuating drink"--flip. Flip was made of home-brewed beer, sugar, and a liberal dash of Jamaica rum, and was mixed with a "logger-head"--a great iron "stirring-stick" which was heated in the fire until red hot and then thrust into the liquid. This seething iron made the flip boil and bubble and imparted to it a burnt, bitter taste which was its most attractive attribute. I doubt not that many a "loggerhead" was kept in New England noon-houses and left heating and gathering insinuating goodness in the glowing coals, while the pious owner sat freezing in the meeting-house, also gathering goodness, but internally keeping warm at the thought of the bitter nectar he should speedily brew and gladly imbibe at the close of the long service.

The comfort of a hot midday dinner on the Sabbath was not regarded with much favor, though perhaps with secret envy, by the neighbors of the luxury-loving farmer, who saw in it too close an approach to "profanation of the Sabbath." The heating and boiling of the flip with the red hot "loggerhead" hardly came under the head of "unnecessary Sabbath cooking" even in the minds of the most straight-laced descendants of the Puritans.

When stoves were placed and used in the New England meeting-houses, the noon-day lunches were eaten within the pews inside the sanctuary, and the noon-houses, no longer being needed, followed the law of cause and effect, and like many other institutions of the olden times quickly disappeared.

X
The Deacon's Office

The deacons in the early New England churches had, besides their regular duties on the Lord's Day, and their special duties on communion Sabbaths, the charge of prudential concerns, and of providing for the poor of the church. They also "dispensed the word" on Sabbaths to the congregation during the absence of the ordained minister. Judge Sewall thus describes in his diary under the date of November, 1685, the method at that time of appointing or ordaining a deacon:--

> "In afternoon Mr. Willard ordained our Brother Theophilus Frary to the office of a Deacon. Declared his acceptance January 11th first now again. Propounded him to the congregation at Noon. Then in even propounded him if any of the church of other had to object they might speak. Then took the Church's Vote, then call'd him up to the Pulpit, laid his Hand on's head, and said I ordain Thee, etc., etc., gave him his charge, then Prayed & sung 2nd Part of 84th Psalm."

The deacons always sat near the pulpit in a pew, which was generally raised a foot or two above the level of the meeting-house floor, and which contained, usually, several high-backed chairs and a table or a broad swinging-shelf for use at the communion service. These venerable men were a group of awe-inspiring figures, who, next to the parson, received the respect of the community. In Bristol, Connecticut, the deacons wore starched white linen caps in the meeting-house to indicate their office,--a singular local custom. One of their duties in many communities was naturally to furnish the sacramental wines, and the money for the payment thereof was allowed to them from the church-rates, or was raised by special taxation. In Farmington, Connecticut, in 1669, each male inhabitant was ordered to pay a peck of wheat or one shilling to the deacons of the church to defray the expenses of the sacrament. In Groton church, in 1759, "4 Coppers for every Sacrament for 1 year" was demanded from each communicant. In Springfield the "deacon's rate" was paid in "wampam,"--sixpence in "wampam" or a peck of Indian corn from each family in the town. This special tax was somewhat modified in case a man had no wife, or if he were not a church-member, but in the latter case he still had to pay some dues, though of course he could not take part in the communion service. In 1734 the Milton church ordered the deacons to procure "good Canary Wine for the Communion Table." Abuses sometimes arose,--abominably poor wines were furnished, though full rates were paid for the purchase of wine of good quality; and in Newbury the man who was appointed to furnish the sacramental wines, sold, under that religious cover, wine and liquors at retail.

The deacons also had charge of the vessels used in the communion service. These vessels were frequently stored, when not in use, under the pulpit in a little closet which opened into "the Ministers wives pue," and which was fabled to be at the disposal of the tithingmen and deacons for the darksome incarceration of unruly and Sabbath-breaking boys. The communion vessels were not always of valuable metal; John Cotton's first church had wooden chalices; the wealthier churches owned pieces of silver which had been given to them, one piece at a time, by members or friends of the church; but communion services of pewter were often seen.

The church in Hanover, Massachusetts, bought a pewter service in 1728, and the record of the purchase still exists. It runs thus:--

3 Pewter Tankards marked C. T. 10 shillings.

5 " Beakers " C. B. 6 sh. 6d. each.

2 " Platters " C. P. 5 sh. each.

1 " Basin for Baptisms.

This pewter service is still owned by the Hanover church, a highly prized relic. Until 1753 the church in Andover used a pewter communion service, but when a silver service was given to it, the Andover church sent the vessels of baser metal to a sister church in Methuen. In Haverhill the will of a church-member named White gave to the church absolutely the pewter dishes which were used at the sacrament, and which had been his personal property. The "ffirst church" of Hartford had "one Puter fflagon, ffower pewter dishes, and a bason" left to it by the bequest of one of its members. When the Danvers church was burned in 1805, the pewter communion vessels were saved while the silver ones were either burnt or stolen. As pewter was, in the early days of New England, far from being a despised metal, and as pewter dishes and plates were seen on the tables of the wealthiest families, were left by will as precious possessions, were engraved with initials and stamped with coats of arms, and polished with as much care as were silver vessels, a communion service of pewter was doubtless felt to be a thoroughly satisfactory acquisition and appointment to a Puritan church.

The deacons of course took charge of the church contributions. Lechford, in his "Plaine Dealing," thus describes the manner of giving in the Boston church in 1641:--

> "Baptism being ended, follows the contribution, one of the deacons saying, 'Brethren of the Congregation, now there is time left for contribution, whereof as God has prospered you so freely offer.' The Magistrates and chief gentlemen first, and then the Elders and all the Congregation of them, and most of them that are not of the church, all single persons, widows and women in absence of their husbands, came up one after another one way, and bring their offering to the deacon at his seat, and put it into a box of wood for the purpose, if it be money or papers. If it be any other Chattel they set or lay it down before the deacons; and so pass on another way to their seats again; which money and goods the Deacons dispose towards the maintenance of the Minister, and the poor of the Church, and the Churches occasions without making account ordinarily."

Lechford also said he saw a "faire gilt cup" given at the public contribution; and other gifts of value to the church and minister were often made. Libellous verses too were thrown into the contribution boxes, and warning and gloomy messages from the Quakers; and John Rogers, in derision of a pompous New London minister, threw in the insulting contribution of an old periwig. One Puritan goodwife, sternly unforgiving, never saw a contribution taken for proselyting the Indians without depositing in the contribution-box a number of leaden bullets, the only tokens she wished to see ever dispersed among the red men.

Even our pious forefathers were not always quite honest in their church contributions, and had to be publicly warned, as the records show, that they must deposit "wampum without break or deforming spots," or "passable peage without breaches." The New Haven church was particularly tormented by canny Puritans who thus managed to dispose of their broken and worthless currency with apparent Christian generosity. In 1650 the New Haven "deacons informed the Court that the wampum which is putt into the Church Treasury is generally so bad that the Elders to whom they pay it cannot pay it away."

In 1651, as the bad wampum was still paid in by the pious New Haven Puritans, it was ordered that "no money save silver or bills" be accepted by the deacons. After this order the deacons and elders found tremendous difficulty in getting any contributions at all, and many are the records of the actions and decisions of the church in regard to the perplexing matter.

It should be said, in justice to the New Haven colonists, though they were the most opulent of the New England planters, save the wealthy settlers of Narragansett, that money of all kinds was scarce, and that the Indian money, wampum-peag, being made of a comparatively frail sea-shell, was more easily disfigured and broken than was metal coin; and that there was little transferable wealth in the community anyway, even in "Country Pay." The broken-wampum-giver of the seventeenth century, who contributed with intent to defraud and deceive the infant struggling church was the direct and lineal ancestor of the sanctimonious button-giver of nineteenth-century country churches.

In Revolutionary times, after the divine service, special contributions were taken for the benefit of the Continental Army. In New England large quantities of valuable articles were thus collected. Not only money, but finger-rings, earrings, watches, and other jewelry, all kinds of male attire,--stockings, hats, coats, breeches, shoes,--produce and groceries of all kinds, were brought to the meeting-house to give to the soldiers. Even the leaden weights were taken out of the window-sashes, made into bullets, and brought to meeting. On one occasion Madam Faith Trumbull rose up in Lebanon meeting-house in Connecticut, when a collection was being made for the army, took from her shoulders a magnificent scarlet cloak, which had been a present to her from Count Rochambeau, the commander-in-chief of the French allied army, and advancing to the altar, gave it as her offering to the gallant men, who were fighting not only the British army, but terrible want and suffering. The fine cloak was cut into narrow strips and used as red trimmings for the uniforms of the soldiers. The romantic impressiveness of Madam Trumbull's patriotic act kindled warm enthusiasm in the congregation, and an enormous collection was taken, packed carefully, and sent to the army.

One early duty of the deacons which was religiously and severely performed was to watch that no one but an accepted communicant should partake of the holy sacrament. One stern old Puritan, having been officially expelled from church-membership for some temporal rather than spiritual offence, though ignored by the all-powerful deacon, still refused to consider himself excommunicated, and calmly and doggedly attended the communion service bearing his own wine and bread, and in the solitude of his own pew communed with God, if not with his fellow-men. For nearly twenty years did this austere man rigidly go through this lonely and sad ceremonial, until he conquered by sheer obstinacy and determination, and was again admitted to church-fellowship.

A very extraordinary custom prevailed in several New England churches. Through it the deacons were assigned a strange and serious duty which appeared to make them all-important and possibly self-important, and which must have weighed heavily upon them, were they truly godly, and conscientious in the performance of it. In the rocky little town of Pelham in the heart of Massachusetts, toward the close of the eighteenth century and during the pastorate of the notorious thief, counterfeiter, and forger, Rev. Stephen Burroughs, that remarkable rogue organized and introduced to his parishioners the custom of giving during the month a metal check to each worthy and truly virtuous church-member, on presentation of which the check-bearer was entitled to partake of the communion, and without which he was temporarily excommunicated. The duty of the deacon in this matter was to walk up and down the aisles of the church at the close of each service and deliver to the proper persons (proper in the deacon's halting human judgment) the significant checks. The deacon had also to see that this religionistic ticket was presented on the communion Sabbath. Great must have been the disgrace of one who found himself checkless at the end of the month, and greater even than the heart-burnings over seating the meeting must have been the jealousies and church quarrels that arose over the communion-checks. And yet no records of the protests or complaints of indignant or grieving parishioners can be found, and the existence of the too worldly, too business-like custom is known to us only through tradition.

Many of the little chips called "Presbyterian checks" are, however, still in existence. They are oblong discs of pewter, about an inch and a half long, bearing the initials "P. P.," which stand, it is said, for "Pelham Presbyterian." I could not but reflect, as I looked at the simple little stamped slips of metal, that in a community so successful in the difficult work of counterfeiting coin, it would have been very easy to form a mould and cast from it spurious checks with which to circumvent the deacons and preserve due dignity in the meeting.

The Presbyterian checks have never been attributed in Massachusetts to other than the Pelham church, and are usually found in towns in the vicinity of Pelham; and there the story of their purpose and use is universally and implicitly believed. A clergyman of the Pelham church gave to many of his friends these Presbyterian checks, which he had found among the disused and valueless church-properties, and the little relics of the old-time deacons and services have been carefully preserved.

In New Hampshire, however, a similar custom prevailed in the churches of Londonderry and the neighboring towns.. The Londonderry settlers were Scotch-Irish Presbyterians (and the Pelham planters were an off-shoot of the Londonderry settlement), and they followed the custom of the Scotch

Presbyterians in convening the churches twice a year to partake of the Lord's Supper. This assembly was always held in Londonderry, and ministers and congregations gathered from all the towns around. Preparatory services were held on Thursday, Friday, and Saturday. Long tables were placed in the aisles of the church on the Sabbath; and after a protracted and solemn address upon the deep meaning of the celebration and the duties of the church-members, the oldest members of the congregation were seated at the table and partook of the sacrament. Thin cakes of unleavened bread were specially prepared for this sacred service. Again and again were the tables refilled with communicants, for often seven hundred church-members were present. Thus the services were prolonged from early morning until nightfall. When so many were to partake of the Lord's Supper, it seemed necessary to take means to prevent any unworthy or improper person from presenting himself. Hence the tables were fenced off, and each communicant was obliged to present a "token." These tokens were similar to the "Presbyterian checks;" they were little strips of lead or pewter stamped with the initials "L. D.," which may have stood for "Londonderry" or "Lord's Day." They were presented during the year by the deacons and elders to worthy and pious church-members. This bi-annual celebration of the Lord's Supper-- this gathering of old friends and neighbors from the rocky wilds of New Hampshire to join, in holy communion--was followed on Monday by cheerful thanksgiving and social intercourse, in which, as in every feast, our old friend, New England rum, played no unimportant part. The three days previous to the communion Sabbath were, however, solemnly devoted to the worship of God; a Londonderry man was reproved and prosecuted for spreading grain upon a Thursday preceding a communion Sunday, just as he would have been for doing similar work upon the Sabbath. The use of these "tokens" in the Londonderry church continued until the year 1830.

In the coin collection of the American Antiquarian Society are little pewter communion-checks, or tokens, stamped with a heart. These were used in the Presbyterian church in Philadelphia, and were delivered to pious church-members at the Friday evening prayer-meeting preceding the communion Sabbath. Long tables were set in the aisles, as at Londonderry. In practice, belief, and origin, the New Hampshire and Pennsylvania churches were sisters.

The deacons had many minor duties to perform in the different parishes. Some of these duties they shared with the tithingman. They visited the homes of the church-members to hear the children say the catechism, they visited and prayed with the sick, and they also reported petty offences, though they were not accorded quite so powerful legal authority as the tithingmen and constables.

It was much desired by several of the first-settled ministers that there should be deaconesses in the New England Puritan church, and many good reasons were given for making such appointments. It was believed that for the special duty of visiting the sick and afflicted in the community deaconesses would be more useful than deacons. There had been an aged deaconess in the Puritan church in Holland, who with a "little birchen rod" had kept the children in awe and order in meeting, and who had also exercised "her guifts" in speaking; but when she died no New England successor was appointed to fill her place.

XI
The Psalm-Book of the Pilgrims

We read in "The Courtship of Miles Standish," of the fair Priscilla, when John Alden came to woo her for his friend, the warlike little captain, that

> "Open wide on her lap lay the well-worn psalm-book of Ainsworth, Printed in Amsterdam, the words and the music together; Rough-hewn, angular notes, like stones in the wall of a churchyard, Darkened and overhung by the running vine of the verses. Such was the book from whose pages she sang the old Puritan anthem."

One of these "well-worn psalm-books of Ainsworth" lies now before me, perhaps the very one from which the lonely Priscilla sang as she sat a-spinning.

There is something especially dear to the lover and dreamer of the olden time, to the book-lover and antiquary as well, in an old, worn psalm or hymn book. It speaks quite as eloquently as does an old Bible of loving daily use, and adds the charm of interest in the quaint verse to reverence for the sacred word. A world of tender fancies springs into life as I turn over the pages of any old psalm-book "reading between the lines," and as I decipher the faded script on the titlepage. But this "psalm-book of Ainsworth," this book loved and used by the Pilgrims, brought over in one of those early ships, perhaps in the "Mayflower" itself, this book so symbolic of those early struggling days in New England, has a romance, a charm, an interest which thrills every drop of Puritan blood in my veins.

It is pleasing, too, this "Ainsworth's Version," aside from any thought of its historic associations; its square pages of diversified type are well printed, and have a quaint unfamiliar look which is intensely attractive, and to which the odd, irregular notes of music, the curiously ornamented head and tail pieces, and the occasional Hebrew or Greek letters add their undefinable charm.

It is a square quarto of three hundred and forty-eight closely printed pages, bound in time-stained but well-preserved parchment, and even the parchment itself is interesting, and lovely to the touch. The titlepage is missing, but I know that this is the edition printed, as was Priscilla's, in Amsterdam in 1612 (not "in England in 1600" as a note written in the last blank page states). The full title was "The Book of Psalms. Englished both in Prose and Metre. With annotations opening the words and sentences by conference with other Scriptures. Eph. v: 18,19. Bee yee filled with the Spirit speaking to yourselves in Psalms and Hymns and Spiritual-Songs singing and making melodie in your hearts to the Lord." The book contains besides the Psalms and Annotations, on its first pages, a "Preface declaring the reason and use of the Book;" and at the last pages a "Table directing to some principal things observed in the Annotations of the Psalms," a list of "Hebrew phrases observed which are somewhat hard and figurative," and also some "General Observations touching the Psalms."

I can well imagine what a pious delight this book was to our Pilgrim Fathers; and what a still greater delight it was to our Pilgrim Mothers, in that day and country of few books. They possessed in it, not only a wonderful new metrical version of the Psalms for singing, but a prose version for comparison as well; and the deeply learned and profoundly worded annotations placed at the end of each Psalm were doubtless of special interest to such "scripturists with all their hearts" as they were.

There were also, "for the use and edification of the saints," printed above each psalm the airs of appropriate tunes. The "rough-hewn, angular notes" are irregularly lozenge-shaped, like the notes or "pricks" in Queen Elizabeth's "Virginal-Book," and are placed on the staff without bars. Ainsworth, in his preface, says, "Tunes for the Psalms I find none set of God: so that ech people is to use the most grave decent and comfortable manner that they know how, according to the general rule. The singing notes I have most taken from our Englished psalms when they will fit the mesure of the verse: and for the other long verses I have also taken (for the most part) the gravest and easiest tunes of the French and Dutch psalmes." Easy the tunes certainly are, to the utmost degree of simplicity.

Great diversity too of type did the Pilgrims find in their Psalm-book: Roman type, Italics, black-letter, all were used; the verse was printed in Italics, the prose in Roman type, and the annotation in black-letter and small Roman text with close-spaced lines. This variety though picturesque makes the text rather difficult to read; for while one can decipher black-letter readily enough when reading whole pages of it, when it is interspersed with other type it makes the print somewhat confusing to the unaccustomed eye.

One curious characteristic of the typography is the frequent use of the hyphen, compound words or rather compound phrases being formed apparently without English rule or reason. Such combinations as these are given as instances: "highly-him-preferre," "renowned-name," "repose-me-quietlie," "in-mind-uplay," "turn-to-ashes," "my-alonely-soul," "beat-them-final," "pouring-out-them-hard," "inveyers-mak-streight," and "condemn-thou-them-as-guilty,"--which certainly would make fit verses to be sung to the accompaniment of Master Mace's "excellent-large-plump-lusty-fullspeaking-organ."

Ainsworth's Version when read proves to be a scholarly book, exhibiting far better grammar and punctuation and more uniformity of spelling than "The New England Psalm-book," which at a later date displaced Ainsworth in the affections and religious services of the New England Puritans and Pilgrims. Both versions are somewhat confused in sense, and of uncouth and grotesque versification; though the metre of Ainsworth is better than the rhyme. It is all written in "common metre," nearly all in lines of eight and six syllables alternately.

The name of the author of this version was Henry Ainsworth; he was the greatest of all the Holland Separatists, a typical Elizabethan Puritan, who left the church in which he was educated and attached himself to the Separatists, or Brownists, as they were called. He went into exile in Amsterdam in 1593, and worked for some time as a porter in a book-seller's shop, living (as Roger Williams wrote) "upon ninepence in the weeke with roots boyled." He established, with the Reverend Mr. Johnson, the new church in Holland; and when it was divided by dissension, he became the pastor of the "Ainsworthian Brownists" and so remained for twelve years. He was a most accomplished scholar, and was called the "rabbi of his age." Governor Bradford, in his "Dialogue," written in 1648, says of Ainsworth, "He had not his better for the Hebrew tongue in the University nor scarce in Europe." Hence, naturally, he was constantly engaged upon some work of translating or commentating, and still so highly prized is some of his work that it has been reprinted during this century. He also, being a skilful disputant, wrote innumerable controversial pamphlets and books, many of which still exist. It is said that he once had a long and spirited controversy with a brother divine as to whether the ephod of Aaron were blue or green. I fear we of to-day have lost much that the final, decisive judgment from so learned scholars and students as to the correct color has not descended to us, and now, if we wish to know, we shall have to fight it all over again.

In spite of his power of argument (or perhaps on account of it) the most prominent part which Ainsworth seemed to take in Amsterdam for many years was that of peacemaker, as many of his contemporaries testify: for they quarrelled fiercely among themselves in the exiled church, though they had such sore need of unity and good fellowship; and they had many church arguments and judgments and lawsuits. They quarrelled over the exercise of power in the church; over the true meaning of the text Matthew xviii. 17; whether the members of the congregation should be allowed to look on their Bibles during the preaching or on their Psalm-books during the singing; whether they should sing at all in their meetings; over the power of the office of ruling elder (a fruitful source of dissension and disruption in the New England congregations likewise) and above all, they quarrelled long and bitterly over the unseemly and gay dress of the parson's wife, Madam Johnson. These were the terrible accusations that were brought against that bedizened Puritan: that she wore "her bodies tied to the petticote with points as men do their doublets and hose; contrary to I Thess. v: 22, conferred with Deut. xx: 11;" that she also wore "lawn coives," and "busks," and "whalebones in the petticote bodies," and a "veluet hoode," and a "long white brest;" and that she "stood gazing bracing and vaunting in the shop dores;" and that "men called her a bounceing girl" (as if she could help that!). And one of her worst and most bitterly condemned offences was that she wore "a topish hat." This her husband vehemently denied; and long discussions and explanations followed on the hat's topishness,--"Mr. Ainsworth dilating much upon a greeke worde" (as of course so learned a man would). For the benefit of unlearned modern children of the Puritans let me give the old Puritan's precise explanation and classification of topishness. "Though veluet in its nature were not topish, yet if common mariners should weare such it would be a sign of pride and topishness in them. Also a gilded raper and a feather are not topish in their nature, neither in a captain to weare them, and yet if a minister should weare them they would be signs of great vanity topishness and lightness." I wonder that topish hat had not undone the whole Puritan church in Holland.

In settling all these and many other disputes, in translating, commentating, and versifying, did Henry Ainsworth pass his days; until, worn out by hard labor, and succumbing to long continued weakness, he died in 1623. This romantic story of his death is told by Neal. "It was sudden and not without suspicion of violence; for it is reported that, having found a diamond of very great value in the streets of Amsterdam, he advertised it in print; and when the owner, who was a Jew, came to demand it, he offered him any acknowledgment he would desire, but Ainsworth though poor would accept of nothing but conference with some of his rabbis upon the prophecies of the Old Testament relating to the Messiah, which the other promised, but not having interest enough to obtain it he was poisoned." This rather ambiguous sentence means that Ainsworth was poisoned, not the Jew. Brooks's account of the story is that the conference took place, the Jews were vanquished, and in revenge poisoned the champion of Christianity afterwards. Dexter most unromantically throws cold water on this poisoning story, and adduces much circumstantial testimony to prove its improbability; but it could hardly have been invented in cold blood by the Puritan historians, and must have had some foundation in truth. And since he is dead, and the thought cannot harm him, I may acknowledge that I firmly believe and I like to believe that he died in so romantic a way.

The Puritans were psalm-singers ever; and in Holland the Brownist division of the church came under strong influences from Geneva and Wittenberg, the birth-places of psalm-singing, that made them doubly fond of "worship in song." Hence the Pilgrim Fathers, Brewster, Bradford, Carver, and Standish, for love of music as well as in affectionate testimony to their old pastor and friend, brought to the New World copies of his version of the Psalms and sang from it with delight and profit to themselves, if not with ease and elegance.

Dexter says very mildly of Ainsworth's literary work that "there are diversities of gifts, and it is no offence to his memory to conclude that he shone more as an exegete than as a poet." Poesy is a gift of the gods and cometh not from deep Hebrew study nor from vast learning, and we must accept Ainsworth's pious enthusiasm in the place of poetic fervor. Of the quality of his work, however, it is best to judge for one's self. Here is his rendition of the Nineteenth Psalm, so well known to us in verse by Addison's glorious "The spacious firmament on high." The prose version is printed in one column and the verse by its side.

1. To the Mayster of the Musik: A Psalm of David

2. The heavens, doo tel the glory of God: and the out-spred firmament shevveth; the work of his hand.

3. Day unto day uttereth speech: and night unto night manifesteth knowledge:

4. No speech, and no words: not heard is their voice

5. Through all the earth, gone-forth is their line: and unto the utmost-end of the world their speakings: he hath put a tent in them for the sun.

6. And he; as a bridegroom, going-forth out of his privy-chamber: joyes as a mighty-man to run a race

7. From the utmost end of the heavens is his egress; and his compassing-regress is unto the utmost-ends of them: and none *is* hidd, from his heat.

2. The heav'ne, doo tel the glory of God and his firmament dooth preach.

3. work of his hands. Day unto day dooth largely-utter speach and night unto night dooth knowledge shew

4. No speach, and words are none.

5. thier voice it-is not heard. Thier line through all the earth is gone: and to the worlds end, thier speakings: in them he did dispose,

6. tent for the Sun. Who-bride-groom-like out of his chamber goes: joyes strong-man-like, to run a race

7. From heav'ns end, his egress: and his regress to the end of them hidd from his heat, none is:

In order to show the proportion of annotation in the book, and to indicate the mental traits of the author, let me state that this psalm, in both prose and metrical versions, occupies about one page; while the closely printed annotations fill over three pages; which is hardly "explaining with brevitie," as Ainsworth says in his preface. With this psalm the notes commence thus:--

"2. (the out-spred-firmament) the whole cope of heaven, with the aier which though it be soft and liquid and spred over the Earth, yet it is fast and firm and therefore called of us according to the common Greek version a firmament: the holy Ghost expresseth it by another term Mid-heaven. This out-spred-firmament of expansion God made amidds the waters for a separation and named it Heaven, which of David is said to be stretched out as courtayn and elsewhere is said to be as firm as moulten glass. So under this name firmament be commised the orbs of the heav'ns and the aier and the whole spacious country above the earth."

These annotations must have formed to the Pilgrims not only a dictionary but a perfect encyclopædia of useful knowledge. Things spiritual and things temporal were explained therein. Scientific, historic, and religious information were dispensed impartially. Much and varied instruction was given in Natural History, though viewed of course from a strictly religious point of view. The little Pilgrims learned from their Psalm-Book that the "Leviathan is the great whalefish or seadragon, so called of the fast joyning together of his scales as he is described Job 40: 20, 41 and is used to resemble great tyrants." They also learned that "Lions of sundry-kinds have sundry-names. Tear-in-pieces like a lion. That he ravin not, make-a-prey; called a plueker Renter or Tearer, and elsewhere Laby that is, Harty and couragious; Kphir, this lurking, Couchant. The reason of thier names is shewed, as The renting-lion as greedy to tear, and the lurking-Lion as biding in covert places. Other names are also given to this kind as Shachal, of ramping, of fierce nature; and Lajith of subduing his prey. Psalm LVI Lions called here Lebain, harty, stowt couragious, Lions. Lions are mentioned in the Scriptures for the stowtness of thier hart, boldnes, and grimnes of thier countenance."

Here are other annotations taken at hap-hazard. The lines,

> "Al they that doo upon me look
> a scoff at me doe make
> they with the lip do make-a-mow
> the head they scornful-shake,"

Ainsworth thus explains: "Make-a-mow, making-an-opening with the lip which may be taken both for mowing and thrusting out of the lip and for licentious opening thereof to speak reproach." The expression "Keep thou me as the black of the apple of the eye" is thus annotated: "The black, that is, the sight in the midds of the eye wherein appeareth the resemblance of a little man, and thereupon seemeth to be called in Hebrew Ishon which is a man. And as that part is blackish so this word is also used for other black things as the blackness of night. The apple so we call that which the Hebrew here calleth bath and babath that is the babie or little image appearing in the eye." Anger receives this definition: "ire, outward in the face, grauue, grimnes or fiercenes of countenance. The original Aph signifieth both the nose by which one breatheth, and Anger which appeareth in the snuffing or breathing of the nose."

Before the Holland exiles had this version of Ainsworth's to sing from, they used the book known as "Sternhold and Hopkins' Psalms." They gave it up gladly to show honor to the work of their loved pastor, and perhaps also with a sense of pleasure in not having to sing any verses which had been used and authorized by the Church of England. In doing this they had to abandon, however, such spirited lines as Sternhold's--

> "The earth did shake, for feare did quake
> the hills their bases shook.
> Removed they were, in place most fayre
> at God's right fearfull looks.
>
> "He rode on hye, and did soe flye Upon the cherubins
> He came in sight and made his flight Upon the winges of windes."

They sung instead,--

> "And th' earth did shake and quake and styrred bee
> grounds of the mount: & shook for wroth was hee
> Smoke mounted, in his wrath, fyre did eat
> out of his mouth: from it burned-with heat."

Alas, poor Priscilla! how could she sing with ease or reverence such confused verses? The tune, too, set in the psalm-book seems absolutely unfitted to the metre. I fear when she sang from the pages "the old Puritan anthem" that she was forced to turn it into a chant, else the irregular lines could never have been brought within the compass of the melody; and yet, the metre is certainly better than the sense.

It may be thought that these selections of the Psalms have been chosen for their crudeness and grotesqueness. I have tried in vain to find othersome that would show more elegant finish or more of the spirit of poetry; the most poetical lines I can discover are these, which are beautiful for the reason that the noble thoughts of the Psalmist cannot be hidden, even by the wording of the learned Puritan minister:--

1. Jehovah feedeth me: I shall not lack

2. In grassy fields, he downe dooth make me lye: he gently-leads mee, quiet-Waters by.

3. He dooth return my soul: for his name-sake in paths of justice leads-me-quietly.

4. Yea, though I walk in dale of deadly-shade ile fear none yll, for with me thou wilt be thy rod, thy staff eke, they shall comfort mee.

But few of these psalm-books of Ainsworth are now in existence; but few indeed came to New England. Elder Brewster owned one, as is shown by the inventory of the books in his library. Not every member of the congregation, not every family possessed one; many were too poor, many "lacked skill to read," and in some communities only one psalm-book was owned in the entire church. Hence arose the odious custom of "deaconing" or "lining" the psalm, by which each line was read separately by the deacon or elder and then sung by the congregation. There is no doubt, however, that this Ainsworth's Version was used in many of the early New England meetings. Reverend Thomas Symmes, in his "Joco-Serious Dialogue," printed in 1723, wrote: "Furthermore the Church of Plymouth made use of Ainsworths Version of the Psalms until the year 1692. For altho' our New England version of the Psalms was compiled by sundry hands and completed by President Dunster about the year 1640; yet that church did not use it, it seems, 'till two and fifty years after but stuck to Ainsworth; and until about 1682 their excellent custom was to sing without reading the lines."

John Cotton's account of the Salem church written in 1760, says, "On June 19, 1692, the pastor propounded to the church that seeing many of the psalms in Mr. Ainsworth's translation which had hitherto been sung in the congregation had such difficult tunes that none in the church could set, they would consider of some expedient that they might sing all the psalms. After some time of consideration on August 7 following, the church voted that when the tunes were difficult in the translation then used, they would make use of the New England psalm-book, long before received in the churches of the Massachusetts colony, not one brother opposing the conclusion. But finding it inconvenient to use two psalm-books, they at length, in June 1696 agreed wholly to lay aside Ainsworth and with general consent introduced the other which is used to this day, 1760. And here it will be proper to observe that it was their practice until the beginning of October, 1681 to sing the psalms without reading the lines; but then, at the motion of a brother who otherwise could not join in the ordinance [I suppose because he could not read] they altered the custom, and reading was introduced, the elder performing that service after the pastor had first expounded the psalm, which were usually sung in course."

On the blank leaf of the copy of Ainsworth now lying before me are written these words, "This was used in Salem half-a-century from the first settlement." In a record of the Salem church is this entry of a church meeting: "4 of 5th month, 1667. The pastor having formerly propounded and given reason for the use of the Bay Psalm Book in regard to the *difficulty of the tunes* and that we could not sing them so well as formerly and *that there was a singularity in our using Ainsworths tunes*: but especially because we had not the liberty of singing all the scripture Psalms according to Col. iii. 16. He did not again propound the same, and after several brethren had spoken, there was at last a unanimous consent with respect to the last reason mentioned, that the Bay Psalm Book should be used together with Ainsworth to supply the defects of it."

It is significant enough of the "low state of the musik in the meetings" when we find that the simple tunes written in Ainsworth's Version were too difficult for the colonists to sing. To such a condition had church-music been reduced by "lining the psalm" and by the lack of musical instruments to guide and control the singers. It was not much better in old England; for we find in the preface of Rous' Psalms (which were published in 1643 and authorized to be used in the English Church) references to the "difficulty of Ainsworth's tunes."

Hood says, "There is almost a certainty that no other version than Ainsworth was ever used in the colonies until the New England Version was published. But if any one was used in one or two of the churches it was

Sternhold and Hopkins." I cannot feel convinced of this, but believe that both Ravenscroft's and Sternhold and Hopkins' Versions were used at first in many of the Bay settlements. Salem church had a peculiar connection in its origin with the church of Plymouth, which would account, doubtless, for its protracted use of the version so loved by the Pilgrims; but the Puritans of the Bay, coming directly from England, must have brought with them the version which they had used in England, that of Sternhold and Hopkins; and they would hardly have wished, nor would it have been possible for them to acquire speedily in the new land the Ainsworth's Version used by the Pilgrims from Holland.

The second edition of Ainsworth's Version was printed in 1617, a third in 1618; the fourth, in London in 1639, was a folio; and the sixth, in Amsterdam in 1644, was an octavo. A little 24mo copy is in the Essex Institute in Salem, and an octavo is in the Prince Library, now in the custody of the Public Library of the City of Boston. The latter copy has a note in it written by the Rev. Thomas Prince: "Plymouth, May 1, 1732. I have seen an edition of this version of 1618; and this version was sung in Plymouth Colony and I suppose in the rest of New England 'till the New England Version was printed."

There is a copy of the first edition of Ainsworth in the Bodleian Library and one in the library of Trinity College, Dublin. The American Antiquarian Society and the Lenox Library are the only public libraries in America that possess copies, so far as I know. The one in the library of the American Antiquarian Society was presented to it in 1815 by the Rev. William Bentley of Salem, Massachusetts, to whom also belonged the copy of the Bay Psalm Book now in the library at Worcester. He was a divine and a bibliophile and an antiquary, but there also ran in his veins blood of warmer flow. During the war of 1812, when the report came, in meeting-time, that the frigate "Constitution" was being chased into Marblehead harbor, the loyal parson Bentley locked up his church, and tucked up his gown, and sallied forth with his whole flock of parishioners to march to Marblehead with the soldiers, ready to "fight unto death" if necessary. Being short and fat, and the mercury standing at eighty-five degrees, the doctor's physical strength gave out, and he had to be hoisted up astride a cannon to ride to the scene of conflict,--martial in spirit though weak in the legs.

But this association with the old book is comparatively of our own day; and the most pleasing fancy which the "psalm-book of Ainsworth" brings to my mind, the most sacred and reverenced thought, is of a far more remote, a more peaceful and quiet scene; though men of warlike blood and fighting stock were there present and took part therein. It is with that Sabbath Day before the Landing at Plymouth which was spent by the Pilgrims, as Mather says, "in the devout and pious exercises of a sacred rest." And though Matthew Arnold thought that the Mayflower voyagers would have been intolerable company for Shakespeare and Virgil, yet in that quiet day of devout prayer and praise they show a calm religious peace and trust that is, perhaps, the highest spiritual type of "sweetness and light." And from this quaint old book their lips found words and music to express in song their pure and holy faith.

XII
The Bay Psalm-Book

It seems most proper that the first book printed in New England should be now its rarest one, and such is the case. It was also meet that the first book published by the Puritan theocracy should be a psalm-book. This New England psalm-book, being printed by the colony at Massachusetts Bay, is familiarly known as "The Bay Psalm-Book," and was published two hundred and fifty years ago with this wording on the titlepage: "The Whole Book of Psalmes Faithfully Translated into English Metre. Whereunto is prefixed a discourse declaring not only the lawfullnes, but also the necessity of the Heavenly Ordinance of Singing Psalmes in the Churches of God.

"Coll. III. Let the word of God dwell plenteously in you in all wisdome, teaching, and exhorting one another in Psalmes, Himnes, and spirituall Songs, singing to the Lord with grace in your hearts.

"James V. If any be afflicted, let him pray; and if any be merry let him sing psalmes. Imprinted 1640."

The words "For the Use, Edification, and Comfort of the Saints in Publick and Private especially in New England," though given in Thomas's "History of Printing," Lowndes's "Bibliographers Manual," Hood's "History of Music in New England," and many reliable books of reference, as part of the correct title, were in fact not printed upon the titlepage of this first edition, but appeared on subsequent ones. Mr. Thomas, at the time he wrote his history, knew of but one copy of the first edition; "an entire copy except the title-page is now in the possession of rev. mr. Bentley of Salem." The titlepage being missing, he probably fell into the error of copying the title of a later edition, and other cataloguers and manualists have blindly followed him.

There were in 1638 thirty ministers in New England, all men of intelligence and education; and to three of them, Richard Mather, Thomas Welde, and John Eliot was entrusted the literary part of the pious work. They managed to produce one of the greatest literary curiosities in existence. The book was printed in the house of President Dunster of Harvard College upon a "printery," or printing-press, which had cost £50, and was the gift of friends in Holland to the new community in 1638, the name-year of Harvard College. Governor Winthrop in his journal tells us that the first sheet printed on this press was the Freeman's Oath, certainly a characteristic production; the second an almanac for New England, and the third, "The Bay Psalm-Book." Some, who deem an almanac a book, call this psalm-book the second book printed in British America.

A printer named Steeven Daye was brought over from England to do the printing on this new press. Now Steeven must have been given entire charge of the matter, and could not have been a very literate fellow (as we know positively he was a most reprehensible one), or the three reverend versifiers must have been most uncommonly careless proof-readers, for certainly a worse piece of printer's work than "The Bay Psalm Book" could hardly have been struck off. Diversity and grotesqueness of spelling were of course to be expected, and paper might have been coarse without reproof, in that new and poor country; but the type was good and clear, the paper strong and firm, and with ordinary care a very presentable book might have been issued. The punctuation was horrible. A few commas and periods and a larger number of colons were "pepered and salted" à la Timothy Dexter, apparently quite by chance, among the words. Periods were placed in the middle of sentences; words of one syllable were divided by hyphens; capitals and italics were used after the fashion of the time, apparently quite at random; and inverted letters were common enough. The pages were unnumbered, and on every left-hand page the word "Psalm" in the title was spelled correctly, while on the right-hand page it is uniformly spelled "Psalme." But after all, these typographical blemishes might be forgiven if the substance, the psalms themselves, were worthy; but the versification was certainly the most villainous of all the many defects, though the sense was so confused that many portions were unintelligible save with the friendly aid of the prose version of the Bible; and the grammatical construction, especially in the use of pronouns, was also far from correct. Such amazing verses as these may be found:--

> "And sayd He would not them waste: had not
> Moses stood (whom He chose)
> 'fore him i' th' breach; to turne his wrath
> lest that he should waste those."

Cotton Mather, in his "Magnalia," gives thus the full story of the production of "The Bay Psalm-book":--

> "About the year 1639, the New-English reformers, considering that their churches enjoyed the other ordinances of Heaven in their scriptural purity were

willing that the 'The singing of Psalms' should be restored among them unto a share of that *purity*. Though they blessed God for the religious endeavours of them who translated the Psalms into the *meetre* usually annexed at the end of the Bible, yet they beheld in the translation so many *detractions* from, *additions* to, and *variations* of, not only the text, but the very *sense* of the psalmist, that it was an offense unto them. Resolving then upon a new translation, the chief divines in the country took each of them a portion to be translated; among whom were Mr. Welds and Mr. Eliot of Eoxbury, and Mr. Mather of Dorchester. These like the rest were so very different a *genius* for their poetry that Mr. Shephard, of Cambridge, on the occasion addressed them to this purpose:

> You Roxb'ry poets keep clear of the crime
> Of missing to give us very good rhime.
> And you of Dorchester, your verses lengthen
> And with the text's own words, you will them
strengthen.

The Psalms thus turned into *meetre* were printed at Cambridge, in the year 1640. But afterwards it was thought that a little more of art was to be employed upon them; and for that cause they were committed unto Mr. Dunster, who revised and refined this translation; and (with some assistance from Mr. Richard Lyon who being sent over by Sir Henry Mildmay as an attendant unto his, son, then a student at Harvard College, now resided in Mr. Dunster's house:) he brought it the condition wherein our churches have since used it. Now though I heartily join with those gentlemen who wish that the *poetry* thereof were mended, yet I must confess, that the Psalms have never yet seen a *translation* that I know of nearer to the Hebrew original; and I am willing to receive the excuse which our translators themselves do offer us when they say: 'If the verses are not always so elegant as some desire or expect, let them consider that God's altar needs not our pollishings; we have respected rather a plain translation, than to smooth our verses with the sweetness of any paraphrase. We have attended conscience rather than elegance, fidelity rather than ingenuity, that so we may sing in Zion the Lord's songs of praise, according unto his own will, until he bid us enter into our Master's joy to sing eternal hallelujahs.'"

I have never liked Cotton Mather so well as after reading this calm and kindly account of the production of "The Bay-Psalm-Book." He was a scholarly man, and doubtless felt keenly and groaned inwardly at the inelegance, the appalling and unscholarly errors in the New England version; and yet all he mildly said was that "it was thought that a little more of art was to be employed upon them," and that he "wishes the poetry hereof was mended." Such justice, such self-repression, such fairness make me almost forgive him for riding around the scaffold on which his fellow-clergyman was being executed for witchcraft, and urging the crowd not to listen to the poor martyr's dying words. I can even almost overlook the mysterious fables, the outrageous yarns which he imposed upon us under the guise of history.

The three reverend versifiers who turned out such questionable poetry are known to have been writers of clear, scholarly, and vigorous prose. They were all graduated at Emanuel College, Cambridge, the nursery of Puritans. Mr. Welde soon returned to England and published there two intelligent tracts vindicating the purity of the New England worship. Richard Mather was the general prose-scribe for the community; he drafted the "Cambridge Platform" and other important papers, and was clear and scholarly enough in all his work *except* the "Bay Psalm-Book." From his pen came the tedious, prolix preface to the work; and the first draft of it in his own handwriting is preserved in the Prince Library. The other co-worker was John Eliot, that glory of New England Puritanism, the apostle to the Indians. His name heads my list of the saints of the Puritan calendar; but I confess that when I consider his work in "The Bay Psalm-Book," I have sad misgivings lest the hymns which he wrote and published in the Indian language may not have proved to the poor Massachusetts Indians all that our loving and venerating fancy has painted them. It is said also that Francis Quarles, the Puritan author of "Divine Emblems," sent across the Atlantic some of his metrical versions of the psalms as a pious contribution to the new version of the new church in the new land.

The "little more of art" which was bestowed by the improving President Dunster left the psalms still improvable, as may be seen by opening at random at any page of the revised editions. Mr. Lyon conferred also upon the New England church the inestimable boon of a number of hymns or "Scripture-Songs placed in order as in the Bible." They were printed in that order from the third until at least the sixteenth edition, but in subsequent editions the hymns were all placed at the end of the book after the psalms. I doubt not that the Puritan youth, debarred of merry catches and roundelays, found keen delight in these rather astonishing renditions of the songs of Solomon, portions of Isaiah, etc. Those Scripture-Songs should be read quite through to be fully appreciated, as no modern Christian could be full enough of grace to sing them. Here is a portion of the song of Deborah and Barak:--

24. Jael the Kenite Hebers wife
'bove women blest shall be:
Above the women in the tent
a blessed one is she.
25. He water ask'd: she gave him milk
him butter forth she fetch'd
26. In lordly dish: then to the nail
she forth her left hand stretched.

Her right the workman's hammer held
and Sisera struck dead:
She pierced and struck his temple through
and then smote off his head.
27. He at her feet bow'd, fell, lay down
he at her feet bow'd, where
He fell: ev'n where he bowed down
he fell destroyed there.

28. Out of a window Sisera
his mother looked and said
The lattess through in coming why
so long his chariot staid?
His chariot wheels why tarry they?
29. her wise dames, answered
Yea she turned answer to herself
30. and what have they not sped?

31. The prey by poll; a maid or twain
what parted have not they?
Have they not parted, Sisera,
a party-colour'd prey
A party-colour'd neildwork prey
of neildwork on each side
That's party-colour'd meet for necks
of them that spoils divide?

Our Pilgrim Fathers accepted these absurd, tautological verses gladly, and sang them gratefully; but we know the spirit of poesy could never have existed in them, else they would have fought hard against abandoning such majestic psalms as Sternhold's--

"The Lord descended from above
and bow'd the heavens hye
And underneath his feete he cast
the darkness of the skye.

"On cherubs and on cherubines
full royally he road
And on the winges of all the windes
came flying all abroad."

They gave up these lines of simple grandeur, to which they were accustomed, for such wretched verses as these of the New England version:--

9. Likewise the heavens he downe-bow'd and he descended, & there was under his feet a gloomy cloud
10. And he on cherub rode and flew; yea, he flew on the wings of winde.
11. His secret place hee darkness made his covert that him round confide.

I cannot understand why they did not sing the psalms of David just as they were printed in the English Bible; it would certainly be quite as practicable as to sing this latter selection.

President Dunster's improving hand and brain evolved this rendition:--

"Likewise the heavens he down-bow'd
and he descended: also there
Was at his feet a gloomy cloud
and he on cherubs rode apace.
Yea on the wings of wind he flew
he darkness made his secret place
His covert round about him drew."

Though the grotesque wording and droll errors of these old psalm-books can, after the lapse of centuries, be pointed out and must be smiled at, there is after all something so pathetic in the thought of those good, scholarly old New England saints, hampered by poverty, in dread of attack of Indians, burdened with hard work, harassed by "eighty-two pestilent heresies," still laboring faithfully and diligently in their strange new home at their unsuited work,--something so pathetic, so grand, so truly Christian, that when I point out any of the absurdities or failures in their work, I dread lest the shades of Cotton, of Sewall, of Mather, of Eliot, brand me as of old, "in capitall letters," as "AN OPEN AND OBSTINATE CONTEMNER OF GOD'S HOLY ORDINANCES," or worse still, with that mysterious, that dread name, "A WANTON GOSPELLER."

The second edition of the "New England Psalm-Book" was published in 1647; the one copy known to exist has sold for four hundred and thirty-five dollars. The third edition was the one revised by President Dunster and Mr. Lyon, and was printed in 1650. In 1691 the unfortunate book was again "pollished" by a committee of ministers, who thus altered the last two stanzas of the Song of Deborah and Barak:--

28. Out of a window Sisera
  His mother look'd and said
  The lattess through in coming why
  So long's chariot staid?
  His chariot-wheels why tarry they?
  Her ladies wise reply'd
29. Yea to herself the answer made,
30. Have they not speed? she cry'd.

31. The prey to each a maid or twain
  Divided have not they?
  To Sisera have they not shar'd
  A divers-colour'd prey?
  Of divers-colour'd needle-work
  Wrought curious on each side
  Of various colours meet for necks
  Of those who spoils divide?

Rev. Elias Nason wittily says of "The Bay Psalm-Book," "Welde, Eliot, and Mather mounted the restive steed Pegasus, Hebrew psalter in hand, and trotted in warm haste over the rough roads of Shemitic roots and metrical psalmody. Other divines rode behind, and after cutting and slashing, mending and patching, twisting and turning, finally produced what must ever remain the most unique specimen of poetical tinkering in our literature."

Other editions quickly followed these "pollishings" until, in 1709, sixteen had been printed. Mr. Hood stated that at least seventy editions in all were brought out. Some of these were printed in England and Scotland, in exceedingly fine and illegible print, and were intended to be bound up with the Bible; and occasionally duodecimo Bibles were sent from Scotland to New England with "The Bay Psalm-Book" bound at the back part of the book. Strange as it may seem, the poor, halting New England version was used in some of the English dissenting congregations and Scotch kirks, instead of the smoother verses composed in England for the English churches.

The Reverend Thomas Prince, after two years of careful work thereon, published in 1758 a revised edition of the much-published book, and it was adopted by his church, the Old South, of Boston, the week previous to his death. It was used by his congregation until 1786. He clung closely to the form of the old editions, changing only an occasional word. In his preface Dr. Prince says that "The Bay Psalm-Book" "had the honor of being the first book printed in North America, and as far as I can find, in this New World." We have fuller means of information now-a-days than had the reverend reviser, and we know that as early as 1535 a book called "The Book of St. John Climacus or The Spiritual Ladder" had been printed in the Spanish tongue, in Mexico; and no less than one hundred and sixteen other Spanish works in the sixteenth century, as the "Bibliografia Mexicana" testifies.

If the printing of all these various editions was poor, and the diction worse, the binding certainly was good and could be copied in modern times to much advantage. No flimsy cloth or pasteboard covers, no weak paper backs, no ill-pasted leaves, no sham-work of any kind was given; securely sewed, firmly glued, with covers of good strong leather, parchment, kid, or calfskin, these psalm-books endured constant *daily* (not weekly) use for years, for decades, for a century, and are still whole and firm. They were carried about in pockets, in saddle-bags, and were opened, and handled, and conned, as often as were the Puritan Bibles, and they bore the usage well. They were distinctively characteristic of the unornamental, sternly pious, eminently honest, and sturdily useful race that produced them.

Judge Sewall makes frequent mention in his famous diary of "the New Psalm Book." He bought one "bound neatly in Kids Leather" for "3 shillings & sixpence" and gave it to a widow whom he was wooing. Rather a serious lover's gift, but characteristic of the giver, and not so gloomy as "Dr. Mathers Vials of Wrath," "Dr. Sibbs Bowels," "Dr. Preston's Church Carriage," and "Dr. Williard's Fountains opened," all of which he likewise presented to her.

The Judge frequently gave a copy as a bridal gift, after singing from it "Myrrh aloes," to the gloomy tune of Windsor, at the wedding.

> 8. Myrrh Aloes and Cussias *smell*
>   all of thy garments *had*
>   Out of the yvory pallaces
>   whereby they made thee glad:

> 9. Amongst thine honourable maids
>   kings daughters present were
>   The Queen is set at thy right hand
>   in fine gold of Ophir.

But his most frequent mention of the "new psalm-book" is in his "Humbell acknowledgement" made to God of the "great comfort and merciful kindness received through singing of His Psalmes;" and the pages of the diary bear ample testimony that whatever the book may appear to us now, it was to the early colonists the very Word of God.

As years passed on, however, and singing-schools multiplied, it became much desired, and even imperative that there should be a better style and manner of singing, and open dissatisfaction arose with "The Bay Psalm-Book;" the younger members of the congregations wished to adopt the new and smoother versions of Tate and Brady, and of Watts. Petitions were frequently made in the churches to abolish the century-used book. Here is an opening sentence of one church-letter which is still in existence; it was presented to the ministers and elders of the Roxbury church September 11th, 1737, and was signed by many of the church members:--

"The New England Version of Psalms however useful it may formerly have been, has now become through the natural variableness of Language, not only very uncouth but in many Places unintelligible; whereby the mind instead of being Raised and spirited in Singing The Praises of Almighty God and thereby being prepared to Attend to other Parts of Divine Service is Damped and made Spiritless in the Performance of the Duty at least such is the Tendency of the use of that Version," etc., etc.

Great controversy arose over the abolition of the accustomed book, and church-quarrels were rife; but the end of the century saw the dearly loved old version consigned to desuetude, uever again to be opened, alas! but by critical or inquisitive readers.

There is owned by the American Antiquarian Society, and kept carefully locked in the iron safe in the building of that Society in Worcester, a copy of the first edition of "The Bay Psalm Book." It is a quarto (not octavo, as Thomas described it in his "History of Printing") and is in very good condition, save that the titlepage is missing. It is in the original light-colored, time-stained parchment binding, and contains the autograph of Stephen Sewall. It also bears on the inside of the front cover the book-plate of Isaiah Thomas, and at the back, in the veteran printer's clear and beautiful handwriting, this statement: "After advertising for another copy of this book and making enquiry in many places in New England &c. I was not able to obtain or even hear of another. This copy is therefore invaluable and must be preserved with the greatest care. Isaiah Thomas, Sep. 20. 1820." His "History of Printing," was published in 1810, and the Society had acquired through the gift of "the rev. mr. Bentley" the copy which Thomas mentioned in his book.

It is strange that Thomas should have been ignorant of the existence of other copies of the first edition of "The Bay Psalm-Book," for there were at that time six copies belonging to the Prince Library in the possession of the Old South Church of Boston. One would fancy that the Prince Library would have been one of his first objective points of search, save that a dense cloud of indifference had overshadowed that collection for so long a time. Five of those copies remained in the custody of the deacons and pastor of the Old South Church until 1860, and they were at one time all deposited in the Public Library of the City of Boston. Two still remain in that suitable place of deposit; they are almost complete in paging, but are in modern bindings. The other three copies were surrendered by Lieut-Gov. Samuel Armstrong (who, as one of the deacons of the Old South Church, had joint custody of the Prince Library), severally, to Mr. Edward Crowninshield of Boston, Dr. Nathaniel B. Shurtleff of Boston, and Mr. George Livermore of Cambridge. Governor Armstrong surrendered these three books in consideration of certain modern books being given to the Prince Library, and of the modern bindings bestowed on the two other copies; which seems to us hardly a brilliant or judicious exchange.

In Dr. Shurtleff "The Bay Psalm-Book" found a congenial and loving owner; and under his careful superintendence an exact reprint was published in 1862 in the Riverside Press at Cambridge. He wrote for it a preface. It was published by subscription; one copy on India paper, fifteen on thick paper, and fifty on common paper. Copies on the last named paper have sold readily for thirty dollars each. All the typographical errors of the original were carefully reproduced in this reprint.

At Dr. Shurtleffs death, his "Bay Psalm-Book" was catalogued with the rest of his library, which was to be sold on Dec. 2, 1875; but an injunction was obtained by the deacons of the Old South Church, to prevent the sale of the old psalm-book. They were rather late in the day however, to try to obtain again the too easily parted with book, and the ownership of it was adjudged to the estate. The book was sold Oct. 12, 1876, at the Library salesroom, Beacon Street, Boston, for one thousand and fifty dollars. It is now in the library of Mrs. John Carter Brown, of Providence, Rhode Island. Special interest attaches to this copy, because it was "Richard Mather, His Book" as several autographs in it testify; and the author's own copy is always of extra value. Cotton Mather, a grandson of Richard, was the close friend of the Reverend Thomas Prince, who founded the Prince Library, and who left it by will to the Old South Church in 1758. Mr. Prince's book-plate is on the reverse of the titlepage of this copy of "The Bay Psalm-Book," and is in itself a rarity. It reads thus:--

> "This Book belongs to
> The New England Library
> Begun to be collected by Thomas Prince
> upon his ent'ring Harvard-College July 6
> 1703, and was given by said Prince, to
> remain therein forever."

There was a sixth copy of "The Bay Psalm-Book" in the Prince Library in 1830 when Dr. Wisner wrote his four sermons on the Old South Church of Boston,--a copy annotated by Dr. Prince and used by him while he was engaged on his revision. It has disappeared, together with many other important books and manuscripts belonging to the same library. The vicissitudes through which this most valuable collection has passed--lying neglected for years on shelves, in boxes, and in barrels in the steeple-room of the Old South Church, depleted to use for lighting fires, injured by British soldiery, but injured still more by the neglect and indifference of its custodians--are too painful to contemplate or relate. They contribute to the scholarly standing and honor of neither pastors nor congregations during those years. It is enough to state, however, that it is to the noble and ill-requited forethought of Dr. Prince that we owe all but three of the copies of the Bay Psalm-Book which are now known to be in existence.

There is also a perfect copy of the first edition of the old book in the Lenox Library in New York, and the manner in which it was acquired (and also some further accounts of two of our old friends of the Prince Library, the acquisitions of Messrs. Crowninshield and Liverraore) is told so entertainingly by Henry Stevens, of Vermont, in his charming book, "Recollections of Mr. James Lenox" that it is best to quote his account in full:--

> "For nearly ten years Mr. Lenox had entertained a longing de to possess a perfect copy of 'The Bay Psalm Book.' He gave me to understand that if an opportunity occurred of securing a copy for him I might go as far as one hundred guineas. Accordingly from 1847 till his death, six years later, my good friend William Pickering and I put our heads and book-hunting forces together to run down this rarity. The only copy we knew of on this side the Atlantic was a spotless one in the Bodleian Library, which had lain there unrecognized for ages, and even in the printed catalogue of 1843 its title was recorded without distinction among the common herd of Psalms in verse. I had handled it several times with great reverence, and noted its many peculiar points, but, as agreed with Mr. Pickering, without making

any sign or imparting any information to our good and obliging friend Dr. Bandinel, Bodley's Librarian. We thought that when we had secured a copy for oursel it would be time enough to acquaint the learned Doctor that he was entertaining unawares this angel of the New World.

"Under these circumstances, therefore, only an experienced collector can judge of my surprise and inward satisfaction, when on the 12 January, 1855, at Sotheby's, at one of the sales of Pickering's stock, after untying parcel after parcel to see what I might chance to see, and keeping ahead of the auctioneer, Mr. Wilkinson, on resolving to prospect in one parcel more before he overtook me, my eye rested an instant only on the long-lost Benjamin, clean and unspotted. I instantly closed the parcel (which was described in the Catalogue as Lot '531 Psalmes, other editions, 1630 to 1675 black letter, a parcel') and tightened the string just as Alfred came to lay it on the table. A cool-blooded coolness seized me, and advancing to the table behind Mr. Lilly I quietly bid, in a perfectly natural tone, 'Sixpence,' and so the bids went on increasing by sixpence until half a crown was reached, and Mr. Lilly had loosened the string. Taking up this very volume he turned to me and remarked that 'This looks a rare edition, Mr. Stevens, don't you think so? I do not remember having seen it before,' and raised the bid to five shillings. I replied that I had little doubt of its rarity though comparatively a late edition of the Psalms, at the same time gave Mr. Wilkinson a six-penny nod. Thenceforth a 'spirited competition' arose between Mr. Lilly and myself, until finally the lot was knocked down to 'Stevens' for nineteen shillings. I then called out with perhaps more energy than discretion, 'Delivered!' On pocketing this volume, leaving the other seven to take the usual course, Mr. Lilly and others inquired with some curiosity, 'What rarity have you got now?' 'Oh, nothing,' said I, 'but the first English book printed in America.' There was a pause in the sale, while all had a good look at the little stranger. Some said jocularly, 'There has evidently been a mistake; put up the lot again.' Mr. Stevens, with the book again safely in his pocket, said, 'Nay, if Mr. Pickering, whose cost mark of [3s] did not recognize the prize he had won, certainly the cataloguer might be excused for throwing it away into the hands of the right person to rescue, appreciate, and preserve it. I am now fully rewarded for my long and silent hunt of seven years.'

"On reaching Morley's I eagerly collated the volume, and at first found it right witli all the *usual* signatures correct. The leaves were not paged or folioed. But on further collation I missed sundry of the Psalms, enough to fill four leaves. The puzzle was finally solved when it was discovered that the inexperienced printer had marked the sheet with the signature w after v, which is very unusual.

"This was a very disheartening disappointment, but I held my tongue, and knowing that my old friend and correspondent, George Liverm of Cambridge, N. E., possessed an imperfect copy, which he and Mr. Crowninshield, after the noble example of the 'Lincoln Nosegay,' had won from the Committee of the 'Old South' together with another and perfect copy, I proposed an advantageous exchange and obtained four missing leaves. Mr. Crowninshield strongly advised Mr. Livermore against parting with his four leaves, because, as he said, 'They would enable Stevens to complete his copy and to place it in the library of Mr. Lenox, who would then crow over us because he also had a perfect copy of "The Bay-Psalm Book."'

"Having thus completed my copy and had it bound by Francis Bedford in his best style, I sent it to Mr. Lenox for £80. Five years later I bought the Crowninshield Library in Boston for $10,000, mainly to obtain his perfect copy of 'The Bay Psalm Book,' and brought the whole library to London. This second copy, after being held several months, was at the suggestion of Mr. Thomas Watts, offered to the British Museum for £150. The Keeper of the Printed Books, however, never had the courage to send it before the Trustees for approval and payment; so after waiting five or six years longer the volume was withdrawn, bound by Bedford, taken to America in 1868, and sold to Mr. George Brinley for 150 guineas. At the Brinley sale, in March, 1878, it was bought by Mr. Cornelius Vanderbilt for $1200, or more than three times the cost of my first copy to Mr. Lenox."

We hear the expression of a book being "worth its weight in gold." "The Bay Psalm-Book," in the Library of the American Antiquarian Society, weighs nine ounces, hence Mr. Vanderbilt paid at least seven times its weight in gold for his precious book. Lowndes's "Bibliographers' Manual" says, "This volume, which is extremely rare and would at an auction in America produce from four to six thousand dollars, is familiarly termed 'The Bay Psalm Book.'" This must have been intended to be printed four to six hundred dollars, and is about as correct as the remainder of the description in that manual.

The copy which is spoken of by Mr. Stevens as being in the Bodleian Library at Oxford was once the property of Bishop Tanner, the famous antiquary. Thus it is seen that there are seven copies at least of the first edition of "The Bay Psalm-Book" now in existence in America, instead of "five or at the most six," as a recent writer in "The Magazine of American History" states.

And of all the manifold later editions of the New England Psalm-Book comparatively few copies now remain. Occasionally one is discovered in an old church library or seen in the collection of an antiquary. It is usually found to bear on its titlepage the name of its early owner, and often, also, in a different handwriting, the simple record and date of his death. Tender little memorial postils are frequently written on the margins of the pages: "Sung this the day Betty was baptized"--"This Psalm was sung at Mothers Funeral" "Gods Grace help me to heed this word." Sometimes we see on the blank pages, in a fine, cramped handwriting, the record of the births and deaths of an entire family. More frequently still we find the familiar and hackneyed verses of ancient titlepage lore, such as are usually seen on the blank leaves of old Bibles. This script was written in a "Bay Psalm-Book" of the sixteenth edition, and with the characteristic indifference of our New England forefathers for tiresome repetition, or possibly with their disdain of novelty, was seen on each and every blank page of the book:--

> "Israel Balch, His Book,
> God give him Grace theirin to look
> And when the Bell for him doth toal
> May God have mearcy on his Sole."

What the diction lacked in variety is quite made up, however, in the spelling, which was painstakingly different on each page.

Another Psalm-Book bore, inscribed in an elegant, minute handwriting, these lines, which were probably intended for verse, since the first word of each line commenced with a capital letter:--

> "Abednego Prime His Book
> When he withein these pages looks
> May he find Grace to sing therein
> Seventeen hundred and forty-seven."

This is certainly pretty bad poetry,--bad enough to be worthy a place in "The Bay Psalm Book,"--but is also a most noble, laudable, and necessary aspiration; for power of Grace was plainly needed to enable Abednego or any one else to sing from those pages; and our pious New England forefathers must have been under special covenant of grace when they persevered against such obstacles and under such overwhelming disadvantages in having singing in their meetings.

Another copy of the old New England Psalm-Book was thus inscribed:--

> "Elam Noyes His Book
> You children of the name of Noyes
> Make Jesus Christ your only choyse."

The early members of the Noyes family all seemed to be exceedingly and properly proud of this rhyming couplet; it formed a sort of patent of nobility. They wrote the pious injunction to their descendants in their Psalm-Books and their Bibles, in their wills, their letters; and they, with the greatest unanimity of feeling, had it cut upon their several tombstones. It was their own family motto,--their totem, so to speak.

In a New England Psalm-Book in the possession of the American Antiquarian Society there is written in the distinct handwriting of Isaiah Thomas these explanatory words:--

"This was the Pocket Psalm-book of John Symmons who died at Salem at 100 years. He was born at North Salem went a-fishing in his youth was a prisoner with the Indians in Nova Scotia afterwards followed his labours in a Shipyard and till great old age laboured upon his lands and died without pain Aet 100. 31 October, 1791. He was a worthy conscientious and well-informed man and agreeable until the last hour of his life."

I can think of no pleasanter tribute to be given to the character of any one than the simple words, "He was agreeable until the last hour of his life." What share in the production and maintenance of that amiable and enviable condition of disposition may be attributed to the ever-present influence of the Pocket Psalm-Book cannot be known; but the constant study of the holy though clumsy verses may have largely caused that sweet agreeability which so characterized John Symmons.

There lies now before me a copy of one of the early editions of "The Bay Psalm-Book." As I open the little dingy octavo volume, with its worn and torn edges, I am conscious of that distinctive, penetrating, *old-booky* smell,--that ancient, that fairly *obsolete* odor that never is exhaled save from some old, infrequently opened, leather-bound volume, which has once in years far past been much used and handled. A book which has never been familiarly used and loved cannot have quite the same antique perfume. The mouldering, rusty, flaky leather comes off in a yellow-brown powder on my fingers as I take up the book; and the cover nearly breaks off as I open it, though with tender, book-loving usage. The leather, though strong and honest, has rotted or disintegrated until it has almost fallen into dust. Across the yellow, ill-printed pages there runs, zig-zagging sideways and backwards crab-fashion on his crooked brown legs, one of those pigmy book-spiders,--those ugly little bibliophiles that seem flatter even than the close-pressed pages that form their home.

Fair Puritan hands once held this dingy little book, honest Puritan eyes studied its ill-expressed words, and sweet Puritan lips sang haltingly but lovingly from its pages. This was "Cicely Morse Her Book" in the year 1710, and bears on many a page her name and the simple little couplet:--

> "In youth I praise
> And walk thy ways."

And pretty it were to see Cicely in her praiseful and godly-walking youth, as she stood primly clad in her sad-colored gown and long apron, with a quoif or ciffer covering her smooth hair, and a red whittle on her slender shoulders, a-singing in the old New England meeting-house through the long, tedious psalms, which were made longer and more tedious still by the drawling singing and the deacons' "lining." Truly that were a pretty sight for our eyes, and for other eyes than ours, without doubt. Staid Puritan youth may have glanced soberly across the old meeting-house at the fair girl as she sung the Song of Solomon, with its ardent wording, without any very deep thought of its symbolic meaning:--

> "Let him with kisses of his mouth
>   be pleased me to kiss,
> Because much better than the wine
>   thy loving-kindness is.
> To troops of horse in Pharoahs coach,
>   my love, I thee compare,
> Thy neck with chains, with jewels new,
>   thy cheeks full comely are.
> Borders of gold with silver studs
>   for thee make up we will,
> Whilst that the king at's table sits
>   my spikenard yields her smell.
>
> Like as of myrrh a bundle is
>   my well-belov'd to be,
> Through all the night betwixt my breasts
>   his lodging-place shall be;

My love as in Engedis vines
    like camphire-bunch to me,
So fair, my love, thou fair thou art
    thine eyes as doves eyes be."

Love and music were ever close companions; and the singing-school--
that safety-valve of young New England life--had not then been established
or even thought of, and I doubt not many a warm and far from Puritanical
love-glance was cast from the "doves-eyes" across the "alley" of the old
meeting-house at Cicely as she sung.

But Cicely vas not young when she last used the old psalm-book. She
may have been stately and prosperous and seated in the dignified "foreseat;"
she may have been feeble and infirm in her place in the "Deaf Pue;" and
she may have been careworn and sad, tired of fighting against poverty,
worn with dread of fierce Indians, weary of the howls of the wolves in the
dense forests so near, and home-sick and longing for the yonderland, her
"faire Englishe home;" but were she sad or careworn or heartsick, in her
treasured psalm-book she found comfort,--comfort in the halting verses as
well as in the noble thoughts of the Psalmist. And the glamour of eternal,
sweet-voiced youth hangs around the gentle Cicely, through the power of
the inscription in the old psalm-book,--

    "In youth I praise
    And walk thy ways,"--

the romance of the time when Cicely, the Puritan commonwealth, the
whole New World was young.

XIII
Sternhold and Hopkins' Version of the Psalms

The metrical translation of the Psalms known as Sternhold and Hopkins' Version was doubtless used in the public worship of God in many of the early New England settlements, especially those of the Connecticut River Valley, though the old register of the town of Ipswich is the only local record that gives positive proof of its use in the Puritan church. In 1693 an edition of Sternhold and Hopkins was printed in Cambridge, Massachusetts. It was not a day nor a land where a whole edition of such a book would be printed for reference or comparison only; and to thus publish the work of the English psalmists in the very teeth of the popularity of "The Bay Psalm Book" is to me a proof that Sternhold and Hopkins' Version was employed far more extensively in the colonial churches and homes than we now have records of, and than many of our church historians now fancy. Certainly the familiar English psalm-books must have been brought across the ocean and used temporarily until the newly landed colonists could acquire the version of Ainsworth or of the New England divines.

An everlasting interest attaches to this metrical arrangement of the Psalms, to Americans as well as to Englishmen, because it was the earliest to be adopted in public worship in England. According to Strype, in his Memorial, the singing of psalms was allowed in England as early as 1548, but it was not until 1562 that the versified psalms of Sternhold and Hopkins were appended to the Book of Common Prayer. Sternhold and Hopkins' Version was also the first to give all the psalms of David in English verse to the English public.

Very little is known of the authors of this version. Sternhold was educated at Oxford; was Groom of the Robes to Henry VIII. and Edward VI., was a "bold and busy Calvinist," and died in 1549. The little of interest told of John Hopkins is that he was a minister and schoolmaster, and that he assisted the work of Sternhold.

The full reason for Sternhold's pious work is thus given by an old English author, Wood: "Being a most zealous reformer and a very strict liver he became so scandalyzed at the loose amorous songs used in the court that he forsooth turned into English metre fifty-one of Davids Psalms, and caused musical notes to be set to them, thinking thereby that the courtiers would sing them instead of their sonnets; but they did not, only some few excepted." The preface printed in the book stated Sternhold's wish and intention that the verses should be sung by Englishmen, not only in church, but "moreover in private houses for their godly solace and comfort; laying apart all ungodly Songs & Ballads which tend only to the nourishment of vice & corrupting of youth."

The first edition contained nineteen psalms only, which were all versified by Sternhold. It was published in 1548 or 1549, under this title, "Certayn Psalmes chosen out of the Psalter of Daid and drawn into English Metre by Thomas Sternhold Groom of ye Kynges Maiesties Roobes." I believe no copy of this edition is now known to exist.

The praise which Sternhold received for his pious rhymes had the same effect upon him as did similar encomiums upon his predecessor, the French psalm-writer Marot,--it encouraged him to write more psalm-verses.

The second edition was printed in 1549, and contained thirty-seven psalms by Sternhold and seven by Hopkins. It bore this title, "Al such Psalmes of David as Thomas Sternehold late grome of his maiesties robes did in his lyfe tyme drawe into English metre." It was a well-printed book and copies are still preserved in the British Museum and the Public Library of Cambridge, England. This second and enlarged edition was dedicated, in a four-page preface, to King Edward VI., and a pretty story is told of the young king's interest in the verses. The delicate and gentle boy of twelve heard Sternhold when "singing them to his organ" as Strype says, and wandered in to hear the music and listen to the words. So great was his awakened interest in the sacred songs that Sternhold resolved to write in verse for him still further of the psalms. The dedication reads: "Seeing that your tender and godly zeale dooth more delight in the holye songs of veritie than in any fayncd rymes of vanytie, I am encouraged to travayle further in the said booke of Psalmes." This young king restored to the English people the free reading of the Bible, which his wicked father, Henry VIII., had forbidden them, and he was of a sincerely religious nature. He also was a music-lover, and encouraged the art as much as his short life and troubled reign permitted.

Hopkins also wrote a preface for his share of the work, in which he spoke with much modesty of himself and much praise of Sternhold. He said his own verses were not "in any parte to bee compared with his [Sternhold's] most exquisite dooynges." He thinks, however, that his owne are "fruitfull though they bee not fyne."

The third edition, in 1556, contained fifty-one psalms; the fourth, in 1560, had sixty-seven psalms; the fifth, in 1561, increased the number to eighty-seven; and in 1562 or 1563 the whole book of psalms appeared. Other authors had some share in this work: Norton, Whyttyngham (a Puritan divine who married Calvin's sister), Kethe, who wrote the 100th Psalm, "All people that on earth do dwell," which is still seen in some of our hymn-books. Of all these men, sly old Thomas Fuller truthfully and quaintly said, "They were men whose piety was better than their poetry, and they had drunk more of Jordan than of Helicon."

For over one hundred years from the first publication there was a steady outpour of editions of these Psalms. Before the year 1600 there were seventy-four editions,--a most astonishing number for the times; and from 1600 to 1700 two hundred and thirty-five editions. In 1868 six hundred and one editions were known, including twenty-one in this nineteenth century and doubtless there were still others uncatalogued and forgotten. Among other editions this version had in the time of Charles II. two in shorthand, one printed by "Thos. Cockerill at the Three Legs and Bible in the Poultry." Two copies of these editions are in the British Museum. They are tiny little 64mos, of which half a dozen could be laid side by side on the palm of the hand. Sternhold and Hopkins' Version had also in 1694 the honor of having arranged for it a Concordance.

Upon no production of the religious Muse in the English tongue has greater diversity of criticism been displayed or more extraordinary or varied judgment been rendered than upon Sternhold and Hopkins' Psalms. A world of testimony could be adduced to fortify any view which one chose to take of them. At the time of their early publication they induced a swarm of stinging lampoons and sneering comments, that often evince most plainly that a difference in religious belief or scorn for an opposing sect brought them forth. The poetry of that and the succeeding century abounds in allusions to them. Phillips wrote:--

> "Singing with woful noise
> Like a crack'd saints bell jarring in the steeple,
> Tom Sternhold's wretched prick-song for the people."

Another poet, a courtier, wrote:--

> "Sternhold and Hopkins had great qualms
> When they translated David's psalms."

But I see no signs of qualmishness; they show to me rather a healthy sturdiness as one of their strongest characteristics.

Pope at a later day wrote:--

"Not but there are who merit other palms
    Hopkins and Sternhold glad the heart with psalms.
The boys and girls whom charity maintains
    Implore your help in these pathetic strains.
How could devotion touch the country pews
    Unless the gods bestowed a proper muse."

Wesley sneered at this version, saying, "When it is seasonable to sing praises to God we do it, not in the scandalous doggrel of Hopkins and Sternhold, but in psalms and hymns which are both sense and poetry, such as would provoke a *critic* to turn *Christian* rather than a *Christian* to turn *critic*."

The edition of 1562 was printed with the notes of melodies that were then called Church Tunes. They formed the basis of all future collections of psalm-music for over a century. They soon were published in harmony in four parts, "which may be sung to all musical instrumentes set forth for the encrease of vertue and abolyshing of other vayne and tryfling ballads." In 1592 a very important collection of psalm-tunes was published to use with Sternhold and Hopkins' words. It is called "The Whole Booke of Psalmes: with their wonted tunes as they are sung in Churches composed into four parts." This book is noteworthy because in it the tunes are for the first time named after places, as is still the custom. The music contained square or oblong notes and also lozenge-shaped notes. The square note was a "semy-brave," the lozenge-shaped note was a "prycke" or a "mynymme," and "when there is a prycke by the square note, that prycke is half as much as the note that goeth before."

Music at that time was said to be pricked, not printed,--the word being derived from the prick or dot which formed the head of the note. Any song which was printed in various parts was called a prick-song, to distinguish it from one sung extemporaneously or by ear. The word prick-song occurs not only in all the musical books, but in the literature of the time, and in Shakespeare. "Tom Sternhold's" songs were entitled to be called prick-songs because they had notes of music printed with them. Many of the tunes in this collection were taken from the Genevan Psalter and Luther's Psalm-Book, or from Marot and Beza's French Book of Psalms. Hence they were irreverently called "Genevan Jiggs," and "Beza's Ballets."

There is much difference shown in the wording of these various editions of Sternhold and Hopkins' Psalms. The earlier ones were printed as Sternhold wrote them; but with the Genevan editions began great and astonishing alterations. Warton, who was no lover of Sternhold and Hopkins' verses, calling them "the disgrace of sacred poetry," said of these attempted improvements, with vehemence, that "many stanzas already too naked and weak like a plain old Gothic edifice stripped of its signatures of antiquity, have lost that little and almost only strength and support which they derived from ancient phrases." Other old critics thought that Sternhold, could he return to life, would hardly know his own verses.

This is Sternhold's rendering of the Psalm in the edition of 1549:--

> 1. The heavens & the fyrmamente
>   do wondersly declare
>   The glory of God omnipotent
>   his workes and what they are.
>
> 2. Ech daye declareth by his course
>   an other daye to come
>   And By the night we know lykwise
>   a nightly course to run.
>
> 3. There is no laguage tong or speche
>   where theyr sound is not heard,
>   In al the earth and coastes thereof
>   theyr knowledge is conferd.
>
> 4. In them the lord made royally
>   a settle for the sunne
>   Where lyke a Gyant joyfully
>   he myght his iourney runne.
>
> 5. And all the skye from ende to ende
>   he compast round about
>   No man can hyde hym from his heate
>   but he wll fynd hym out

In order to show the liberties taken with the text we can compare with it the Genevan edition printed in 1556. The second verse of that presumptuous rendering reads,--

> "The wonderous works of God appears
>   by every days success
>   The nyghts which likewise their race runne
>   the selfe same thinges expresse."

The fourth,--

> "In them the lorde made for the sunne
>   a place of great renoune

> Who like a bridegrome rady-trimed
> doth from his chamber come."

The expression "rady-trimed," meaning close-shaven, is often instanced as one of the inelegancies of Sternhold, but he surely ought not to be held responsible for the "improvements" of the Genevan edition published after his death.

The Genevan editors also invented and inserted an extra verse:--

> "And as a valiant champion
> who for to get a prize
> With joye doth hast to take in hande
> some noble enterprise."

The fifth verse is thus altered:--

> "And al the skye from ende to ende
> he compasseth about,
> Nothing can hyde it from his heate
> but he wil finde it out."

I cannot express the indignation with which I read these belittling and weakening alterations and interpolations; they are so unjust and so degrading to the reputation of Sternhold. It seems worse than forgery-- worse than piracy; for instead of stealing from the defenceless dead poet, it foists upon him a spurious and degrading progeny; there is no word to express this tinkering libellous literary crime.

Cromwell had a prime favorite among these psalms; it was the one hundred and ninth and is known as the "cursing psalm." Here are a few lines from it:--

> "As he did cursing love, it shall
>   betide unto him so,
> And as he did not blessing love
>   it shall be farre him fro,
> As he with cursing clad himselfe
>   so it like water shall
> Into his bowels and like oyl
>   Into his bones befall.
> As garments let it be to him
>   to cover him for aye
> And as a girdle wherewith he
>   may girded be alway."

Another authority gives the "cursing psalm" as the nineteenth of King James's version; but there is nothing in "The heavens declare the glory of God," &c. to justify the nickname of "cursing."

It is said when the tyrannical ruler Andros visited New Haven and attended church there that (Sternhold and Hopkins' Version being used) the fearless minister very inhospitably gave out the fifty-second psalm to be sung. The angry governor, who took it as a direct insult, had to listen to the lining and singing of these words, and I have no doubt they were roared out with a lusty will:--

1. Why dost thou tyrant boast thyself
   thy wicked deeds to praise
   Dost thou not know there is a God
   whose mercies last alwaies?

2. Why doth thy mind yet still deuise
   such wisked wiles to warp?
   Thy tongue untrue, in forging lies
   is like a razer sharp.

4. Thou dost delight in fraude & guilt
   in mischief bloude and wrong:
   Thy lips have learned the flattering stile
   O false deceitful tongue.

5. Therefore shall God for eye confounde
   and pluck thee from thy place.
   Thy seed and root from out the grounde
   and so shall thee deface;

6. The just when they behold thy fall
   with feare will praise the Lord:
   And in reproach of thee withall
   cry out with one accord.

When the unhappy King Charles fled from Oxford to a camp of troops he also was insulted by having the same psalm given out in his presence by the boorish chaplain of the troops. After the cruel words were ended the heartsick king rose and asked the soldiers to sing the fifty-sixth psalm. Whenever I read the beautiful and pathetic words, as peculiarly appropriate as if they had been written for that occasion only, I can see it all before me,--the great camp, the angry minister, the wretched but truly royal king; and I can hear the simple and noble song as it pours from the lips of hundreds of rude soldiers:

1. Have mercy Lord on mee I pray
   for man would mee devour.
   He fighteth with me day by day
   and troubleth me each hour.

2. Mine enemies daily enterprise
   to swallow mee outright
   To fight against me many rise
   O thou most high of might

5. What things I either did or spake
   they wrest them at thier wil:
   And all the councel that they take
   is how to work me il.

6. They all consent themselves to hide
   close watch for me to lay:
   They spie my pathes, and snares have layd
   to take my life away.

7. Shall they thus scape on mischief set,
   thou God on them wilt frowne:
   For in his wrath he will not let
   to throw whole kingdomes downe.

It would perhaps be neither just nor conducive to proper judgment to gather only a florilege of noble verses from Sternhold and Hopkins' Version and point out none of the "weedy-trophies," the quaint and even uncouth lines which disfigure the work. We must, however, in considering and judging them, remember that many words and even phrases which at present seem rather ludicrous or undignified had, in the sixteenth century, significations which have now become obsolete, and which were then neither vulgar nor unpoetical. I also have been forced to take my selections from a copy of Sternhold and Hopkins printed in 1599, and bound up with a "Breeches Bible;" for I have access to no earlier edition. Sternhold and Hopkins themselves may not be in truth responsible for many of the crudities. Hopkins, in his rendition of the 12th verse of the seventy-fourth Psalm, thus addresses the Deity:--

"Why doost withdraw thy hand abacke
   and hide it in thy lappe?
O pluck it out and bee not slacke
   to give thy foes a rap."

"Rap" may have meant a heavier, a mightier blow then than it does now-a-days.

Here is another curious verse from the seventieth psalm,--

"Confounde them that apply
  and seeke to make my shame
And at my harme doe laugh & crye
  So So there goeth the game."

The sixth verse of the fifty-eighth psalm is rendered thus:--

"O God breake thou thier teeth at once
  within thier mouthes throughout;
The tuskes that in thier great jawbones
  like Lions whelpes hang out."

Another verse reads thus:--

"The earth did quake, the raine pourde down
  Heard men great claps of thunder
And Mount Sinai shooke in such state
  As it would cleeve in sunder."

One verse of the thirty-fifth psalm reads thus:--

"The belly-gods and flattering traine
  that all good things deride
At me doe grin with greate disdaine
  and pluck thier mouths aside.
Lord when wilt thou amend this geare
  why dost thou stay & pause?
O rid my soul, my onely deare,
  out of these Lions clawes."

The word tush occurs frequently and quaintly: "Tush I an sure to fail;" "Tush God forgetteth this."

"And with a blast doth puff against
  such as would him correct
Tush Tush saith he I have no dread."

Here are some of the curious expressions used:--

"Though gripes of grief and pangs full sore
  shall lodge with us all night."

"For why their hearts were nothing lent
to Him nor to His trade."

"Our soul in God hath joy and game."

"They are so fed that even for fat
thier eyes oft-times out start."

"They grin they mow they nod thier heads."

"While they have war within thier hearts."
as butter are thier words."

"Divide them Lord & from them pul
thier devilish double-tongue."

"My silly soul uptake."

"And rained down Manna for them to eat
a food of mickle-wonder."

"For joy I have both gaped & breathed."

But it is useless to multiply these selections, which, viewed individually, are certainly absurd and inelegant. They often indicate, however, the exact thought of the Psalmist, and are as well expressed as the desire to be literal as well as poetic will permit them to be. Sternhold's verses compare quite favorably, when looked at either as a whole or with regard to individual lines, with those of other poets of his day, for Chaucer was the only great poet who preceded him.

I must acknowledge quite frankly in the face of critics of both this and the past century that I always read Sternhold and Hopkins' Psalms with a delight, a satisfaction that I can hardly give reasons for. Many of the renderings, though unmelodious and uneven, have a rough vigor and a sweeping swing that is to me wonderfully impressive, far more so than many of the elegant and polished methods of modern versifiers. And they are so thoroughly antique, so devoid of any resemblance to modern poems, that I love them for their penetrating savor of the olden times; and they seem no more to be compared and contrasted with modern verses than should an old castle tower be compared with a fine new city house. We prefer the latter for a habitation, it is infinitely better in every way, but we can admire also the rough grandeur of the old ruin.

XIV
Other Old Psalm-Books

There are occasionally found in New England on the shelves of old libraries, in the collections of antiquaries, or in the attics of old farm-houses, hidden in ancient hair-trunks or painted sea-chests or among a pile of dusty books in a barrel,--there are found dingy, mouldy, tattered psalm-books of other versions than the ones which we know were commonly used in the New England churches. Perhaps these books were never employed in public worship in the new land; they may have been brought over by some colonist, in affectionate remembrance of the church of his youth, and sung from only with tender reminiscent longing in his own home. But when groups of settlers who were neighbors and friends in their old homes came to America and formed little segregated communities by themselves, there is no doubt that they sung for a time from the psalm-books that they brought with them.

A rare copy is sometimes seen of Marot and Beza's French Psalm-book, brought to America doubtless by French Huguenot settlers, and used by them until (and perhaps after) the owners had learned the new tongue. Some of the Huguenots became members of the Puritan churches in America, others were Episcopalians. In Boston the Fancuils, Baudoins, Boutineaus, Sigourneys, and Johannots were all Huguenots, and attended the little brick church built on School Street in 1704, which was afterwards occupied by the Twelfth Congregational Society of Boston, and in 1788 became a Roman Catholic church.

The pocket psalm-book of Gabriel Bernon, the builder of the old French Fort at Oxford, is one of Marot and Beza's Version, and is still preserved and owned by one of his descendants; other New England families of French lineage cherish as precious relics the French psalm-books of their Huguenot ancestors. There has been in France no such incessant production of new metrical versions of the psalms as in England. From the time of the publication of the first versified psalms in 1540, through nearly three centuries the psalm-book of all French Protestants has been that of Marot and Beza. This French version of the psalms is of special interest to all thoughtful students of the history of Protestantism, because it was the first metrical translation of the psalms ever sung and used by the people; and it was without doubt one of the most powerful influences that assisted in the religious awakening of the Reformation.

Clement Marot was the "Valet of the Bed-chamber to King Francis I.," and was one of the greatest French poets of his time; in fact, he gave his name to a new school of poetry,--"Marotique." He had tried his hand at an immense variety of profane verse, he had written ballades, chansons, pastourelles, vers équivoques, eclogues, laments, complaints, epitaphs, chants-royals, blasons, contreblasons, dizains, huitains, envois; he had been, Warton says, "the inventor of the rondeau and the restorer of the madrigal;" and yet, in spite of his well-known ingenuity and versatility, it occasioned much surprise and even amusement when it was known that the gay poet had written psalm-songs and proposed to substitute them for the love-songs of the French court. I doubt if Marot thought very deeply of the religious influence of his new songs, in spite of Mr. Morley's belief in the versifier's serious intent. He was doubtless interested and perhaps somewhat infected by "Lutheranisme," though perhaps he was more of a free-thinker than a Protestant. He himself said of his faith:--

> "I am not a Lutherist
> Nor Zuinglian and less Anabaptist,
> I am of God through his son Jesus Christ.
> I am one who has many works devised
> From which none could extract a single line
> Opposing itself to the law divine."

And again:--

> "Luther did not come down from heaven for me
> Luther was not nailed to the cross to be
> My Saviour; for my sins to suffer shame,
> And I was not baptized in Luther's name.
> The name I was baptized in sounds so sweet
> That at the sound of it, what we entreat
> The Eternal Father gives."

In the year 1540, at the instigation of King Francis, Marot presented a manuscript copy of his thirty new psalm-songs to Charles V., king of Spain, receiving therefor two hundred gold doubloons. Francis encouraged him by further gifts, and so praised his work that the author soon published the thirty in a book which he dedicated to the king; and to which he also prefixed a metrical address to the ladies of France, bidding these fair dames to place their

> "doigts sur les espinettes
> Pour dire sainctes chansonnettes."

These "sainctes chansonnettes" became at once the rage; courtiers and princes, lords and ladies, ever ready for some new excitement, seized at once upon the novel psalm-songs, and having no special or serious music for them, cheerfully sang the sacred words to the ballad-tunes of the times, and to their gailliards and measures, without apparently any very deep thought of their religious meaning. Disraeli says that each of the royal family and each nobleman chose for his favorite song a psalm expressive of his own feeling or sentiments. The Dauphin, as became a brave huntsman, chose

> "Ainsi qu'on vit le cerf bruyre,"

> "As the hart panteth after the water-brook,"

and he gayly and noisily sang it when he went to the chase. The Queen chose

> "Ne vueilles pas, ô sire,
> Me reprendre en ton ire."

> "Rebuke me not in thine indignation."

Antony, king of Navarre, sung

> "Revenge moy prens la querelle,"

> "Stand up, O Lord! to revenge my quarrel,"

to the air of a dance of Poitou. Diane de Poictiers chose

> "Du fond de ma pensée."

> "From the depth of my heart."

But when from interest in her psalm-song she wished to further read and study the Bible, she was warned from the danger with horror by the Cardinal of Lorraine. This religious awakening and inquiry was of course deprecated and dreaded by the Romish Church; to the Sorbonne all this rage for psalm-singing was alarming enough. What right had the people to sing God's word, "I will bless the Lord at all times, His praise shall be continually in my mouth"? The new psalm-songs were soon added to the list of "Heretical Books" forbidden by the Church, and Marot fled to Geneva in 1543. He had ere this been under ban of the Church, even under condemnation of death; had been proclaimed a heretic at all the cross-ways throughout the kingdom, and had been imprisoned. But he had been too good a poet and courtier to be lost, and the king had then interested himself and obtained the release of the versatile song writer. The fickle king abandoned for a second time the psalm versifier, who never again returned to France.

The austere and far-seeing Calvin at once adopted Marot's version of the Psalms, now enlarged to the number of fifty, and added them to the Genevan Confession of Faith,--recommending however that they be sung with the grave and suitable strains written, for them by Guillaume Frane.

The collection was completed with the assistance of Theodore Beza, the great theologian, and the demand for the books was so great that the printers could not supply them quickly enough. Ten thousand copies were sold at once,--a vast number for the times.

But Marot was not happy in Geneva with Calvin and the Calvinists, as we can well understand. Beza, in his "History of the French Reformed Churches" said, "He (Marot) had always been bred up in a very bad school, and could not live in subjection to the reformation of the Gospel, and therefore went and spent the rest of his days in Piedmont, which was then in the possession of the king, where he lived in some security under the favor of the governor." He lived less than a year, however, dying in 1544.

These psalms of Marot's passed through a great number and variety of editions. In addition to the Genevan publications, an immense number were printed in England. Nearly all the early editions were elegant books; carefully printed on rich paper, beautifully bound in rich moroccos and leathers, often emblazoned with gold on the covers, and with corners and clasps of precious metals,--they show the wealth and fashion of the owners. When, however, it came to be held an infallible sign of "Lutheranisme" to be a singer of psalms, simpler and cheaper bindings appear; hence the dress of the French Psalm-Book found in New England is often dull enough, but invariably firm and substantial.

These psalms of Marot's are written in a great variety of song-measures, which seem scarcely as solemn and religious as the more dignified and even metres used by the early English writers. Some are graceful and smooth, however, and are canorous though never sonorous. They are pleasing to read with their quaint old spelling and lettering.

In the old Sigourney psalm-book the nineteenth psalm was thus rendered:--

"Les cieux en chaque lieu
La puissance de Dieu
    Racourent aux humains
Ce grand entour espars
Publie en toutes parts
    L'ouvrage de ses mains.

"Iour apres iour coulant
Du Saigneur va parlant
    Par longue experience.
La nuict suivant la nuict,
Nous presche et nous instruicst
    De sa grád sapience"

Another much-employed metre was this, of the hundred and thirty-third psalm:--

"Asais aux bors do ce superbe fleuve
Que de Babel les campagnes abreuve,
Nos tristes coeurs ne pensoient qu' à Sion.
Chacun, helas, dans cette affliction
Les yeux en pleurs la morte peinte au visage
Pendit sa harpe aux saules du rivage."

A third and favorite metre was this:--

"Mais sa montagne est un sainct lieu:
Qui viendra done au mont de Dieu?
    Qui est-ce qui là tiendra place?
Le homine de mains et coeur lavé,
En vanité non éslevé
    Et qui n'a juré en fallace."

Marot wrote in his preface to the psalms:--

"Thrice happy they who shall behold
And listen in that age of gold
As by the plough the laborer strays
And carman 'mid the public ways
And tradesman in his shop shall swell
The voice in psalm and canticle,
Sing to solace toil; again
From woods shall come a sweeter strain,
Shepherd and shepherdess shall vie
In many a tender Psalmody,
And the Creator's name prolong
As rock and stream return their song."

Though these words seem prophetic, the gay and volatile Marot could never have foreseen what has proved one of the most curious facts in religious history,--that from the airy and unsubstantial seed sown by the French courtier in such a careless, thoughtless manner, would spring the great-spreading and deep-rooted tree of sacred song.

Little volumes of the metrical rendering of the Psalms, known as "Tate and Brady's Version," are frequently found in New England. It was the first English collection of psalms containing any smoothly flowing verses. Many of the descendants of the Puritans clung with affection to the more literal renderings of the "New England Psalm-Book," and thought the new verses were "tasteless, bombastic, and irreverent." The authors of the new book were certainly not great poets, though Nahum Tate was an English Poet-Laureate. It is said of him that he was so extremely modest that he was never able to make his fortune or to raise himself above necessity. He was not too modest, however, to dare to make a metrical version of the Psalms, to write an improvement of King Lear, and a continuation of Absalom and Achitophel. Brady--equally modest--translated the Aeneid in rivalry of Dryden. "This translation," says Johnson, "when dragged into the world did not live long enough to cry."

Such commonplace authors could hardly compose a version that would have a stable foundation or promise of long existence. But few of Tate and Brady's hymns are now seen in our church-collections of Hymns and Psalms. To them we owe, however, these noble lines, which were written thus:--

> "Be thou, O God, exalted High,
> And as thy glory fills the Skie
> So let it be on Earth displaid
> Till thou art here as There obeyed."

The hymn commencing,--

> "My soul for help on God relies,
> From him alone my safety flows,"

is also of their composition.

The first edition of these psalms was printed in 1696, and bore this title, "The Book of Psalms, a new version in metre fitted to the tunes used in Churches. By N. Tate and N. Brady." It was dedicated to King William, and though its use was permitted in English churches, it never supplanted Sternhold and Hopkins' Version. In New England Tate and Brady's Psalms became more universally popular,--not, however, without fierce opposing struggles from the older church-members at giving up the venerated "Bay Psalm-Book."

Another version of Psalms which is occasionally found in New England is known as "Patrick's Version." The title is "The Psalms of David in Metre Fitted to the Tunes used in Parish Churches by John Patrick, D.D. Precentor to the Charter House London." A curious feature of this octavo edition of 1701, which I have, is, "An Explication of Some Words of less Common Use For the Benefit of the Common People." Here are a few of the "explications:"--

"Celebrate--Make renown'd.
Climes--Countries differing in length of days.
Detracting--Lessening one's credit.
Fluid--Yielding.
Infest--Annoy.
Theam--Matter of Discourse.
Uncessant--Never ceasing.
Stupemlious--Astonishing."

Baxter said of Patrick, "His holy affection and harmony hath so far reconciled the Nonconformists that diverse of them use his Psalms in their congregation." I doubt if the version were used in New England Nonconformist congregations. Some of his verses read thus:--

"Lord hear the pray'rs and mournfull cries
   Of mine afflicted estate,
And with thy Comforts chear my soul,
   Before it is too late.

"My days consume away like Smoak
   Mine anguish is so great,
My bones are not unlike a hearth
   Parched & dry with heat.

"Such is my grief I little else
   Can do but sigh and groan.
So wasted is my flesh I'm left
   Nothing but skin and bone.

"Like th' Owl and Pelican that dwell
   In desarts out of sight,
I sadly do bemoan myself,
   In solitude delight.

"The wakeful bird that on Housetops
   Sits without company
And spends the night in mournful cries
   Leads such a life as I.

"The Ashes I rowl in when I eat
   Are tasted with my bread,
And with my Drink are mixed the tears
   I plentifully shed."

A version of the Psalms which seems to have demanded and deserved more attention than it received was written by Cotton Mather. He was doomed to disappointment in seeing his version adopted by the New England churches just as his ambitions and hopes were disappointed in many other ways. This book was published in 1718. It was called "Psalterium Americanum. A Book of Psalms in a translation exactly conformed unto the Original; but all in blank verse. Fitted unto the tunes commonly used in the Church." By a curious arrangement of brackets and the use of two kinds of print these psalms could be divided into two separate metres and could be sung to tunes of either long or short metre. After each psalm were introduced explanations written in Mather's characteristic manner,--a manner both scholarly and bombastic. I have read the "Psalterium Americanum" with care, and am impressed with its elegance, finish, and dignity. It is so popular, however, even now-a-days, to jibe at poor Cotton Mather, that his Psalter does not escape the thrusts of laughing critics. Mr. Glass, the English critic, holds up these lines as "one of the rich things:"--

"As the Hart makes a panting cry
  For cooling streams of water,
So my soul makes a panting cry
  For thee--O Mighty God."

I have read these lines over and over again, and fail to see anything very ludicrous in them, though they might be slightly altered to advantage. Still they may be very absurd and laughable from an English point of view.

So superior was Cotton Mather's version to the miserable verses given in "The Bay Psalm-Book" that one wonders it was not eagerly accepted by the New England churches. Doubtless they preferred rhyme--even the atrocious rhyme of "The Bay Psalm Book." And the fact that the "Psalterium Americanum" contained no musical notes or directions also militated against its use.

Other American clergymen prepared metrical versions of the psalms that were much loved and loudly sung by the respective congregations of the writers. The work of those worthy, painstaking saints we will neither quote nor criticise,--saying only of each reverend versifier, "Truly, I would the gods had made thee poetical." Rev. John Barnard, who preached for fifty-four years in Marblehead, published at the age of seventy years a psalm-book for his people. Though it appeared in 1752, a time when "The Bay Psalm Book" was being shoved out of the New England churches,

Barnard's Version of the Psalms was never used outside of Marblehead. Rev. Abijah Davis published another book of psalms in which he copied whole pages from Watts without a word of thanks or of due credit, which was apparently neither Christian, clerical nor manly behavior.

Watts's monosyllabic Hymns, which were not universally used in America until after the Revolution, are too well known and are still too frequently seen to need more than mention. Within the last century a flood of new books of psalms of varying merit and existence has poured out upon the New England churches, and filled the church libraries and church, pews, the second-hand book shops, the missionary boxes, and the paper-mills.

XV
The Church Music

Of all the dismal accompaniments of public worship in the early days of New England, the music was the most hopelessly forlorn,--not alone from the confused versifications of the Psalms which were used, but from the mournful monotony of the few known tunes and the horrible manner in which those tunes were sung. It was not much better in old England. In 1676 Master Mace wrote of the singing in English churches, "'T is sad to hear what whining, toling, yelling or shreaking there is in our country congregations."

A few feeble efforts were made in America at the beginning of the eighteenth century to attempt to guide the singing. The edition of 1698 of "The Bay Psalm-Book" had "Some few Directions" regarding the singing added on the last pages of the book, and simple enough they were in matter if not in form. They commence, "*First*, observe how many note-compass the tune is next the place of your first note, and how many notes above and below that so as you may begin the tune of your first note, as the rest may be sung in the compass of your and the peoples voices without Squeaking above or Grumbling below."

This "Squeaking above and Grumbling below" had become far too frequent in the churches; Judge Sewall writes often with much self-reproach of his failure in "setting the tune," and also records with pride when he "set the psalm well." Here is his pathetic record of one of his mistakes: "He spake to me to set the tune. I intended Windsor and fell into High Dutch, and then essaying to set another tune went into a Key much to high. So I pray'd to Mr. White to set it which he did well. Litchfield Tune. The Lord Humble me and Instruct me that I should be the occasion of any interruption in the worship of God."

The singing at the time must have been bad beyond belief; how much of its atrocity was attributable to the use of "The Bay Psalm-Book," cannot now be known. The great length of many of the psalms in that book was a fatal barrier to any successful effort to have good singing. Some of them were one hundred and thirty lines long, and occupied, when lined and sung, a full half-hour, during which the patient congregation stood. It is told of Dr. West, who preached in Dartmouth in 1726, that he forgot one Sabbath Day to bring his sermon to meeting. He gave out a psalm, walked a quarter of a mile to his house, got his sermon, and was back in his pulpit long before the psalm was finished. The irregularity of the rhythm in "The Bay Psalm Book" must also have been a serious difficulty to overcome. Here is the rendering given of the 133d Psalm:--

1. How good and sweet to see
   i'ts for bretheren to dwell
   together in unitee:

2. Its like choice oyle that fell
   the head upon
   that down did flow
   the beard unto
   beard of Aron:
   The skirts of his garment
   that unto them went down:

3. Like Hermons dews descent
   Sions mountains upon
   for there to bee
   the Lords blessing
   life aye lasting
   commandeth hee.

How this contorted song could have been sung even to the simplest tune by unskilled singers who possessed no guiding notes of music is difficult to comprehend. Small wonder that Judge Sewall was forced to enter in his diary, "In the morning I set York tune and in the second going over, the gallery carried it irresistibly to St. Davids which discouraged me very much." We can fancy him stamping his foot, beating time, and roaring York at the top of his old lungs, and being overcome by the strong-voiced gallery, and at last sadly succumbing to St. David's. Again he writes: "I set York tune and the Congregation went out of it into St. Davids in the very 2nd going over. They did the same 3 weeks before. This is the 2nd Sign. It seems to me an intimation for me to resign the Praecentor's Place to a better Voice. I have through the Divine Long suffering and Favour done it for 24 years and now God in his Providence seems to call me off, my voice being enfeebled." Still a third time he "set Windsor tune;" they "ran over into Oxford do what I would." These unseemly "running overs" became so common that ere long each singer "set the tune" at his own will and the loudest-voiced carried the day. A writer of the time, Rev. Thomas Walter, says of this reign of *concordia discors*: "The tunes are now miserably tortured and twisted and quavered, in some Churches, into a horrid Medly of confused and disorderly Voices.

Our tunes are left to the Mercy of every unskilful Throat to chop and alter, to twist and change, according to their infinitely divers and no less Odd Humours and Fancies. I have myself paused twice in one note to take breath. No two Men in the Congregation quaver alike or together, it sounds in the Ears of a Good Judge like five hundred different Tunes roared out at the same Time, with perpetual Interfearings with one another."

Still, confused and poor as was the singing, it was a source of pure and unceasing delight to the Puritan colonists,--one of the rare pleasures they possessed,--a foretaste of heaven;

"for all we know
Of what the blessed do above
Is that they sing and that they love."

And to even that remnant of music--their few jumbled cacophonous melodies--they clung with a devotion almost phenomenal.

Nor should we underrate the cohesive power that psalm-singing proved in the early communities; it was one of the most potent influences in gathering and holding the colonists together in love. And they reverenced their poor halting tunes in a way quite beyond our modern power of fathoming. Whenever a Puritan, even in road or field, heard at a distance the sound of a psalm-tune, though the sacred words might be quite undistinguishable, he doffed his hat and bowed his head in the true presence of God. We fain must believe, as Arthur Hugh Clough says,--

"There is some great truth, partial, very likely, but
needful, Lodged, I am strangely sure, in the tones of an
English psalm-tune."

Judge Sewall often writes with tender and simple pathos of his being moved to tears by the singing,--sometimes by the music, sometimes by the words. "The song of the 5th Revelation was sung. I was ready to burst into tears at the words, *bought with thy blood.*" He also, with a vehemence of language most unusual in him and which showed his deep feeling, wrote that he had an intense passion for music. And yet, the only tunes he or any of his fellow-colonists knew were the simple ones called Oxford, Litchfield, Low Dutch, York, Windsor, Cambridge, St. David's and Martyrs.

About the year 1714 Rev. John Tufts, of Newbury, who had previously prepared "A very Plain and Easy Introduction to the Art of Singing Psalm-tunes," issued a collection of tunes in three parts. These thirty-seven tunes, all of which but one were in common metre, were bound often with "The Bay Psalm-Book." They were reprinted from Playford's "Book of Psalms" and the notes of the staff were replaced with letters and dots, and the bars marking the measures were omitted. To the Puritans, this great number of new tunes appeared fairly monstrous, and formed the signal for bitter objections and fierce quarrels.

In 1647 a tract had appeared on church-singing which had attracted much attention. It was written by Rev John Cotton to attempt to influence the adoption and universal use of "The Bay Psalm-Book." This tract thoroughly considered the duty of singing, the matter sung, the singers, and the manner of singing, and, like all the literature of the time, was full of Biblical allusion and quotation. It had been said that "man should sing onely and not the women. Because it is not permitted to a woman to speake in the Church, how then shall they sing? Much lesse is it permitted to them to prophecy in the church and singing of Psalms is a kind of Prophecying." Cotton fully answered and contradicted these false reasoners, who would have had to face a revolution had they attempted to keep the Puritan women from singing in meeting. The tract abounds in quaint expressions, such as, "they have scoffed at Puritan Ministers as calling the people to sing one of *Hopkins-Jiggs* and so *hop* into the pulpit." Though he wrote this tract to encourage good singing in meeting, his endorsement of "lining the Psalm" gave support to the very element that soon ruined the singing. His reasons, however, were temporarily good, "because many wanted books and skill to read." At that time, and for a century later, many congregations had but one or two psalm-books, one of which was often bound with the church Bible and from which the deacon lined the psalm.

So villanous had church-singing at last become that the clergymen arose in a body and demanded better performances; while a desperate and disgusted party was also formed which was opposed to all singing. Still another band of old fogies was strong in force who wished to cling to the same way of singing that they were accustomed to; and they gave many objections to the new-fangled idea of singing by note, the chief item on the list being the everlasting objection of all such old fossils, that "the old way was good enough for our fathers," &c. They also asserted that "*the names of the notes were blasphemous;*" that it was "popish;" that it was a contrivance to get money; that it would bring musical instruments into the churches; and that "no one could learn the tunes any way." A writer in the "New England Chronicle" wrote in 1723, "Truly I have a great jealousy that if we begin to *sing* by *rule*, the next thing will be to *pray* by rule and *preach* by rule and *then comes popery.*"

It is impossible to overestimate the excitement, the animosity, and the contention which arose in the New England colonies from these discussions over "singing by rule" or "singing by rote." Many prominent clergymen wrote essays and tracts upon the subject; of these essays "The

Reasonableness of Regular Singing," also a "Joco-serious Dialogue on Singing," by Reverend Mr. Symmes; "Cases of Conscience," compiled by several ministers; "The Accomplished Singer," by Cotton Mather, were the most important. "Singing Lectures" also were given in many parts of New England by various prominent ministers. So high was party feud that a "Pacificatory Letter" was necessary, which was probably written by Cotton Mather, and which soothed the troubled waters. The people who thought the "old way was the best" were entirely satisfied when they were convinced that the oldest way of all was, of course, by note and not by rote.

This naive extract from the records of the First Church of Windsor, Connecticut, will show the way in which the question of "singing by rule" was often settled in the churches, and it also gives a very amusing glimpse of the colonial manner of conducting a meeting:--

"July 2. 1736. At a Society meeting at which Capt. Pelatiah Allyn Moderator. The business of the meeting proceeded in the following manner Viz. the Moderator proposed as to the consideration of the meeting in the 1st Place what should be done respecting that part of publick Woiship called Singing viz. whether in their Publick meetings as on Sabbath day, Lectures &c they would sing the way that Deacon Marshall usually sung in his lifetime commonly called the 'Old Way' or whether they would sing the way taught by Mr. Beal commonly called 'Singing by Rule,' and when the Society had discoursed the matter the Moderator pioposed to vote for said two ways as followeth viz. that those that were for singing in publick in the way practiced by Deacon Marshall should hold up their hands and be counted, and then that those that were desirous to sing in Mr. Beals way called 'by Rule' would after show their minds by the same sign which method was proceeded upon accordingly. But when the vote was passed there being many voters it was difficult to take the exact number of votes in order to determine on which side the major vote was; whereupon the Moderator ordered all the voters to go out of the seats and stand in the alleys and then those that were for Deacon Marshalls way should go into the mens seats and those that were for Mr. Beals way should go into the womens seat and after much objections made against that way, which prevailed not with the Moderator, it was complied with, and then the Moderator desired that those that were of the mind that the way to be practiced for singing for the future on the Sabbath &c should be the way sung by Deacon Marshall as aforesaid would signify the same by holding up their hands and be counted, and then the Moderator and myself went and counted the voters and the Moderator asked me how many there was. I answered 42 and he said there was 63 or 64 and then we both counted again and agreed the number being 43. Then the Moderator was about to count the number of votes for Mr.

Beals way of Singing called 'by Rule' but it was offered whether it would not be better to order the voters to pass out of the Meeting House door and there be counted who did accordingly and their number was 44 or 45. Then the Moderator proceeded and desired that those who were for singing in Public the way that Mr. Beal taught would draw out of their seats and pass out of the door and be counted. They replied they were ready to show their minds in any proper way where they were if they might be directed thereto but would not go out of the door to do the same and desired that they might be led to a vote where they were and they were ready to show their minds which the Moderator refused to do and thereupon declared that it was voted that Deacon Marshalls way of singing called the 'Old Way' should be sung in Publick for the future and ordered me to record the same as the vote of the Said Society which I refused to do under the circumstances thereof and have recorded the facts and proceedings."

Good old lining, droning Deacon Marshall! though you were dead and gone, you and your years of psalm-singings were not forgotten. You lived, an idealized memory of pure and pious harmony, in the hearts of your old church friends. Warmly did they fight for your "way of singing;" with most undeniable and open partiality, with most dubious ingenuousness and rectitude, did your old neighbor, Captain Pelatiah Allyn, conduct that hot July music-meeting, counting up boldly sixty-three votes in favor of your way, when there were only forty-three voters on your side of the alley, and crowding a final decision in your favor. It is sad to read that when icy winter chilled the blood, warm partisanship of old friends also cooled, and innovative Windsor youth carried the day and the music vote, and your good old way was abandoned for half the Sunday services, to allow the upstart new fashion to take control.

One happy result arose throughout New England from the victory of the ardent advocates of the "singing by rule,"--the establishment of the New England "singing-school,"--that outlet for the pent-up, amusement-lacking lives of young people in colonial times. What that innocent and happy gathering was in the monotonous existence of our ancestors and ancestresses, we of the present pleasure-filled days can hardly comprehend.

Extracts from the records of various colonial churches will show how soon the respective communities yielded to the march of improvement and "seated the taught singers" together, thus forming choirs. In 1762 the church at Rowley, Massachusetts, voted "that those who have learned the art of Singing may have liberty to sit in the front gallery." In 1780 the same parish "requested Jonathan Chaplin and Lieutenant Spefford to assist the deacons in Raising the tune in the meeting house." In Sutton, in 1791, the Company of Singers were allowed to sit together, and $13 was voted to pay for "larning to sing by Rule." The Roxbury "First Church" voted in 1770 "three seats in the back gallery for those inclined to sit together for the purpose of singing" The church in Hanover, in 1742, took a vote to see whether the "church will sing in the new way" and appoint a tuner. In Woodbury, Connecticut, in 1750 the singers "may sitt up Galery all day if they please but to keep to there own seat & not to Infringe on the Women Pues." In 1763, in the Ipswich First Parish, the singers were allowed to sit "two back on each side of the front alley." Similar entries may be found in nearly every record of New England churches in the middle or latter part of that century.

The musical battle was not finished, however, when the singing was at last taught by rule, and the singers were allowed to sit together and form a choir. There still existed the odious custom of "lining" or "deaconing" the psalm. To this fashion may be attributed the depraved condition of church-singing of which Walters so forcibly wrote, and while it continued the case seemed hopeless, in spite of singing-schools and singing-teachers. It would be trying to the continued uniformity of pitch of an ordinary church choir, even now-a-days, to have to stop for several seconds between each line to listen to a reading and sometimes to an explanation of the following line.

The Westminster Assembly had suggested in 1664 the alternate reading and singing of each line of the psalm to those churches that were not well supplied with psalm-books. The suggestion had not been adopted without discussion, It was in 1680 much talked over in the church in Plymouth, and was adopted only after getting the opinion of each male church member. When once taken into general use the custom continued everywhere, through carelessness and obstinacy, long after the churches possessed plenty of psalm-books. An early complaint against it was made by Dr. Watts in the preface of his hymns, which were published by Benjamin Franklin in 1741. As Watts' Psalms and Hymns were not, however, in general use in New England until after the Revolution, this preface with its complaint was for a long time little seen and little heeded.

It is said that the abolition came gradually; that the impetuous and well-trained singers at first cut off the last word only of the deacon's "lining;" they then encroached a word or two further, and finally sung boldly on without stopping at all to be "deaconed." This brought down a tempest of indignation from the older church-members, who protested, however, in vain. A vote in the church usually found the singers victorious, and whether the church voted for or against the "lining," the choir would always by stratagem vanquish the deacon. One old soldier took his revenge, however. Being sung down by the rampant choir, he still showed battle, and rose at the conclusion of the psalm and opened his psalm-book, saying calmly, "*Now* let the *people of the Lord sing.*"

The Rowley church tried diplomacy in their struggle against "deaconing," by instituting a gradual abolishing of the custom. In 1785 the choir was allowed "to sing once on the Lord's Day without reading by the Deacon." In five years the Rowley singers were wholly victorious, and "lining out" the psalm was entirely discontinued.

In 1770, dissatisfaction at the singing in the church was rife in Wilbraham, and a vote was taken to see whether the town would be willing to have singing four times at each service; and it was voted to "take into consideration the Broken State of this Town with regard to singing on the Sabbath Day." Special and bitter objection was made against the leader beating time so ostentatiously. A list of singers was made and a singing-master appointed. The deacon was allowed to lead and line and beat time in the forenoon, while the new school was to have control in the afternoon; and "whoever leads the singing shall be at liberty to use the motion of his hand while singing for the space of three months only." It is needless to state who came off victorious in the end. The deacon left as a parting shot a request to "make Inquiry into the conduct of those who call themselves the Singers in this town."

In Worcester, in 1779, a resolution adopted at the town meeting was "that the mode of singing in the congregation here be without reading the psalms line by line." "The Sabbath succeeding the adoption of this resolution, after the hymn had been read by the minister, the aged and venerable Deacon Chamberlain, unwilling to abandon the custom of his fathers and his own honorable prerogative, rose and read the first line according to his usual practice. The singers, previously prepared to carry the desired alteration into effect, proceeded in their singing without pausing at the conclusion of the line. The white-haired officer of the church with the full power of his voice read on through the second line, until the loud notes of the collected body of singers overpowered his attempt to resist the progress of improvement. The deacon, deeply mortified at the triumph of the musical reformation, then seized his hat and retired from the meeting-house in tears." His conduct was censured by the church, and he was for a time deprived of partaking in the communion, for "absenting himself from the public services of the Sabbath;" but in a few weeks the unhouselled deacon was forgiven, and never attempted to "line" again.

Though the opponents of "lining" were victorious in the larger villages and towns, in smaller parishes, where there were few hymn-books, the lining of the psalms continued for many years. Mr. Hood wrote, in 1846, the astonishing statement that "the habit of lining prevails to this day over three-fourths of the United States." This I can hardly believe, though I know that at present the practice obtains in out of the way towns with poor and ignorant congregations. The separation of the lines often gives a very strange meaning to the words of a psalm; and one wonders what the Puritan children thought when they heard this lino of contradictions that Hood points out:--

"The Lord will come and He will not,"

and after singing that line through heard the second line,--

"Keep silence, but speak out."

Many new psalm-books appeared about the time of the Revolutionary War, and many church petitions have been preserved asking permission to use the new and more melodious psalm and hymn books. Books of instruction also abounded,--books in which the notes were not printed on the staff, and books in which there were staffs but no notes, only letters or other characters (these were called "dunce notes"); books, too, in which the notes were printed so thickly that they could scarcely be distinguished one from the other.

"A dotted tribe with ebon heads
That climb the slender fence along,
As black as ink, as thick as weeds,
Ye little Africans of song."

One book--perhaps the worst, since it was the most pretentious--was "The Compleat Melody or Harmony of Sion," by William Tansur,--"Ingenious Tans'ur Skilled in Musicks Art." It was a most superficial, pedantic, and bewildering composition. The musical instruction was given in the form of a series of ill-spelled dialogues between a teacher and pupil, interspersed with occasional miserable rhymes. It was ill-expressed at best, and such musical terms as "Rations of Concords," "Trilloes," "Trifdiapasons," "Leaps," "Binding cadences," "Disallowances," "Canons," "Prime Flower of Florid," "Consecutions of Perfects," and "Figurates," make the book exceedingly difficult of comprehension to the average reader, though possibly not to a student of obsolete musical phraseology.

A side skirmish on the music field was at this time fought between the treble and the tenor parts. Ravenscroft's Psalms and Walter's book had given the melody, or plain-song, to the tenor. This had, of course, thrown additional difficulties in the way of good singing; but when once the trebles obtained the leading part, after the customary bitter opposition, the improved singing approved the victory.

Many objections, too, were made to the introduction of "triple-time" tunes. It gave great offence to the older Puritans, who wished to drawl out all the notes of uniform length; and some persons thought that marking and accenting the measure was a step toward the "Scarlet Woman." The time was called derisively, "a long leg and a short one."

These old bigots must have been paralyzed at the new style of psalm-singing which was invented and introduced by a Massachusetts tanner and singing-master named Billings, and which was suggested, doubtless, by the English anthems. It spread through the choirs of colonial villages and towns like wild-fire, and was called "fuguing." Mr. Billings' "Fuguing Psalm Singer" was published in 1770. It is a dingy, ill-printed book with a comically illustrated frontispiece, long pages of instruction, and this motto:--

"O, praise the Lord with one consent
And in this grand design
Let Britain and the Colonies
Unanimously join."

The succeeding hymn-books, and the patriotic hymns of Billings in post-Revolutionary years have no hint of "Britain" in them. The names "Federal Harmony," "Columbian Harmony," "Continental Harmony," "Columbian Repository," and "United States Sacred Harmony" show the new nation. Billings also published the "Psalm Singer's Amusement," and other singing-books. The shades of Cotton, of Sewall, of Mather must have groaned aloud at the suggestions, instructions, and actions of this unregenerate, daring, and "amusing" leader of church-singing.

It seems astonishing that New England communities in those times of anxious and depressing warfare should have so delightedly seized and adopted this unusual and comparatively joyous style of singing, but perhaps the new spirit of liberty demanded more animated and spirited expression; and Billings' psalm-tunes were played with drum and fife on the battlefield to inspire the American soldiers. Billings wrote of his fuguing invention, "It has more than twenty times the power of the old slow tunes. Now the solemn bass demands their attention, next the manly tenor, now the lofty counter, now the volatile treble. Now here! Now there! Now here again! Oh ecstatic, push on, ye sons of harmony!" Dr. Mather Byles wrote thus of fuguing:--

"Down starts the Bass with Grave Majestic Air,
And up the Treble mounts with shrill Career,
With softer Sounds in mild melodious Maze
Warbling between, the Tenor gently plays
And, if th' inspiring Altos joins the Force
See! like the Lark it Wings its towering Course
Thro' Harmony's sublimest Sphere it flies
And to Angelic Accents seems to rise."

A more modern poet in affectionate remembrance thus sings the fugue:--

> "A fugue let loose cheers up the place,
>   With bass and tenor, alto, air,
> The parts strike in with measured grace,
>   And something sweet is everywhere.
>
> "As if some warbling brood should build
>   Of bits of tunes a singing nest;
> Each bringing that with which it thrilled
>   And weaving it with all the rest."

All public worshippers in the meetings one hundred years ago did not, however, regard fuguing as "something sweet everywhere," nor did they agree with Billings and Byles as to its angelic and ecstatic properties. Some thought it "heartless, tasteless, trivial, and irreverent jargon." Others thought the tunes were written more for the absurd inflation of the singers than for the glory of God; and many fully sympathized with the man who hung two cats over Billings's door to indicate his opinion of Billings's caterwauling. An old inhabitant of Roxbury remembered that when fuguing tunes were introduced into his church "they produced a literally fuguing effect on the older people, who went out of the church as soon as the first verse was sung." One scandalized and belligerent old clergyman, upon the Sabbath following the introduction of fuguing into his church, preached upon the prophecy of Amos, "The songs of the temple shall be turned into howling," while another took for his text the sixth verse of the seventeenth chapter of Acts, "Those that have turned the world upside down, are come hither also." One indignant and disgusted church attendant thus profanely recorded in church his views:--

"Written out of temper on a Pannel in one of the Pues in Salem Church:--

> "Could poor King David but for once
>   To Salem Church repair;
> And hear his Psalms thus warbled out,
>   Good Lord, how he would swear
>
> "But could St Paul but just pop in,
>   From higher scenes abstracted,
> And hear his Gospel now explained,
>   By Heavens, he'd run distracted."

These lines were reprinted in the "American Apollo" in 1792.

The repetition of a word or syllable in fuguing often lead to some ridiculous variations in the meanings of the lines. Thus the words--

"With reverence let the saints appear
And bow before the Lord,"

were forced to be sung, "And bow-wow-wow, And bow-ow-ow," and so on until bass, treble, alto, counter, and tenor had bow-wowed for about twenty seconds; yet I doubt if the simple hearts that sung ever saw the absurdity.

It is impossible while speaking of fuguing to pass over an extraordinary element of the choir called "singing counter." The counter-tenor parts in European church-music were originally written for boys' voices. From thence followed the falsetto singing of the part by men; such was also the "counter" of New England. It was my fortune to hear once in a country church an aged deacon "sing counter". Reverence for the place and song, and respect for the singer alike failed to control the irrepressible start of amazement and smile of amusement with which we greeted the weird and apparently demented shriek which rose high over the voices of the choir, but which did not at all disconcert their accustomed ears. Words, however chosen, would fail in attempting to describe the grotesque and uncanny sound.

It is very evident, when once choirs of singers were established and attempts made for congregations to sing the same tune, and to keep together, and upon the same key, that in some way a decided pitch must be given to them to start upon. To this end pitch-pipes were brought into the singers' gallery, and the pitch was given sneakingly and shamefacedly to the singers. From these pitch-pipes the steps were gradual, but they led, as the Puritan divines foresaw, to the general introduction of musical instruments into the meetings.

This seemed to be attacking the very foundations of their church; for the Puritans in England had, in 1557, expressly declared "concerning singing of psalms we allow of the people joining with one voice in a plain tune, but not in tossing the psalms from one side to the other with mingling of organs." The Round-heads had, in 1664, gone through England destroying the noble organs in the churches and cathedrals. They tore the pipes from the organ in Westminster Abbey, shouting, "Hark! how the organs go!" and, "Mark what musick that is, that is lawful for a Puritan to dance," and they sold the metal for pots of ale. Only four or five organs were left uninjured in all England. 'Twas not likely, then, that New England Puritans would take kindly to any musical instruments. Cotton Mather declared that there was not a word in the New Testament that authorized the use of such aids to devotion. The ministers preached often and long on the text from the prophecy of Amos, "I will not hear the melody of thy viols;" while, Puritan-fashion, they ignored the other half of the verse, "Take thou away from me the noise of thy songs." Disparaging comparisons were made with Nebuchadnezzar's idolatrous concert of cornet, flute, dulcimer, sackbut, and psaltery; and the ministers, from their overwhelming store of Biblical knowledge, hurled text after text at the "fiddle-players."

Some of the first pitch-pipes were comical little apple-wood instruments that looked like mouse-traps, and great pains was taken to conceal them as they were passed surreptitiously from hand to hand in the choir. I have seen one which was carefully concealed in a box that had a leather binding like a book, and which was ostentatiously labelled in large gilt letters "Holy Bible;" a piece of barefaced and unnecessary deception on the part of some pious New England deacon or chorister.

Little wooden fifes were also used, and then metal tuning-forks. A canny Scotchman, who abhorred the thought of all musical instruments anywhere, managed to have one fling at the pitch-pipe. The pitch had been given but was much too high, and before the first verse was ended the choir had to cease singing. The Scotchman stood up and pointed his long finger to the leader, saying in broad accents of scorn, "Ah, Johnny Smuth, now ye can have a chance to blaw yer braw whustle agaen." At a similar catastrophe owing to the mistake of the leader in Medford, old General Brooks rose in his pew and roared in an irritated voice of command, "Halt! Take another pitch, Bailey, take another pitch."

In 1713 there was sent to America an English organ, "a pair of organs" it was called, which had chanced, by being at the manufacturers instead of in a church, to have escaped the general destruction by the Round-heads. It was given by Thomas Brattle to the Brattle Street Church in Boston. The congregation voted to refuse the gift, and it was then sent to King's Chapel, where it remained unpacked for several months for fear of hostile demonstrations, but was finally set up and used. In 1740 a Bostonian named Bromfield made an organ, and it was placed in a meeting-house and used weekly. In 1794 the church in Newbury obtained an organ, and many unpleasant and disparaging references were made by clergymen of other parishes to "our neighbor's box of whistles," "the tooting tub."

Violoncellos, or bass-viols, as they were universally called, were almost the first musical instruments that were allowed in the New England churches. They were called, without intentional irreverence, "Lord's fiddles." Violins were widely opposed, they savored too much of low, tavern dance-music. After much consultation a satisfactory compromise was agreed upon by which violins were allowed in many meetings, if the performers "would play the fiddle wrong end up." Thus did our sanctimonious grandfathers cajole and persuade themselves that an inverted fiddle was not a fiddle at all, but a small bass-viol. An old lady, eighty years old, wrote thus in the middle of this century, of the church of her youth: "After awhile there was a bass-viol Introduced and brought into meeting and did not suit the Old people; one Old Gentleman got up, took his hat off the peg and marched off. Said they had begun fiddling and there would be dancing soon." Another church-member, in derisive opposition to a clarinet which had been "voted into the choir," brought into meeting a fish-horn, which he blew loud and long to the complete rout of the clarinet-player and the singers. When reproved for this astounding behavior he answered stoutly that "if one man could blow a horn in the Lord's House on the Sabbath day he guessed he could too," and he had to be bound over to keep the peace before the following Sunday. A venerable and hitherto decorous old deacon of Roxbury not only left the church when the hated bass-viol began its accompanying notes, but he stood for a long time outside the church door stridently "caterwauling" at the top of his lungs. When expostulated with for this unseemly and unchristianlike annoyance he explained that he was "only mocking the banjo." To such depths of rebellion were stirred the Puritan instincts of these religious souls.

Many a minister said openly that he would like to walk out of his pulpit when the obnoxious and hated flutes, violins, bass-viols, and bassoons were played upon in the singing gallery. One clergyman contemptuously announced "We will now sing and fiddle the forty-fifth Psalm." Another complained of the indecorous dress of the fiddle-player. This had reference to the almost universal custom, in country churches in the summer time, of the bass-viol player removing his coat and playing "in his shirt sleeves." Others hated the noisy tuning of the bass-viol while the psalm was being read. Mr. Brown, of Westerly, sadly deplored that "now we have only catgut and resin religion."

In 1804 the church in Quincy, being "advanced," granted the singers the sum of twenty-five dollars to buy a bass-viol to use in meeting, and a few other churches followed their lead. From the year 1794 till 1829 the church in Wareham, Massachusetts, was deeply agitated over the question of "Bass-Viol, or No Bass-Viol." They voted that a bass-viol was "expedient," then they voted to expel the hated abomination; then was obtained "Leave for the Bass Viol to be brought into ye meeting house to be Played On every other Sabbath & to Play if chosen every Sabbath in the Intermission between meetings & not to Pitch the Tunes on the Sabbaths that it don't Play" Then, they tried to bribe the choir for fifty dollars not to use the "bars-vile," but being unsuccessful, many members in open rebellion stayed away from church and were disciplined therefor. Then they voted that the bass-viol could not be used unless Capt. Gibbs were previously notified (so he and his family need not come to hear the hated sounds); but at last, after thirty years, the choir and the "fiddle-player" were triumphant in Wareham as they were in other towns.

We were well into the present century before any cheerful and also simple music was heard in our churches; fuguing was more varied and surprising than cheerful. Of course, it was difficult as well as inappropriate to suggest pleasing tunes for such words as these:--

"Far in the deep where darkness dwells,
 The land of horror and despair,
Justice hath built a dismal hell,
 And laid her stores of vengeance there:

"Eternal plagues and heavy chains,
 Tormenting racks and fiery coals,
And darts to inflict immortal pains,
 Dyed in the blood of damned souls."

But many of the words of the old hymns were smooth, lively, and encouraging; and the young singers and perhaps the singing-masters craved new and less sober tunes. Old dance tunes were at first adapted; "Sweet Anne Page," "Babbling Echo," "Little Pickle" were set to sacred words. The music of "Few Happy Matches" was sung to the hymn "Lo, on a narrow neck of land;" and that of "When I was brisk and young" was disguised with the sacred words of "Let sinners take their course." The jolly old tune, "Begone dull care," which began,--

"My wife shall dance, and I will sing,
 And merrily pass the day."

was strangely appropriated to the solemn words,--

"If this be death, I soon shall be
 From every pain and sorrow free,"

and did not seem ill-fitted either.

"Sacred arrangements," "spiritual songs," "sacred airs," soon followed, and of course demanded singers of capacity and education to sing them. From this was but a step to a paid quartette, and the struggle over this last means of improvement and pleasure in church music is of too recent a date to be more than referred to.

I attended a church service not many years ago in Worcester, where an old clergyman, the venerable "Father" Allen, of Shrewsbury, then too aged and feeble to preach, was seated in the front pew of the church.

When a quartette of singers began to render a rather operatic arrangement of a sacred song he rose, erect and stately, to his full gaunt height, turned slowly around and glanced reproachfully over the frivolous, backsliding congregation, wrapped around his spare, lean figure his full cloak of quilted black silk, took his shovel hat and his cane, and stalked indignantly and sadly the whole length of the broad central aisle, out of the church, thus making a last but futile protest against modern innovations in church music. Many, in whom the Puritan instincts and blood are still strong, sympathize internally with him in this feeling; and all novelty-lovers must acknowledge that the sublime simplicity and deep piety in which the old Puritan psalm-tunes abound, has seldom been attained in the modern church-songs. Even persons of neither musical knowledge, taste, nor love, feel the power of such a tune as Old Hundred; and more modern and more difficult melodies, though they charm with their harmony and novelty, can never equal it in impressiveness nor in true religious influence.

XVI
The Interruptions of the Services

Though the Puritans were such a decorous, orderly people, their religious meetings were not always quiet and uninterrupted. We know the torment they endured from the "wretched boys," and they were harassed by other annoying interruptions. For the preservation of peace and order they made characteristic laws, with characteristic punishments. "If any interrupt or oppose a preacher in season of worship, they shall be reproved by the Magistrate, and on repetition, shall pay £5, or stand two hours on a block four feet high, with this inscription in Capitalls, 'A WANTON GOSPELLER.'" As with other of their severe laws the rigid punishment provoked the crime, for Wanton Gospellers abounded. The Baptists did not hesitate to state their characteristic belief in the Puritan meetings, and the Quakers or "Foxians," as they were often called, interrupted and plagued them sorely. Judge Sewall wrote, in 1677, "A female quaker, Margaret Brewster, in sermon-time came in, in a canvass frock, her hair dishevelled loose like a Periwig, her face as black as ink, led by two other quakers, and two other quakers followed. It occasioned the greatest and most amazing uproar that I ever saw." More grievous irruptions still of scantily clad and even naked Quaker women were made into other Puritan meetings; and Quaker men shouted gloomily in through the church windows, "Woe! Woe! Woe to the people!" and, "The Lord will destroy thee!" and they broke glass bottles before the minister's very face, crying out, "Thus the Lord will break thee in pieces!" and they came into the meeting-house, in spite of the fierce tithingman, and sat down in other people's seats with their hats on their heads, in ash-covered coats, rocking to and fro and groaning dismally, as if in a mournful obsession. Quaker women managed to obtain admission to the churches, and they jumped up in the quiet Puritan assemblies screaming out, "Parson! thou art an old fool," and, "Parson! thy sermon is too long," and, "Parson! sit down! thee has already said more than thee knows how to say well," and other unpleasant, though perhaps truthful personalities. It is hard to believe that the poor, excited, screaming visionaries of those early days belonged to the same religious sect as do the serene, low-voiced, sweet-faced, and retiring Quakeresses of to-day. And there is no doubt that the astounding and meaningless freaks of these half-crazed fanatics were provoked by the cruel persecutions which they endured from our much loved and revered, but alas, intolerant and far from perfect Puritan Fathers. These poor Quakers were arrested, fined, robbed, stripped naked, imprisoned, laid neck and heels, chained to logs of wood, branded, maimed, whipped, pilloried, caged, set in the stocks, exiled, sold into slavery and hanged by our stern and cruel ancestors. Perhaps some gentle-hearted but timid Puritan souls may have inwardly felt that the Indian wars, and the destructive fires, and the earthquakes, and the dead cattle, blasted wheat, and wormy peas, were not judgments of God for small ministerial pay and periwig-wearing, but punishments for the heartrending woes of the persecuted Quakers. Others than the poor Quakers spoke out in colonial meetings. In Salem village and in other witch-hunting towns the crafty "victims" of the witches were frequently visited with their mock pains and sham fits in the meeting-houses, and they called out and interrupted the ministers most vexingly. Ann Putnam, the best and boldest actress among those cunning young Puritan witch-accusers, the protagonist of that New England tragedy known as the Salem Witchcraft, shouted out most embarrassingly, "There is a yellow-bird sitting on the minister's hat, as it hangs on the pin in the pulpit." Mr. Lawson, the minister, wrote with much simplicity that "these things occurring in the time of public worship did something interrupt me in my first prayer, being so unusual." But he braced himself up in spite of Ann and the demoniacal yellow-bird, and finished the service. These disorderly interruptions occurred on every Lord's Day, growing weekly more constant and more universal, and must have been unbearable. Some few disgusted members withdrew from the church, giving as reason that "the distracting and disturbing tumults and noises made by persons under diabolical power and delusions, preventing sometimes our hearing and understanding and profiting of the word preached; we having after many trials and experiences found no redress in this case, accounted ourselves under a necessity to go where we might hear the word in quiet." These withdrawing church-members were all of families that contained at least one person that had been accused of practising witchcraft. They were thus severely intolerant of the sacrilegious and lawless interruptions of the shy young "victims," who received in general only sympathy, pity, and even stimulating encouragement from their deluded and excited neighbors.

One very pleasing interruption,--no, I cannot call it by so severe a name,--one very pleasing diversion of the attention of the congregation from the parson was caused by an innocent custom that prevailed in many a country community. Just fancy the flurry on a June Sabbath in Killingly, in 1785, when Joseph Gay, clad in velvet coat, lace-frilled shirt, and white broadcloth knee-breeches, with his fair bride of a few days, gorgeous in a peach-colored silk gown and a bonnet trimmed "with sixteen yards of white ribbon," rose, in the middle of the sermon, from their front seat in the gallery and stood for several minutes, slowly turning around in order to show from every point of view their bridal finery to the eagerly gazing congregation of friends and neighbors. Such was the really delightful and thoughtful custom, in those fashion-plateless days, among persons of wealth in that and other churches; it was, in fact, part of the wedding celebration. Even in midwinter, in the icy church, the blushing bride would throw aside her broadcloth cape or camblet roquelo and stand up clad in a sprigged India muslin gown with only a thin lace tucker over her neck, warm with pride in her pretty gown, her white bonnet with ostrich feathers and embroidered veil, and in her new husband.

The services in the meeting-house on the Sabbath and on Lecture days were sometimes painfully varied, though scarcely interrupted, by a very distressing and harrowing custom of public abasement and self-abnegation, which prevailed for many years in the nervously religious colonies. It was not an enforced punishment, but a voluntary one. Men and women who had committed crimes or misdemeanors, and who had sincerely repented of their sins, or who were filled with remorse for some violation of conscience, or even with regret for some neglect of religious ethics, rose in the Sabbath meeting before the assembled congregation and confessed their sins, and humbly asked forgiveness of God, and charity from their fellows. At other times they stood with downcast heads while the minister read their confession of guilt and plea for forgiveness. A most graphic account of one of those painful scenes is thus given by Governor Winthrop in his "History of New England:"--

> "Captain Underhill being brought by the blessing of God in this church's censure of excommunication, to remorse for his foul sins, obtained, by means of the elders, and others of the church of Boston, a safe conduct under the hand of the governor and one of the council to repair to the church. He came at the time of the court of assistants, and upon the lecture day, after sermon, the pastor called him forth and declared the occasion, and then gave him leave to speak: and in it was a spectacle winch caused many weeping eyes, though it afforded matter of much rejoicing to behold the power of the Lord Jesus in his ordinances, when they are dispensed in his own way, holding forth the authority of his regal sceptre in the simplicity of the gospel came in his worst clothes (being accustomed to take great pride in his

bravery and neatness) without a band, in a foul linen cap pulled close to his eyes; and standing upon a form, he did, with many deep sighs and abundance of tears, lay open his wicked course, his adultery, his hypocrisy, his persecution of God's people here, and especially his pride (as the root of all which caused God to give him over to his other sinful courses) and contempt of the magistrates.... He spake well save that his blubbering &c interrupted him, and all along he discovered a broken and melting heart and gave good exhortations to take heed of such vanities and beginnings of evil as had occasioned his fall; and in the end he earnestly and humbly besought the church to have compassion of him and to deliver him out of the hands of Satan."

What a picture! what a story! "Of all tales 'tis the saddest--and more sad because it makes us smile."

Captain John Underhill was a brave though somewhat bumptious soldier, who had fought under the Prince of Orange in the War of the Netherlands, and had been employed as temporal drill-master in the church-militant in New England. He did good service for the colonists in the war with the Pequot Indians, and indeed wherever there was any fighting to be done. "He thrust about and justled into fame" He also managed to have apparently a very good time in the new land, both in sinning and repenting. When he stood up on the church-seat before the horrified, yet wide-open eyes of pious Boston folk, in his studiously and theatrically disarranged garments, and blubbered out his whining yet vain-glorious repentance, he doubtless acted his part well, for he had twice before been through the same performance, supplementing his second rehearsal by kneeling down before an injured husband in the congregation, and asking earthly forgiveness. I wish I could believe that this final repentance of the resilient captain were sincere--but I cannot. Nor did Boston people believe it either, though that noble and generous-minded man, Winthrop, thought he saw at the time of confession evidences of a truly contrite heart. The Puritans sternly and eagerly cast out the gay captain to the Dutch when he became an Antinomian, and he came to live and fight and gallant in a town on the western end of Long Island, where he perhaps found a church-home with members less severe and less sharp-eyed than those of his Boston place of martyrdom, and a people less inclined to resent and punish his frailties and his ways of amusing himself.

In justice to Underhill (or perhaps to show his double-dealing) I will say that he left behind him a letter to Hanserd Knollys, complaining of the ill-treatment he had received; and in it he gives a very different account of this little affair with the Boston Church from that given us by Governor Winthrop. The offender says nothing about his hypocrisy, his public and self-abasing confession, nor of his sanctimonious blubbering and wishes for death. He explains that his offence was mild and purely mental, that in an infaust moment he glanced (doubtless stared soldier-fashion) at "Mistris Miriam Wildbore" as she sat in her "pue" at meeting. The elders, noting his admiring and amorous glances, thereupon accused him of sin in his heart, and severely asked him why he did not look instead at Mistress Newell or Mistress Upham. He replied very spiritedly and pertinently that these dames were "not desiryable women as to temporal graces," which was certainly sufficient and proper reason for any man to give, were he Puritan or Cavalier. Then acerb old John Cotton and some other Boston ascetics (perhaps Goodman Newell and Goodman Upham, resenting for their wives the *spretæ injuria formæ*) at once hunted up some plainly applicable verses from the Bible that clearly proved him guilty of the alleged sin-- and summarily excommunicated him. He also wrote that the pious church complained that the attractive, the temporally graced Mistress Wildbore came vainly and over-bravely clad to meeting, with "wanton open-worked gloves slitt at the thumbs and fingers for the purpose of taking snuff," and he resented this complaint against the fair one, saying no harm could surely come from indulging in the "good creature called tobacco." He would naturally feel that snuff-taking was a proper and suitable church-custom, since his own conversion,--dubious though it was,--his religious belief had come to him, "the spirit fell home upon his heart" while he was indulging in a quiet smoke.

The story of his offences as told b his contemporaries does not assign to him so innocuous a diversion as staring across the meeting-house, but the account is quite as amusing as his own plaintive and deeply injured version of his arraignment.

Other letters of his have been preserved to us,--letters blustering as was Ancient Pistol, and equally sanctimonious, letters fearfully and phonetically spelt. Here is the opening of a letter written while he was under sentence of excommunication from the Boston Church, and of banishment. It is to Governor Winthrop, his friend and fellow-emigrant:--

"Honnored in the Lord,--

"Your silenc one more admirse me. I Youse chrischan playnnes. I know you love it.... Silene can not reduce the hart of youer lovd brother: I would the rightchous would smite me espechah youerslfe & the honnered Depoti to whom I also dereckt this letter.... I would to God you would tender me soule so as to youse playnnes with me. I wrot to you both but now answer:

& here I am dayli abused by malishous tongue. John Baker I here hath wrot to the honnored depoti how as I was drouck & like to be cild & both falc, upon okachon I delt with Wannerton for intrushon & finddmg them resolutli bent to rout all gud a mong us & advanc there superstischous ways & by boystrous words indeferd to fritten men to accomplish his end. & he abusing me to my face, dru upon him with intent to corb his insolent & dastardli sperrite.... Ister daye on Pickeren their Chorch Warden caim up to us with intent to make some of ourse drone as is sospeckted but the Lord sofered him so to misdemen himslfe as he is likli to li by the hielse this too month.... My homble request is that you will be charitable of me.... Let justies and merci be goyned.... You may plese to soggest youer will to this barrer you will find him tracktabel."

My sense of drollery is always most keenly tickled when I read Underhill's epistles, with their amazing and highly-varied letter concoctions, and remember that he also--wrote a book. What that seventeenth-century printer and proof-reader endured ere they presented his "edited" volume to the public must have been beyond expression by words. It was a pretty good book though, and in it, like many another man of his ilk, he tendered to his much-injured wife loud and diffuse praise, ending with these sententious words, "Let no man despise advice and counsel of his wife--though she be a woman."

And yet, upon careful examination we find a method, a system, in Underhill's orthography, or rather in his cacography. He thinks a final tion should be spelt chon--and why not? "proposichon," "satisfackchon," "oblegachon," "persekuchon," "dereckchon," "himelyachon"--thus he spells such words. And his plurals are plain when once you grasp his laws: "poseschouse" and "considderachonse," "facktse," and "respecktse." And his ly is alwajs li, "exacktli," "thorroli," "fidelliti," "charriti," "falsciti." And why is not "indiered," as good as 'endeared,' "pregedic," as 'prejudice,' "obstrucktter" as 'obstructer,' "paschceges," and "prouydentt," and "antyentt," just as clear as our own way of spelling these words? A "painful" speller you surely were, my gay Don Juan Underbill, as your pedantic "writtingse" all show, and the most dramatic and comic figure among all the early Puritans as well, though you scarcely deserve to be called a Puritan; we might rather say of you, as of Malvolio, "The devil a Puritan that he was, or anything constantly but a time-pleaser ... his ground of faith that all who looked on him loved him."

In keen contrast to this sentimental excitement is the presence of noble Judge Sewall, white-haired and benignant, standing up calmly in Boston meeting, with dignified face and demeanor, but an aching and contrite heart, to ask through the voice of his minister humble forgiveness of God and man for his sad share as a judge in the unjust and awful condemnation and cruel sentencing to death of the poor murdered victims of that terrible delusion the Salem Witchcraft. Years of calm and unshrinking reflection, of pleading and constant communion with God had brought to him an overwhelming sense of his mistaken and over-influenced judgment, and a horror and remorse for the fatal results of his error. Then, like the steadfast and upright old Puritan that he was, he publicly acknowledged his terrible mistake. It is one of the finest instances of true nobility of soul and of absolute self-renunciation that the world affords. And the deep strain, the sharp wrench of the step is made more apparent still by the fact of the disapproval of his fellow-judges of his public confession and recantation. The yearly entries in his diary, simply expressed yet deeply speaking, entries of the prayerful fasts which he spent alone in his chamber when the anniversary of the fatal judgment-day returned, show that no half-vain bigotry, no emotional excitement filled and moved him to the open words of remorse. The lesson of his repentance is farther reaching than he dreamed, when the story of his confession can so move and affect this nineteenth-century generation, and fill more than one soul with a nobler idea of the Puritan nature, and with a higher and fuller conception of the absolute truth of the Puritan Christianity.

Some very prosaic and earthly interruptions to the church services are recorded as being made, and possibly by the church-members themselves. In one church, in 1661, a fine of five shillings was imposed on any one "who shot off a gun or led a horse into the meeting-house." These seem to me quite as unseemly, irreverent, and disagreeable disturbances as shouting out, Quaker-fashion, "Parson, your sermon is too long;" but possibly the house of God was turned into a stable on week-days, not on the Sabbath.

In many parishes church-attendants were fined who brought their "doggs" into the meeting-house. Dogs swarmed in the colony, for they had been imported from England, "sufficient mastive dogs, hounds and beagles," and also Irish wolf-hounds; and they caused an interruption in one afternoon service by chasing into the meeting-house one of those pungently offensive, though harmless, animals that abounded even in the earliest colonial days, and whose mephitic odor, in this case, had power to scatter the congregation as effectively as would have a score of armed Indian braves. Officially appointed "Dogg-whippers" and the never idle tithingman expelled the intruding and unwelcome canine attendants from the meeting-house with fierce blows and fiercer yelps. The swarming dogs, though they were trained to hunt the Indians and wolves and tear them in pieces, were much fonder of hunting and tearing the peaceful sheep, and thus became such unmitigated nuisances, out of meeting as well as in, that they had to be muzzled and hobbled, and killed, and land was granted (as in Newbury in 1703) on condition that no dog was ever kept thereon. As late as the year 1820, it was ordered in the town of Brewster that any dog that came into meeting should be killed unless the owner promised to thenceforth keep the intruder out.

Alarms of fire in the neighborhood frequently disturbed the quiet of the early colonial services; for the combustible catted chimneys were a constant source of conflagration, especially on Sundays, when the fireplaces with their roaring fires were left unwatched; and all the men rushed out of the meeting at sound of the alarm to aid in quenching the flames, which could however be ill-fought with the scanty supply of water that could be brought in a few leathern fire-buckets and milk-pails,--though at a very early date as an aid in extinguishing fires each New England family was ordered by law to own a fire-ladder. Occasionally the town's ladder and poles and hooks and cedar-buckets were kept in the meeting-house, and thus were handy for Sunday fires.

Sometimes armed men, bearing rumors of wars and of hostile attacks, rode clattering up to the church-door, and strode with jingling spurs and rattling swords into the excited assembly with appeal for more soldiers to bear arms, or for more help for those already in the army, and the whole congregation felt it no interruption but a high religious privilege and duty, to which they responded in word and deed. On some happy Sabbaths the armed riders bore good news of great victories, and great was the rejoicing thereat in prayer and praise in the old meeting-house.

But usually through the Sabbath services, though the quiet was not that of our modern carpeted, cushioned, orderly churches, but few interrupting sounds were heard. The cry of a waking infant, the scraping of restless feet on the sanded floor, the lumbering noise of the motions of a cramped farmer as he stood up to lean over the pew-door or gallery-rail, the clatter of an overturned cricket, the twittering of swallows in the rafters, and in the summer-time the bumping and buzzing of an invading bumble-bee as he soared through the air and against the walls, were the only sounds within the meeting-house that broke the monotonous "thirteenthly" and "fourteenthly" of the minister's sermon.

XVII
The Observances of the Day

The so-called "False Blue Laws" of Connecticut, which were foisted upon the public by the Reverend Samuel Peter, have caused much indignation among all thoughtful descendants and all lovers of New England Puritans. Three of his most bitterly resented false laws which refer to the observance of the Sabbath read thus:--

"No one shall travel, cook victuals, make beds, sweep house, cut hair, or shave on the Sabbath Day.

"No woman shall kiss her child on the Sabbath or fasting day.

"No one shall ride on the Sabbath Day, or walk in his garden or elsewhere except reverently to and from meeting."

Though these laws were worded by Dr. Peters, and though we are disgusted to hear them so often quoted as historical facts, still we must acknowledge that though in detail not correct, they are in spirit true records of the old Puritan laws which were enacted to enforce the strict and decorous observance of the Sabbath, and which were valid not only in Connecticut and Massachusetts, but in other New England States. Even a careless glance at the historical record of any old town or church will give plenty of details to prove this.

Thus in New London we find in the latter part of the seventeenth century a wicked fisherman presented before the Court and fined for catching eels on Sunday; another "fined twenty shillings for sailing a boat on the Lord's Day;" while in 1670 two lovers, John Lewis and Sarah Chapman, were accused of and tried for "sitting together on the Lord's Day under an apple tree in Goodman Chapman's Orchard,"--so harmless and so natural an act. In Plymouth a man was "sharply whipped" for shooting fowl on Sunday; another was fined for carrying a grist of corn home on the Lord's Day, and the miller who allowed him to take it was also fined. Elizabeth Eddy of the same town was fined, in 1652, "ten shillings for wringing and hanging out clothes." A Plymouth man, for attending to his tar-pits on the Sabbath, was set in the stocks. James Watt, in 1658, was publicly reproved "for writing a note about common business on the Lord's Day, *at least in the evening somewhat too soon.*" A Plymouth man who drove a yoke of oxen was "presented" before the Court, as was also another offender, who drove some cows a short distance "without need" on the Sabbath.

In Newbury, in 1646, Aquila Chase and his wife were presented and fined for gathering peas from their garden on the Sabbath, but upon investigation the fines were remitted, and the offenders were only admonished. In Wareham, in 1772, William Estes acknowledged himself "Gilty of Racking Hay on the Lord's Day" and was fined ten shillings; and in 1774 another Wareham citizen, "for a breach of the Sabbath in puling apples," was fined five shillings. A Dunstable soldier, for "wetting a piece of an old hat to put in his shoe" to protect his foot--for doing this piece of heavy work on the Lord's Day, was fined, and paid forty shillings.

Captain Kemble of Boston was in 1656 set for two hours in the public stocks for his "lewd and unseemly behavior," which, consisted in his kissing his wife "publicquely" on the Sabbath Day, upon the doorstep of his house, when he had just returned from a voyage and absence of three years. The lewd offender was a man of wealth and influence, the father of Madam Sarah Knights, the "fearfull female travailler" whose diary of a journey from Boston to New York and return, written in 1704, rivals in quality if not in quantity Judge Sewall's much-quoted diary. A traveller named Burnaby tells of a similar offence of an English sea-captain who was soundly whipped for kissing his wife on the street of a New England town on Sunday, and of his retaliation in kind, by a clever trick upon his chastisers; but Burnaby's narrative always seemed to me of dubious credibility.

Abundant proof can be given that the act of the legislature in 1649 was not a dead letter which ordered that "whosoever shall prophane the Lords daye by doeing any seruill worke or such like abusses shall forfeite for euery such default ten shillings or be whipt."

The Vermont "Blue Book" contained equally sharp "Sunday laws." Whoever was guilty of any rude, profane, or unlawful conduct on the Lord's Day, in words or action, by clamorous discourses, shouting, hallooing, screaming, running, riding, dancing, jumping, was to be fined forty shillings and whipped upon the naked back not to exceed ten stripes. The New Haven code of laws, more severe still, ordered that "Profanation of the Lord's Day shall be punished by fine, imprisonment, or corporeal punishment; and if proudly, and with a high hand against the authority of God--*with death.*"

Lists of arrests and fines for walking and travelling unnecessarily on the Sabbath might be given in great numbers, and it was specially ordered that none should "ride violently to and from meeting." Many a pious New

Englander, in olden days, was fined for his ungodly pride, and his desire to "show off" his "new colt" as he "rode violently" up to the meeting-house green on Sabbath morn. One offender explained in excuse of his unnecessary driving on the Sabbath that he had been to visit a sick relative, but his excuse was not accepted. A Maine man who was rebuked and fined for "unseemly walking" on the Lord's Day protested that he ran to save a man from drowning. The Court made him pay his fine, but ordered that the money should be returned to him when he could prove by witnesses that he had been on that errand of mercy and duty. As late as the year 1831, in Lebanon, Connecticut, a lady journeying to her father's home was arrested within sight of her father's house for unnecessary travelling on the Sabbath; and a long and fiercely contested lawsuit was the result, and damages were finally given for false imprisonment. In 1720 Samuel Sabin complained of himself before a justice in Norwich that he visited on Sabbath night some relatives at a neighbor's house. His morbidly tender conscience smote him and made him "fear he had transgressed the law," though he felt sure no harm had been done thereby. In 1659 Sam Clarke, for "Hankering about on men's gates on Sabbath evening to draw company out to him," was reproved and warned not to "harden his neck" and be "wholly destrojed." Poor stiff-necked, lonely, "hankering" Sam! to be so harshly reproved for his harmlessly sociable intents. Perhaps he "hankered" after the Puritan maids, and if so, deserved his reproof and the threat of annihilation.

Sabbath-breaking by visiting abounded in staid Worcester town to a most base extent, but was severely punished, as local records show. In Belfast, Maine, in 1776, a meeting was held to get the "Towns Mind" with regard to a plan to restrain visiting on the Sabbath. The time had passed when such offences could be punished either by fine or imprisonment, so it was voted "that if any person makes unnecessary Vizits on the Sabeth, They shall be Look't on with Contempt." This was the universal expression throughout the Puritan colonies; and looked on with contempt are Sabbath-breakers and Sabbath-slighters in New England to the present day. Even if they committed no active offence, the colonists could not passively neglect the Church and its duties. As late as 1774 the First Church of Roxbury fined non-attendance at public worship. In 1651 Thomas Scott "was fyned ten shillings unless he have learned Mr. Norton's 'Chatacise' by the next court" In 1760 the legislature of Massachusetts passed the law that "any person able of Body who shall absent themselves from publick worship of God on the Lord's Day shall pay ten shillings fine." By the Connecticut code ten shillings was the fine, and the law was not suspended until the year 1770. By the New Haven code five shillings was the fine for non-attendance at church, and the offender was often punished as well. Captain Dennison, one of New

Haven's most popular and respected citizens, was fined fifteen shillings for absence from church. William Blagden, who lived in New Haven in 1647, was "brought up" for absence from meeting. He pleaded that he had fallen into the water late on Saturday, could light no fire on Sunday to dry his clothes, and so had lain in bed to keep warm while his only suit of garments was drying. In spite of this seemingly fair excuse, Blagden was found guilty of "sloathefuluess" and sentenced to be "publiquely whipped." Of course the Quakers contributed liberally to the support of the Court, and were fined in great numbers for refusing to attend the church which they hated, and which also warmly abhorred them; and they were zealously set in the stocks, and whipped and caged and pilloried as well,--whipped if they came and expressed any dissatisfaction, and whipped if they stayed away.

Severe and explicit were the orders with regard to the use of the "Creature called Tobacko" on the Sabbath. In the very earliest days of the colony means had been taken to present the planting of the pernicious weed except in very small quantities "for meere necessitie, for phisick, for preseruaceon of health, and that the same be taken privatly by auncient men." In Connecticut a man could by permission of the law smoke once if he went on a journey of ten miles (as some slight solace for the arduous trip), but never more than once a day, and never in another man's house. Let us hope that on their lonely journeys they conscientiously obeyed the law, though we can but suspect that the one unsocial smoke may have been a long one. In some communities the colonists could not plant tobacco, nor buy it, nor sell it, but since they loved the fascinating weed then as men love it now, they somehow invoked or spirited it into their pipes, though they never could smoke it in public unfined and unpunished. The shrewd and thrifty New Haven people permitted the raising of it for purposes of trade, though not for use, thus supplying the "devil's weed" to others, chiefly the godless Dutch, but piously spurning it themselves--in public. Its use was absolutely forbidden under any circumstances on the Sabbath within two miles of the meeting-house, which (since at that date all the homes were clustered around the church-green) was equivalent to not smoking it at all on the Lord's Day, if the lav were obeyed. But wicked backsliders existed, poor slaves of habit, who were in Duxbury fined ten shillings for each offence, and in Portsmouth, not only were fined, but to their shame be it told, set as jail-birds in the Portsmouth cage. In Sandwich and in Boston the fine for "drinking tobacco in the meeting-house" was five shillings for each drink, which I take to mean chewing tobacco rather than smoking it; many men were fined for thus drinking, and solacing the weary hours, though doubtless they were as sly and kept themselves as unobserved as possible. Four Yarmouth men--old sea-dogs, perhaps, who loved their pipe-

-were, in 1687, fined four shillings each for smoking tobacco around the end of the meeting-house. Silly, ostrich-brained Yarmouth men! to fancy to escape detection by hiding around the corner of the church; and to think that the tithingman had no nose when he was so Argus-eyed. Some few of the ministers used the "tobacco weed." Mr. Baily wrote with distress of mind and abasement of soul in his diary of his "exceeding in tobacco." The hatred of the public use of tobacco lingered long in New England, even in large towns such as Providence, though chiefly on account of universal dread lest sparks from the burning weed should start conflagrations in the towns. Until within a few years, in small towns in western Massachusetts, Easthampton and neighboring villages, tobacco-smoking on the street was not permitted either on weekdays or Sundays.

Not content with strict observance of the Sabbathday alone, the Puritans included Saturday evening in their holy day, and in the first colonial years these instructions were given to Governor Endicott by the New England Plantation Company: "And to the end that the Sabeth may be celebrated in a religious man ner wee appoint that all may surcease their labor every Satterday throughout the yeare at three of the clock in the afternoone, and that they spend the rest of the day in chatechizing and preparacoon for the Sabeth as the ministers shall direct." Cotton Mather wrote thus of his grandfather, old John Cotton: "The Sabbath he begun the evening before, for which keeping from evening to evening he wrote arguments before his coming to New England, and I suppose 't was from his reason and practice that the Christians of New England have generally done so too." He then tells of the protracted religious services held in the Cotton household every Saturday night,--services so long that the Sabbath-day exercises must have seemed in comparison like a light interlude.

John Norton described these Cotton Sabbaths more briefly thus: "He [John Cotton] began the Sabbath at evening; therefore then performed family-duty after supper, being longer than ordinary in Exposition. After which he catechized his children and servants and then returned unto his study. The morning following, family-worship being ended, he retired into his study until the bell called him away. Upon his return from meeting he returned again into his study (the place of his labor and prayer) unto his private devotion; where, having a small repast carried him up for his dinner, he continued until the tolling of the bell. The public service being over, he withdrew for a space to his pre-mentioned oratory for his sacred addresses to God, as in the forenoon, then came down, *repeated the sermon in the family*, prayed, after supper sang a Psalm, and towards bedtime betaking himself again to his study he closed the day with prayer. Thus he spent the

Sabbath continually." Just fancy the Cotton children and servants listening to his long afternoon sermon a second time!

All the New England clergymen were rigid in the prolonged observance of Sunday. From sunset on Saturday until Sunday night they would not shave, have rooms swept, nor beds made, have food prepared, nor cooking utensils and table-ware washed. As soon as their Sabbath began they gathered their families and servants around them, as did Cotton, and read the Bible and exhorted and prayed and recited the catechism until nine o'clock, usually by the light of one small "dip candle" only; on long winter Saturdays it must have been gloomy and tedious indeed. Small wonder that one minister wrote back to England that he found it difficult in the new colony to get a servant who "enjoyed catechizing and family duties." Many clergymen deplored sadly the custom which grew in later years of driving, and even transacting business, on Saturday night. Mr. Bushnell used to call it "stealing the time of the Sabbath," and refused to countenance it in any way.

It was very generally believed in the early days of New England that special judgments befell those who worked on the eve of the Sabbath. Winthrop gives the case of a man who, having hired help to repair a milldam, worked an hour on Saturday after sunset to finish what he had intended for the day's labor. The next day his little child, being left alone for some hours, was drowned in an uncovered well in the cellar of his house. "The father freely, in open congregation, did acknowledge it the righteous hand of God for his profaning his holy day."

Visitors and travellers from other countries were forced to obey the rigid laws with regard to Saturday-night observance. Archibald Henderson, the master of a vessel which entered the port of Boston, complained to the Council for Foreign Plantations in London that while he was in sober Boston town, being ignorant of the laws of the land, and having walked half an hour after sunset on Saturday night, as punishment for this unintentional and trivial offence, a constable entered his lodgings, seized him by the hair of his head, and dragged him to prison. Henderson claimed £800 damages for the detention of his vessel during his prosecution. I have always suspected that the gay captain may have misbehaved himself in Boston on that Saturday night in some other way than simply by walking in the streets, and that the Puritan law-enforcers took advantage of the Sabbath-day laws in order to prosecute and punish him. We know of Bradford's complaint of the times; that while sailors brought "a greate deale" of money from foreign parts to New England to spend, they also brought evil ways of spending it--"more sine I feare than money."

The Puritans found in Scripture support for this observance of Saturday night, in these words, "The evening and the morning were the first day," and they had many followers in their belief. In New England country towns to this day, descendants of the Puritans regard Saturday night, though in a modified way, as almost Sunday, and that evening is never chosen for any kind of gay gathering or visiting. As late as 1855 the shops in Hartford were never open for customers upon Saturday night.

Much satire was directed against this Saturday night observance both by English and by American authors. In the "American Museum" for February, 1787, appeared a poem entitled, "The Connecticut Sabbath." After saying at some length that God had thought one day in seven sufficient for rest, but New England Christians had improved his law by setting apart a day and a half, the poet thus runs on derisively:--

> "And let it be enacted further still
> That all our people strict observe our will;
> Five days and a half shall men, and women, too,
> Attend their bus'ness and their mirth pursue,
> But after that no man without a fine
> Shall walk the streets or at a tavern dine.
> One day and half 'tis requisite to rest
> From toilsome labor and a tempting feast.
> Henceforth let none on peril of their lives
> Attempt a journey or embrace their wives;
> No barber, foreign or domestic bred,
> Shall e'er presume to dress a lady's head;
> No shop shall spare (half the preceding day)
> A yard of riband or an ounce of tea."

And many similar rhymes might be given.

Sunday night, being shut out of the Sabbath hours, became in the eighteenth century a time of general cheerfulness and often merry-making. This sudden transition from the religious calm and quiet of the afternoon to the noisy gayety of the evening was very trying to many of the clergymen, especially to Jonathan Edwards, who preached often and sadly against "Sabbath evening dissipations and mirth-making." In some communities singing-schools were held on Sunday nights, which afforded a comparatively decorous and orderly manner of spending the close of the day.

Sweet to the Pilgrims and to their descendants was the hush of their calm Saturday night, and their still, tranquil Sabbath,--sign and token to them, not only of the weekly rest ordained in the creation, but of the eternal rest to come. The universal quiet and peace of the community showed the primitive instinct of a pure, simple devotion, the sincere religion which knew no compromise in spiritual things, no half-way obedience to God's Word, but rested absolutely on the Lord's Day--as was commanded. No work, no play, no idle strolling was known; no sign of human life or motion was seen except the necessary care of the patient cattle and other dumb beasts, the orderly and quiet going to and from the meeting, and at the nooning, a visit to the churchyard to stand by the side of the silent dead. This absolute obedience to the letter as well as to the spirit of God's Word was one of the most typical traits of the character of the Puritans, and appeared to them to be one of the most vital points of their religion.

XVIII
The Authority of the Church and the Ministers

Severely were the early colonists punished if they ventured to criticise or disparage either the ministers or their teachings, or indeed any of the religious exercises of the church. In Sandwich a man was publicly whipped for speaking deridingly of God's words and ordinances as taught by the Sandwich minister. Mistress Oliver was forced to stand in public with a cleft stick on her tongue for "reproaching the elders." A New Haven man was severely whipped and fined for declaring that he received no profit from the minister's sermons. We also know the terrible shock given the Windham church in 1729 by the "vile and slanderous expressions" of one unregenerate Windhamite who said, "I had rather hear my dog bark than Mr. Bellamy preach." He was warned that he would be "shakenoff and givenup," and terrified at the prospect of so dire a fate he read a confession of his sorrow and repentance, and promised to "keep a guard over his tongue," and also to listen to Mr. Bellamy's preaching, which may have been a still more difficult task. Mr. Edward Tomlins, of Boston, upon retracting his opinion which he had expressed openly against the singing in the churches, was discharged without a fine. William Howes and his son were in 1744 fined fifty shillings "apeece for deriding such as sing in the congregation, tearming them fooles." The church music was as sacred to the Puritans as were the prayers, but it must have been a sore trial to many to keep still about the vile manner and method of singing. In 1631 Phillip Ratcliffe, for "speaking against the churches," had his ears cut off, was whipped and banished. We know also the consternation caused in New Haven in 1646 by Madam Brewster's saying that the custom of carrying contributions to the Deacons' table was popish--was "like going to the High Alter," and "savored of the Mass." She answered her accusers in such a bold, highhanded, and defiant manner that her heinous offence was considered worthy of trial in a higher court, whose decision is now lost.

The colonists could not let their affection and zeal for an individual minister cause them to show any disrespect or indifference to the Puritan

Church in general. When the question of the settlement of the Reverend Mr. Lenthal in the church of Weymouth, Massachusetts, was under discussion, the tyranny of the Puritan Church over any who dared oppose or question it was shown in a marked manner, and may be cited as a typical case. Mr. Lenthal was suspected of being poisoned with the Anne Hutchinson heresies, and he also "opposed the way of gathering churches." Hence his ordination over the church in the new settlement was bitterly opposed by the Boston divines, though apparently desired by the Weymouth congregation. One Britton, who was friendly towards Lenthal and who spoke "reproachfully" and slurringly of a book which defended the course of the Boston churches, was whipped with eleven stripes, as he had no money to pay the imposed fine. John Smythe, who "got hands to a blank" (which was either canvassing for signatures to a proxy vote in favor of Lenthal or obtaining signatures to an instrument declaring against the design of the churches), for thus "combining to hinder the orderly gathering" of the Weymouth church at this time, was fined £2. Edward Sylvester for the same offence was fined and disfranchised. Ambrose Martin, another friend of Lenthal's, for calling the church covenant of the Boston divines "a stinking carrion and a human invention," was fined £10, while Thomas Makepeace, another Weymouth malcontent, was informed by those in power that "they were weary of him," or, in modern slang, that "he made them tired." Parson Lenthal himself, being sent for by the convention, weakened at once in a way his church followers must have bitterly despised; he was "quickly convinced of his error and evil." His conviction was followed with his confession, and in open court he gave under his hand a laudable retraction, which retraction he was ordered also to "utter in the assembly at Weymouth, and so no further censure was passed on him." Thus the chief offender got the lightest punishment, and thus did the omnipotent Church rule the whole community.

The names of loquacious, babbling Quakers and Baptists who spoke disrespectfully of some or all of the ordinances of the Puritan church might be given, and would swell the list indefinitely; they were fined and punished without mercy or even toleration.

All profanity or blaspheming against God was severely punished. One very wicked man in Hartford for his "fillthy and prophane expressions," namely, that "hee hoped to meet some of the members of the Church in Hell before long, and he did not question but hee should," was "committed to prison, there to be kept in safe custody till the sermon, and then to stand the time thereof in the pillory, and after sermon to be severely whipped." What a severe punishment for so purely verbal an offence! New England ideas of profanity were very rigid, and New England men had reason to guard well their temper and tongue, else that latter member might be bored with a hot iron; for such was the penalty for profanity. We know what horror Mr. Tomlins's wicked profanity, "Curse ye woodchuck!" caused in Lynn meeting, and Mr. Dexter was "putt in ye billboes ffor prophane saying dam ye cowe." The Newbury doctor was sharply fined also for wickedly cursing. When drinking at the tavern he raised his glass and said,--

> "I'll pledge my friends, and for my foes
> A plague for their heels, and a poxe for their toes."

He acknowledged his wickedness and foolishness in using the "olde proverb," and penitently promised to curse no more.

Sad to tell, Puritan women sometimes lost their temper and their good-breeding and their godliness. Two wicked Wells women were punished in 1669 "for using profane speeches in their common talk; as in making answer to several questions their answer is, The Devil a bit." In 1640, in Springfield, Goody Gregory, being grievously angered, profanely abused an annoying neighbor, saying, "Before God I coulde breake thy heade!" But she acknowledged her "great sine and faulte" like a woman, and paid her fine and sat in the stocks like a man, since she swore like the members of that profane sex.

Sometimes the sins of the fathers were visited on the children in a most extraordinary manner. One man, "for abusing N. Parker at the tavern," was deprived of the privilege of bringing his children to be baptized, and was thus spiritually punished for a very worldly offence. For some offences, such as "speaking deridingly of the minister's powers," as was done in Plymouth, "casting uncharitable reflexions on the minister," as did an Andover man; and also for absenting one's self from church services; for "sloathefulness," for "walking prophanely," for spoiling hides when tanning and refusing explanation thereof; for selling short weight in grain, for being "given too much to Jearings," for "Slanndering," for being a "Makebayte," for "ronging naibors," for "being too Proude," for "suspitions of stealing pinnes," for "pnishouse Squerilouse Odyouse wordes," and for "lyeing," church-members were not only fined and punished but were deprived of partaking of the sacrament. In the matter of lying great distinction was made as to the character and effect of the offence. George Crispe's wife, who "told a lie, not a pernicious lie, but unadvisedly," was simply admonished and remonstrated with. Will Randall, who told a "plain lie," was fined ten shillings. While Ralph Smith, who "lied about seeing a whale," was fined twenty shillings and excommunicated.

In some communities, of which Lechford tells us New Haven was one, these unhouselled Puritans were allowed, if they so desired, to stand outside the meeting-house door at the time of public worship and catch what few words of the service they could. This humble waiting for crumbs of God's word was doubtless regarded as a sign of repentance for past deeds, for it was often followed by full forgiveness. As excommunicated persons were regarded with high disfavor and even abhorrence by the entire pious and godly walking community, this apparently spiritual punishment was more severe in its temporal effects than at first sight appears. From the Cambridge Platform, which was drawn up and adopted by the New England Synod in 1648, we learn that "while the offender remains excommunicated the church is to refrain from all communion with him in civil things," and the members were specially "to forbear to eat and drink with him;" so his daily and even his family life was made wretched. And as it was not necessary to wait for the action of the church to pronounce excommunication, but the "pastor of a church might by himself and authoritatively suspend from the Lord's table a brother *suspected* of scandal" until there was time for full examination, we can see what an absolute power the church and even the minister had over church-members in a New England community.

Nor could the poor excommunicate go to neighboring towns and settlements to start afresh. No one wished him or would tolerate him. Lancaster, in 1653, voted not to receive into its plantation "any excommunicat or notoriously erring agt the Docktrin & Discipline of churches of this Commonwealth." Other towns passed similar votes. Fortunately, Rhode Island--the island of "Aquidnay" and the Providence Plantations--opened wide its arms as a place of refuge for outcast Puritans. Universal freedom and religious toleration were in Rhode Island the foundations of the State. Josiah Quincy said that liberty of conscience would have produced anarchy if it had been permitted in the New England Puritan settlements in the seventeenth century, but the flourishing Narragansett, Providence, and Newport plantations seem to prove the absurdity of that statement. Liberty of conscience was there allowed, as Dr. MacSparran, the first clergyman of the Narragansett Church, complained in his "America Dissected," "to the extent of no religion at all." The Gortonians, the Foxians, and Hutchinsonians, the Anabaptists, the Six Principle Baptists, the Church of

England, apparently all the followers of the eighty-two "pestilent heresies" so sadly enumerated and so bitterly hated and "cast out to Satan" by the Massachusetts Puritan divines,--all the excommunicants and exiles found in Rhode Island a home and friends--other friends than the Devil to whom they had been consigned.

Though the early Puritan ministers had such powerful influence in every other respect, they were not permitted to perform the marriage-service nor to raise their voices in prayer or exhortation at a funeral. Sewall jealously notes when the English burial-service began to be read at burials, saying, "the office for Burial is a Lying very bad office makes no difference between the precious and the vile." The office of marriage was denied the parson, and was generally relegated to the magistrate. In this, Governor Bradford states, they followed "ye laudable custome of ye Low Countries." Not rulers and magistrates only were empowered to perform the marriage ceremony; squires, tavern-keepers, captains, various authorized persons might wed Puritan lovers; any man of dignity or prominence in the community could apparently receive authority to perform that office except the otherwise all-powerful parson.

As years rolled on, though the New Englanders still felt great reverence and pride for their church and its ordinances, the minister was no longer the just man made perfect, the oracle of divine will. The church-members escaped somewhat from ecclesiastical power, and some of them found fault with and openly disparaged their ministers in a way that would in early days have caused them to be pilloried, whipped, caged, or fined; and often the derogatory comments were elicited by the most trivial offences. One parson was bitterly condemned because he managed to amass eight hundred dollars by selling the produce of his farm. Another shocking and severely criticised offence was a game of bowls which one minister played and enjoyed. Still another minister, in Hanover, Massachusetts, was reproved for his lack of dignity, which was shown in his wearing stockings "footed up with another color;" that is, knit stockings in which the feet were colored differently from the legs. He also was found guilty of having jumped over the fence instead of decorously and clerically walking through the gate when going to call on one of his parishioners. Rev. Joseph Metcalf of the Old Colony was complained of in 1720 for wearing too worldly a wig. He mildly reproved and shamed the meddlesome women of his church by asking them to come to him and each cut off a lock of hair from the obnoxious wig until all the complainers were satisfied that it had been rendered sufficiently unworldly. Some Newbury church-members, in 1742, asserted that their minister unclerically wore a colored kerchief instead of a band. This he indignantly denied, saying that he "had never buried a babe even in most tempestuous weather," when he rode several miles, but he always wore a band, and he complained in turn that members of his congregation turned away from him on the street, and "glowered" at him and "sneered at him." Still more unseemly demonstrations of dislike were sometimes shown, as in South Hadley, in 1741, when a committee of disaffected parishioners pulled the Rev. Mr Rawsom out of the pulpit and marched him out of the meeting-house because they did not fancy his preaching. But all such actions were as offensive to the general community then as open expressions of dissatisfaction and contempt are now.

XIX
The Ordination of the Minister

The minister's ordination was, of course, an important social as well as spiritual event in such a religious community as was a New England colonial town. It was always celebrated by a great gathering of people from far and near, including all the ministers from every town for many miles around; and though a deeply serious service, was also an excuse for much merriment. In Connecticut, and by tradition also in Massachusetts, an "ordination-ball" was frequently given. It is popularly supposed that at this ball the ministers did not dance, nor even appear, nor to it in any way give their countenance; that it was only a ball given at the time of the ordination because so many people would then be in the town to take part in the festivity. That this was not always the case is proved by a letter of invitation still in existence written by Reverend Timothy Edwards, who was ordained in Windsor in 1694; it was written to Mr. and Mrs. Stoughton, asking them to attend the ordination-ball which was to be given in his, the minister's house. But whether the parsons approved and attended, or whether they strongly discountenanced it, the ordination-ball was always a great success. It is recorded that at one in Danvers a young man danced so vigorously and long on the sanded floor that he entirely wore out a new pair of shoes. The fashion of giving ordination-balls did not die out with colonial times. In Federal days it still continued, a specially gay ball being given in the town of Wolcott at an ordination in 1811.

There was always given an ordination supper,--a plentiful feast, at which visiting ministers and the new pastor were always present and partook with true clerical appetite. This ordination feast consisted of all kinds of New England fare, all the mysterious compounds and concoctions of Indian corn and "pompions," all sorts of roast meats, "turces" cooked in various ways, gingerbread and "cacks," and--an inevitable feature at the time of every gathering of people, from a corn-husking or apple-bee to a funeral--a liberal amount of cider, punch, and grog was also supplied, which latter compound beverages were often mixed on the meeting-house green or even in punch-bowls on the very door-steps of the church. Beer, too, was specially brewed to honor the feast. Rev. Mr. Thatcher, of Boston, wrote in his diary on the twentieth of May, 1681, "This daye the Ordination

Beare was brewed." Portable bars were sometimes established at the church-door, and strong drinks were distributed free of charge to the entire assemblage. As late as 1825, at the installation of Dr. Leonard Bacon over the First Congregational Church in New Haven, free drinks were furnished at an adjacent bar to all who chose to order them, and were "settled for" by the generous and hospitable society. In considering the extravagant amount of moneys often recorded as having been paid out for liquor at ordinations, one must not fail to remember that the seemingly large sums were often spent in Revolutionary times during the great depreciation of Continental money. Six hundred and sixty-six dollars were disbursed for the entertainment of the council at the ordination of Mr. Kilbourn, of Chesterfield; but the items were really few and the total amount of liquor was not great,--thirty-eight mugs of flip at twelve dollars per mug; eleven gills of rum bitters at six dollars per gill, and two mugs of sling at twenty-four dollars per mug. The church in one town sent the Continental money in payment for the drinks of the church-council in a wheelbarrow to the tavern-keeper, and he was not very well paid either.

It gives one a strange sense of the customs and habits of the olden times to read an "ordination-bill" from a tavern-keeper which is thus endorsed, "This all Paid for exsept the Minister's Rum." To give some idea of the expense of "keeping the ministers" at an ordination in Hartford in 1784, let me give the items of the bill:--

	£	s.	d.
To keeping Ministers	0	2	4
2 Mugs tody	0	5	10
5 Segars	0	3	0
1 Pint wine	0	0	9
3 lodgings	0	9	0
3 bitters	0	0	9
3 breakfasts	0	3	6
15 boles Punch	1	10	0
24 dinners	1	16	0
11 bottles wine	0	3	6
5 mugs flip	0	5	10
3 boles punch	0	6	0
3 boles tody	0	3	6

One might say with Falstaff, "O monstrous! but one half-pennyworth of bread to this intolerable deal of sack!" I sadly fear me that at that Hartford ordination our parson ancestors got grievsously "gilded," to use a choice "red-lattice phrase."

Many accounts of gay ordination parties have been preserved in diaries for us. Reverend Mr. Smith, who was settled in Portland in the early part of the eighteenth century, wrote thus in his journal of an ordination which he attended: "Mr. Foxcroft ordained at New Gloucester. We had a pleasant journey home. Mr. L. was alert and kept us all merry. A *jolly ordination*. We lost all sight of decorum." The Mr. L. referred to was Mr. Stephen Longfellow, greatgrandfather of the poet.

Bills for ordination-expenses abound in items of barrels of rum and cider and metheglin, of bowls of flip and punch and toddy, of boxes of lemons and loaves of sugar, in punches, and sometimes broken punchbowls, and in one case a large amount of Malaga and Canary wine, spices and "ross water," from which was brewed doubtless an appetizing ordination-cup which may have rivalled Josselyn's New England nectar of "cyder, Maligo raisins, spices, and sirup of clove-gillyflowers."

In Massachusetts, in January, 1759, the subject of the frequent disorders and irregularities in connection with ordination-services, especially in country towns, came before the council of the province, who referred its consideration to a convention of ministers. The ministers at that convention were recommended to each give instruction, exhortation, and advice against excesses to the members of his congregation whenever an ordination was about to take place in the vicinity of his church. In this way it was hoped that the reformation would be aided, and temperance, order, and decorum established. The newspapers were free in their condemnation of the feasting and roistering at ordination-services. When Dr. Cummings was ordained over the Old South Church of Boston in February, 1761, a feast took place at the Rev. Dr. Sewall's house which occasioned much comment. A four-column letter of criticism appeared in the Boston Gazette of March 9, 1761, over the signature of "Countryman," which provoked several answers and much newspaper controversy. As Dr. Sewall had been moderator of the meeting of ministers held only two years previously with the hope, and for the purpose of abolishing ordination revelries, it is not strange that the circumstance of the feast being given in his house should cause public comment and criticism.

"Countryman" complained that "the price of provisions was raised a quarter cart in Boston for several days before the instalment by reason of the great preparations therefor, and the readiness of the ecclesiastical caterers to give almost any price that was demanded. Many Boston people complained the town had, by this means, in a few days lost a large sum of money; which was, as it were, levied on and extorted from them. If the poor were the *better for what remained of so plentiful and splendid a feast* I am very glad but yet think it is a pity the charity were not better timed." He reprovingly enumerates, "There were six tables that held one with another eighteen persons each, upon each table a good rich plumb pudding, a dish of boil'd pork and fowls, and a corn'd leg of pork with sauce proper for it, a leg of bacon, a piece of alamode beef, a leg of mutton with caper sauce, a roast line of veal, a roast turkey, a venison pastee, besides chess cakes and tarts, cheese and butter. Half a dozen cooks were employed upon this occasion, upwards of twenty tenders to wait upon the tables; they had the best of old cyder, one barrel of Lisbon wine, punch in plenty before and after dinner, made of old Barbados spirit. The cost of this moderate dinner was upwards of fifty pounds lawful money." This special ordination-feast, even as detailed by the complaining "Countryman," does not seem to me very reprehensible. The standing of the church, the wealth of the congregation, the character of the guests (among whom were the Governor and the judges of the Superior Court) all make this repast appear neither ostentatious nor extravagant. Fifty pounds was certainly not an enormous sum to spend for a dinner with wine for over one hundred persons, and such a good dinner too. Nor is it probable that a city as large as was Boston at that date could through that dinner have been swept of provisions to such an extent that prices would be raised a quarter part. I suspect some personal malice caused "Countryman's" attacks, for he certainly could have found in other towns more flagrant cases to complain of and condemn.

Though no record exists to prove that "the poor were the better for what remained" after this Boston feast, in other towns letters and church-entries show that any fragments remaining after the ordination-dinner were well disposed of. Sometimes they furnished forth the new minister's table. In one case they were given to "a widowed family" ("widowed" here being used in the old tender sense of bereaved). In Killingly "the overplush of provisions" was sold to help pay the arrearages of the salary of the outgoing minister, thus showing a laudable desire to "settle up and start square."

If the church were dedicated at the time of the ordination, that would naturally be cause for additional gayety. A very interesting and graphic account of the feast at the dedication of the Old Tunnel Meeting-House of Lynn in the year 1682 has been preserved. It thus describes the scene:--

"Ye Deddication Dinner was had in ye greate barne of Mr. Hoode which by reason of its goodly size was deemed ye most fit place. It was neatly adorned with green bows and other hangings and made very faire to look upon, ye wreaths being mostly wrought by ye young folk, they meeting together, both maides and young men, and having a merry time in doing ye work. Ye rough stalls and unbowed posts being gaily begirt and all ye corners and cubbies being clean swept and well aired, it truly did appear a meet banquetting hall. Ye scaffolds too from which ye provinder had been removed were swept cleane as broome could make them. Some seats were put up on ye scaffoldes whereon might sitt such of ye antient women as would see & ye maides and children. Ye greate floor was all held for ye company which was to partake of ye feast of fat things, none others being admitted there save them that were to wait upon ye same. Ye kine that were wont to be there were forced to keep holiday in the field."

Then follows a minute account of how the fowls persisted in flying in and roosting over the table, scattering feathers and hay on the parsons beneath.

"Mr. Shepard's face did turn very red and he catched up an apple and hurled it at ye birds. But he thereby made a bad matter worse for ye fruit being well aimed it hit ye legs of a fowl and brought him floundering and flopping down on ye table, scattering gravy, sauce and divers things upon our garments and in our faces. But this did not well please some, yet with most it was a happening that made great merryment. Dainty meats were on ye table in great plenty, bear-stake, deer-meat, rabbit, and fowle, both wild and from ye barnyard. Luscious puddings we likewise had in abundance, mostly apple and berry, but some of corn meal with small bits of sewet baked therein; also pyes and tarts. We had some pleasant fruits, as apples, nuts and wild grapes, and to crown all, we had plenty of good cider and ye inspiring Barbadoes drink. Mr. Shepard and most of ye ministers were grave and prudent at table, discoursing much upon ye great points of ye deddication sermon and in silence laboring upon ye food before them. But I will not risque to say on which they dwelt with most relish, ye discourse or ye dinner. Most of ye young members of ye Council would fain make a jolly time of it. Mr. Gerrish, ye Wenham minister, tho prudent in his meat and drinks, was yet in right merry mood. And he did once grievously scandalize Mr. Shepard, who on suddenly looking up from his dish did spy him, as he thot, winking in an unbecoming way to one of ye pretty damsels on ye scaffold. And thereupon bidding ye godly Mr. Rogers to labor with him aside for his misbehavior, it turned out that ye winking was occasioned by some of ye hay seeds that were blowing about, lodging in his eye; whereat Mr. Shepard felt greatly releaved.

"Ye new Meeting house was much discoursed upon at ye table. And most thot it as comely a house of worship as can be found in the whole Collony save only three or four. Mr. Gerrish was in such merry mood that he kept ye end of ye table whereby he sat in right jovial humour. Some did loudly laugh and clap their hands. But in ye middest of ye merryment a strange disaster did happen unto him. Not having his thots about him he endeavored ye dangerous performance of gaping and laughing at the same time which he must now feel is not so easy or safe a thing. In doing this he set his jaws open in such wise that it was beyond all his power to bring them together again. His agonie was very great, and his joyful laugh soon turned to grievous gioaning. Ye women in ye scaffolds became much distressed for him. We did our utmost to stay ye anguish of Mr. Gerrish, but could make out little till Mr. Rogers who knoweth somewhat of anatomy did bid ye sufferer to sit down on ye floor, which being done Mr. Rogers took ye head atween his legs, turning ye face as much upward as possible and then gave a powerful blow and then sudden press which brot ye jaws into working order. But Mr. Geirish did not gape or laugh much more on that occasion, neither did he talk much for that matter.

"No other weighty mishap occurred save that one of ye Salem delegates, in boastfully essaying to crack a walnut atween his teeth did crack, instead of ye nut, a most usefull double tooth and was thereby forced to appear at ye evening with a bandaged face."

This ended this most amusing chapter of disasters to the ministers, though the banquet was diversified by interrupting crows from invading roosters, fierce and undignified counter-attacks with nuts and apples by the clergymen, a few mortifyingly "mawdlin songs and much roistering laughter," and the account ends, "so noble and savoury a banquet was never before spread in this noble town, God be praised." What a picture of the good old times! Different times make different manners; the early Puritan ministers did not, as a rule, drink to excess, any more than do our modern clergymen; but it is not strange that though they were of Puritan blood and belief, they should have fallen into the universal custom of the day, and should have "gone to their graves full of years, honor, simplicity, and rum." The only wonder is, when the ministers had the best places at every table, at every feast, at every merry-making in New England, that stories of their roistering excesses should not have come down to us as there have of the intemperate clergy of Virginia.

The ordination services within the meeting-houses were not always decorous and quiet scenes. In spite of the reverence which our forefathers had for their church and their ministers, it did not prevent them from bitterly opposing the settlement of an unwished-for clergyman over them, and many towns were racked and divided, then as now, over the important question. As years passed on the church members grew bold enough to dare to offer personal and bodily opposition. At the ordination of the Rev. Peter

Thatcher in the New North Church in Boston, in 1720, there were two parties. The members who did not wish him to be settled over the church went into the meeting-house and made a great disorder and clamor. They forbade the proceedings, and went into the gallery, and threw from thence water and missiles on the friends of the clergymen who were gathered around him at the altar. Perhaps they obtained courage for these sacrilegious acts from the barrels of rum and the bowls of strong punch. And this was in Puritanical Boston, in the year of the hundredth anniversary of the landing of the Mayflower. Thus had one century changed the absolute reverence and affectionate regard of the Pilgrims for their church, their ministers, and their meeting-houses, to irreverent and obstinate desire for personal satisfaction. No wonder that the ministers at that date preached and believed that Satan was making fresh and increasing efforts to destroy the Puritan church. The hour was ready for Whitefield, for Edwards, for any new awakening; and was above all fast approaching for the sadly needed temperance reform.

In the seventeenth century a minister was ordained and re-ordained at each church over which he had charge; but after some years the name of installation was given to each appointment after the first ordination, and the ceremony was correspondingly changed.

XX
The Ministers

The picture which Colonel Higginson has drawn of the Puritan minister is so well known and so graphic that any attempt to add to it would be futile. All the succeeding New England parsons, as years rolled by, were not, however, like the black-gowned, black-gloved, stately, and solemn man whom he has so clearly shown us. Men of rigid decorum, and grave ceremony there were, such as Dr. Emmons and Jonathan Edwards; but there were parsons also of another type,--eccentric, unconventional, and undignified in demeanor and dress. Parson Robinson, of Duxbury, persisted in wearing in the pulpit, as part of his clerical attire, a round jacket instead of the suitable gown or Geneva cloak, and he was known thereby as "Master Jack." With astonishing inconsistency this Master Jack objected to the village blacksmith's wearing his leathern apron into the church, and he assailed the offender again and again with words and hints from his pulpit. He was at last worsted by the grimaces of the victorious smith (where was the Duxbury tithingman?), and indignantly left the pulpit, ejaculating, "I'll not preach while that man sits before me." A remonstrating parishioner said afterward to Master Jack, "I'd not have left if the Devil sat there." "Neither would I" was the quick answer.

Another singular article of attire was worn in the pulpit by Father Mills, of Torrington, though neither in irreverence nor indifference. When his dearly loved wife died he pondered how he, who always wore black, could express to the world that he was wearing mourning; and his simple heart hit upon this grotesque device: he left off his full-flowing wig, and tied up his head in a black silk handkerchief, which he wore thereafter as a trapping of woe.

Parson Judson, of Taunton, was so lazy that he used to preach while sitting down in the pulpit; and was so contemptibly fond of comfort that he would on summer Sundays give out to the sweltering members of his congregation the longest psalm in the psalm-book, and then desert them--piously perspiring and fuguing--and lie under a tree enjoying the cool outdoor breezes until the long psalm was ended, escaping thus not only the heat but the singing; and when we consider the quantity and quality of both, and that he condemned his good people to an extra amount of each, it seems a piece of clerical inhumanity that would be hard to equal. Surely this selfish Taunton sybarite was the prosaic ideal of Hamlet's words:--

"Some ungracious pastors do
Show me the steep and thorny way to Heaven,
Whilst like a puff'd and reckless libertine
Himself the primrose path of dalliance treads,
And recks not his own rede."

But lazy and slothful ministers were fortunately rare in New England. No primrose path of dalliance was theirs; industrious and hard-working were nearly all the early parsons, preaching and praying twice on the Sabbath, and preaching again on Lecture days; visiting the sick and often giving medical and "chyrurgycal" advice; called upon for legal counsel and adjudication; occupied in spare moments in teaching and preparing young men for college; working on their farms; hearing the children say their catechism; fasting and praying long, weary hours in their own study,--truly they were "pious and painful preachers," as Colonel Higginson saw recorded on a gravestone in Watertown. Though I suspect "painful" in the Puritan vocabulary meant "painstaking," did it not? Cotton Mather called John Fiske, of Chelmsford, a "plaine but able painful and useful preacher," while President Dunster, of Harvard College, was described by a contemporary divine as "pious painful and fit to teach." Other curious epithets and descriptions were applied to the parsons; they were called "holy-heavenly," "sweet-affecting," "soul-ravishing," "heaven-piercing," "angel-rivalling," "subtil," "irrefragable," "angelical," "septemfluous," "holy-savoured," "princely," "soul-appetizing," "full of antic tastes" (meaning having the tastes of an antiquary), "God-bearing." Of two of the New England saints it was written:--

"Thier Temper far from Injucundity,
Thier tongues and pens from Infecundity."

Many other fulsome, turgid, and even whimsical expressious of praise might be named, for the Puritans were rich in classic sesquipedalian adjectives, and their active linguistic consciences made them equally fertile in producing new ones.

Ready and unexpected were the solemn Puritans in repartee. A party of gay young sparks, meeting austere old John Cotton, determined to guy him. One of the young reprobates sent up to him and whispered in his ear, "Cotton, thou art an old fool." "I am, I am," was the unexpected answer; "the Lord make both thee and me wiser than we are." Two young men of like intent met Mr. Haynes, of Vermont, and said with mock sad faces,

"Have you heard the news? the Devil is dead." Quick came the answer, "Oh, poor, fatherless children! what will become of you?"

Gloomy and depressed of spirits they were often. The good Warham, who could take faithful and brave charge of his flock in the uncivilized wilds of Connecticut among ferocious savages, was tortured by doubts and "blasphemous suggestions," and overwhelmed by unbelief, enduring specially agonizing scruples about administering and partaking of the Lord's Supper, and was thus perplexed and buffeted until the hour of his sad death. The ministers went through various stages of uncertainty and gloom, from the physical terror of Dr. Cogswell in a thunderstorm, through vacillating and harassing convictions about the Half Way Covenant, through doubt of God, of salvation, of heaven, of eternite, particularly distressing suspicions about the reality of hell and the personality of the Devil, to the stage of deep melancholy which was shown in its highest type in "Handkerchief Moody," who preached and prayed and always appeared in public with a handkerchief over his face, and gave to Hawthorne the inspiration for his story of "The Black Veil." Rev. Mr. Bradstreet, of the First Church of Charlestown, was so hypochondriacal that he was afraid to preach in the pulpit, feeling sure that he would die if he entered therein; so he always delivered his sermons to his patient congregation from the deacons' pew. Mr. Bradstreet was unconventional in many other respects, and was far from being a typical Puritan minister. He seldom wore a coat, but generally appeared in a plaid gown, and was always seen with a pipe in his mouth,--a most disreputable addition to the clerical toilet at that date, or, in truth, at any date. He was a learned and pious man, however, and was thus introduced to a fellow clergyman, "Here is a man who can whistle Greek."

Scarcely one of the early Puritan ministers was free from the sad shadow of doubt and fear. No "rose-pink or dirty-drab views of humanity" were theirs; all was inky-black. And it is impossible to express the gloom and the depression of spirit which fall on one now, after these centuries of prosperous and cheerful years, when one considers thoughtfully the deep and despairing agony of mind endured by these good, brave, steadfast, godly Puritan ministers. Read, for instance, the sentences from the diary of the Rev. John Baily, or of Nathaniel Mather, as given by Cotton Mather in his "Magnalia." Mather says that poor, sad, heart-sick Baily was filled with "desponding jealousies," "disconsolate uneasinesses," gloomy fears, and thinks the words from his diary "may be profitable to some discouraged minds." Profitable! Ah, no; far from it! The overwhelming blackness of despair, the woful doubts and fears about destruction and utter annihilation which he felt so deeply and so continually, fall in a heavy, impenetrable cloud upon us as we read, until we feel that we too are in the "Suburbs of hell" and are "eternally damned."

But in succeeding years they were not always gloomy and not always staid, as we know from the stories of the cheerful parties at ordination-times; and I doubt not the reverend Assembly of Elders at Cambridge enjoyed to the full degree the twelve gallons of sack and six gallons of white wine sent to them by the Court as a testimony of deep respect. And the group of clergymen who were painted over the mantelpiece of Parson Lowell, of Newbury, must have been far from gloom, as the punch-bowl and drinking-cups and tobacco and pipes would testify, and their cheerful motto likewise: "In essentials unity, in non-essentials liberty, in all things charity." And the Rev. Mr. ---- no, I will not tell his name--kept an account with one Jerome Ripley, a storekeeper, and on one page of this account-book, containing thirty-nine entries, twenty-one were for New England rum. It somewhat lessens in our notions the personal responsibility, or the personal potatory capability of the parson, to discover that there was an ordination in town during that rum-paged week, and that the visiting ministers probably drank the greater portion of Jerome Ripley's liquor. But I wish the store-keeper had--to save this parson's reputation among succeeding generations-- called and entered the rum as hay, or tea, or nails, or anything innocent and virtuous and clerical. When we read of all these doings and drinkings of the old New England ministers,--"if ancient tales say true, nor wrong these ancient men"--we feel that we cannot so fiercely resent nor wonder at the degrading coupling in Byron's sneering lines:--

"There's naught, no doubt, so much the spirit calms,
As rum and true religion."

All the cider made by the New England elders did not tend to gloom, and they were celebrated for their fine cider. The best cider in Massachusetts--that which brought the highest price--was known as the Arminian cider, because the minister who furnished it to the market was suspected of having Arminian tendencies. A very telling compliment to the cider of one of the first New England ministers is thus recorded: "Mr. Whiting had a score of appill-trees from which he made delicious cyder. And it hath been said yt an Indyan once coming to hys house and Mistress Whiting giving him a drink of ye cyder, he did sett down ye pot and smaking his lips say yt Adam and Eve were rightlie damned for eating ye appills in ye garden of Eden, they should have made them into cyder." This perverse application of good John Eliot's teaching would have vexed the apostle sorely. Of so much account were the barrels of cider, and so highly were they prized by the ministers, that one honest soul did not hesitate to thank the Lord in the pulpit for the "many barrels of cider vouchsafed to us this year."

Stronger liquors than cider were also manufactured by the ministers,--and by God-fearing, pious ministers also. They did not hesitate to own and operate distilleries. Rev. Nathan Strong, pastor of the First Church of Hartford and author of the hymn "Swell the anthem, raise the song," was engaged in the distilling business and did not make a success of it either. Having become bankrupt, he did not dare show his head anywhere in public for some time, except on Sunday, for fear of arrest. This disreputable and most unclerical affair did not operate against him in the minds of the contemporaneous public, for ten years later he received the degree of Doctor of Divinity from Princeton College; and he did not hesitate to joke about his liquor manufacturing, saying to two of his brother-clergymen, "Oh, we are all three in the same boat together,--Brother Prime raises the grain, I distil it, and Brother Flint drinks it."

Impostors there were--false parsons--in the early struggling days of New England (since "the devil was never weary and never ceasing in disturbing the peace of the new English church"), and they plagued the colonists sorely. The very first shepherd of the wandering flock--Mr. Lyford, who preached to the planters in 1624--was, as Bradford says, "most unsavory salt," a most agonizing and unbearable thorn in the flesh and spirit of the poor homesick Pilgrims; and he was finally banished to Virginia, where it was supposed that he would find congenial and un-Puritanlike companions. Another bold-faced cheat preached to the colonists a most impressive sermon on the text, "Let him that stole steal no more," while his own pockets were stuffed out with stolen money. "Out of the fulness of the heart the mouth speaketh."

Dicky Swayn, "after a thousand rogueries," set up as a parson in Boston. But, unfortunately for him, he prayed too loud and too long on one occasion, and his prayer attracted the attention of a woman whose servant he had formerly been. She promptly exposed his false pretensions and past villanies, and he left Boston and an army of cheated creditors. In 1699 two other attractive and plausible scamps--Kingsbury and May--garbed and curried themselves as ministers, and went through a course of unchecked villany, building only on their agreeable presence. Cotton Mather wrote pertinently of one of these charmers, "Fascination is a thing whereof mankind has more Experience than Comprehension;" and he also wrote very despitefully of the adventurer's scholarly attainments saying there were "eighteen horrid false spells and not one point in one very short note I received from him." As the population increased, so also did the list of dishonest impostors, who made a cloak of religion most effectively to aid them in deceiving the religious community; and sometimes, alas! the ordained clergymen became sad backsliders.

Nor were the pious and godly Puritan divines above the follies and frailties of other men in other places and in other times. It can be said of them, as of the Jew, had they not "eyes, hands, organs, dimensions, senses, affections, passions?"--were they not as other men? It is recorded of Rev. Samuel Whiting, of Lynn, that "once coming among a gay partie of yong people he kist all ye maides and said yt he felt all ye better for it." And who can doubt it? Even that extreme type, that highest pinnacle of American Puritanical bigotry,--solemn and learned Cotton Mather,--had, when he was a mourning widower, a most amusing amorous episode with a rather doubtful, a decidedly shady, young Boston woman, whom he styled an "Ingenious Child," but who was far from being an ingenuous child. "She," as he proudly stated, "became charmed with my person to such a degree that she could not but break in upon me with her most importunate requests." And a very handsome and thoroughly attractive person does his portrait show even to modern eyes. Poor Cotton resisted the wiles of the devil in this alluring form, though he had to fast and pray three consecutive nights ere the strong Puritan spirit conquered the weak flesh, and he could consent and resolve to give up the thought of marrying the siren. His self-denial and firmness deserved a better reward than the very trying matrimonial "venture" that he afterwards made.

Many another Puritan parson has left record of his wooings that are warm to read. And well did the parsons' wives deserve their ardent wooings and their tender love-letters. Hard as was the minister's life, over-filled as was his time, highly taxed as were his resources, all these hardships were felt in double proportion by the minister's wife. The old Hebrew standard of praise quoted by Cotton Mather, "A woman worthy to be the wife of a priest," was keenly epigrammatic; and ample proof of the wise insight of the standard of comparison may be found in the lives of "the pious, prudent, and prayerful" wives of New England ministers. What wonder that their praises were sung in many loving though halting threnodies, in long-winded but tender eulogies, in labored anagrams, in quaintly spelled epitaphs?--for the ministers' wives were the saints of the Puritan calendar.

XXI
The Ministers' Pay

The salaries of New England clergymen were not large in early days, but the £60 or £70 which they each were yearly voted was quite enough to suitably support them in that new country of plain ways and plain living, if they only received it, which was, alas! not always the case. The First Court of Massachusetts, in 1630, set the amount of the minister's annual stipend to be £20 or £30 according to the wealth of the community, and made it a public charge. In 1659 the highest salary paid in Suffolk County was £100 to Mr. Thatcher, and the lowest was £40 to the clergyman at Hull. The minister of the Andover church was voted a salary of £60, and "when he shall have occacion to marry, £10 more." He was very glad, however, to take £42 in hard cash instead of £60 in corn and labor, which were at that time the most popular forms of ministerial remuneration; even though the "hard cash" were in the form of wampum, beaver-skins, or leaden bullets.

Many congregations, though the members were so pious and godly, were pretty sharp in bargaining with their preachers; for instance, the church in New London made its new parson sign a contract that "in case he remove before the year is out, he returneth the £80 paid him." Often clergymen would "supply" (or "Sipploye," or "syploy" or "sipply," or "sciploy," as various records have it) from month to mouth without "settling." As they got the "keepe of a hors," and their own board for Saturday and Sunday, and on Monday morning a cash payment for preaching (though often the amount was only twelve shillings), they were richer than with a small yearly salary that was irregularly and inconveniently paid. Often too they entered by preference into a yearly contract with a church, without any wish for regular settlement or ordination.

A large portion of the stipends in early parishes being paid in corn and labor, the amounts were established by fixed rate upon the inhabitants; and the amount of land owned and cultivated by each church-member was considered in reckoning his assessment. These amounts were called voluntary contributions. If, however, any citizen refused to "contribute," he was taxed; and if he refused to pay his church-tax he could be fined, imprisoned, or pilloried. For one hundred years the ministers' salaries in Boston were paid by these so-called "voluntary contributions." In one church it was voted that "the Deacons have liberty for a quarter of a yeare to git in every mans sume either in a Church way or in a Christian way." I would the process employed in the "Church way" were recorded, since it differed so from the Christian way.

It is one of the Puritan paradoxes that abounded in New England, that the community of New Haven, a "State whose Desire was Religion," and religion alone, was particularly backward in paying the minister who had spiritual charge there. After much trouble in deciding about the form and quality of the currency which should be used in pay, since so much bad wampum was thrust upon the deacons at the public contributions, it was in 1651 enacted that "whereas it is taken notice of that Divers give not into the Treasury at all on the Lords Day, it is decreed that all such if they give not freely, of themselves be rated according to the Jurisdiction order for the Ministers Maintaynance." The delinquents were ordered to bring their "rate" to the Deacon's house at once. A presuming young man ventured to suggest that the recreant members who would not pay in the face of the whole congregation would hardly rush to the Deacon's door to give in their "rate." He was severely ordered to keep silence in the company of wiser and elder people; but time proved his simply wise supposition to be correct; and many and various were the devices and forces which the deacons were obliged to use to obtain the minister's rate in New Haven.

Some few bold Puritan souls dared to protest against being forced to pay the church rate whether they wished to or not. Lieutenant Fuller, of Barnstable, was fined fifty shillings for "prophanely" saying "that the law enacted about the ministers maintenance was a wicked and devilish one, and that the devil sat at the helm when the law was made." Such courageous though profane expressions of revolt but little availed; for not only were members and attendants of the Puritan churches taxed, but Quakers, Baptists, and Church-of-England men were also "rated," and if they refused to pay to help support the church that they abhorred, they were fined and imprisoned. One man, of Watertown, named Briscoe, dared to write a book against the violent enforcement of "voluntary" subscriptions. He was fined £10 for his wickedness; and the printer of the book was also punished. A virago in New London, more openly courageous, threw scalding water on the head of the tithingman who came to collect the minister's rate. Old John Cotton preached long and earnestly upon the necessity and propriety of raising the money for the minister's salary, and for other expenses of the church, wholly by voluntary and eagerly given contributions,--the "Lord having directed him to make it clear by Scripture." He believed that tithes and church-taxes were productive of "pride, contention and sloth," and indicated a declining spiritual condition of the church. But it was a strange voluntary gift he wished, that was forced by dread of the pillory and cage!

Since, as Higginson said, "New England was a plantation of Religion, not a plantation of Trade," the church and its support were of course the first thought in laying out a new town-settlement, and some of the best town-lots were always set aside for the "yuse of the minister." Sometimes these lots were a gift outright to the first settled preacher, in other townships they were set aside as glebes, or "ministry land" as it was called. It was a universal custom to build at once a house for the minister, and some very queer contracts and stipulations for the size, shape, and quality of the parson's home-edifice may be read in church-records. To the construction of this house all the town contributed, as also to the building of the meeting-house; some gave work; some, the use of a horse or ox-team; some, boards; some, stones or brick; some, logs; others, nails; and a few, a very few, money. At the house-raising a good dinner was provided, and of course, plenty of liquor. Some malcontents rebelled against being forced to work on the minister's house. Entries of fines are common enough for "refusing to dig on the Minister's Selor," for neglecting to send "the Minister's Nayles," for refusing to "contribute clay-boards," etc. As with the town-lot, the house sometimes was a gift outright to the clergyman, and ofttimes the ownership was retained by the church, and the free use only was given to each minister.

It was a universal custom to allow free pasturage for the minister's horse, for which the village burial-ground was assigned as a favorite feeding-ground. Sometimes this privilege of free pasturage was abused. In Plymouth, in 1789, Rev. Chandler Robbins was requested "not to have more horses than shall be necessary, for his many horses that had been pastured on 'Burial Hill'" had sadly damaged and defaced the gravestones,--perhaps the very headstones placed over the bones of our Pilgrim Fathers.

The "strangers' money," which was the money contributed by visitors who chanced to attend the services, and which was sometimes specified as "all the silver and black dogs given by strangers," was usually given to the minister. A "black dog" was a "dog dollar."

Often a settlement or a sum of money was given outright to the clergyman when he was first ordained or settled in the parish. At a town meeting in Sharon, January 8, 1755, which was held with regard to procuring a new minister, it was voted "that a committe confer with Mr. Smith, and know which will be more acceptable to him, to have a larger settlement and a smaller salary, or a larger salary and a smaller settlement, and make report to this meeting." On Jan. 15th it was voted "that we give to said Mr. Smith 420 ounces of silver or equivalent in old Tenor bills, for a settlement, to be paid in three years after settlement. That we give to said Mr. Smith 220 Spanish dollars or an equivalent in old Tenor bills for his yearly salary." Mr. Smith was very generous to his new parish, for his acceptance of its call contains this clause: "As it will come heavy upon some perhaps to pay salary and settlement together I have thought of releasing part of the payment of the salary for a time to be paid to me again. The first year I shall allow you out of the salary you have voted me 40 dollars, the 2nd 30 dollars, the 3rd 15, the 4th year 20 to be repaid to me again, the 5th year 20 more, the 6th year 20 more and the 25 dollars that remain, I am willing that the town should keep 'em for its own use." He was apparently "willing to live very low," as Parson Eliot humbly and pathetically wrote in a petition to his church.

The Puritan ministers in New England in the eighteenth century were all good Whigs; they hated the English kings, fully believing that those stupid rulers, who really cared little for the Church of England, were burning with pious zeal to make Episcopacy the established church of the colonies, and knowing that were that deed accomplished they themselves would probably lose their homes and means of livelihood. They were the most eager of Republicans and patriots, and many of them were good and brave soldiers in the Revolution.

When the minister acquired the independence he so longed and fought for, it was not all his fancy painted it. He found himself poor indeed,-- practically penniless. He complained sadly that he was paid his salary in the worthless continental paper money, and he refused to take it. Often he cannily took merchandise of all kinds instead of the low-valued paper money, and he became a good and sharp trader, exchanging his various goods for whatever he needed--and could get. Merchandise was, indeed, far preferable to money. The petition of Rev. Mr. Barnes to his Willsborough people has been preserved, and he thus speaks of his salary: "In 1775 the war comenced & Paper money was emitted which soon began to depreciate and the depreciation was so rappid that in may 1777 your Pastor gave the whole of his years Salary for one sucking Calf, the next year he gave the whole for a small store pig. Your Pastor has not asked for any consideration being willing to try to Scrabble along with the people while they are in low circumstances." His neighbor, Rev. Mr. Sprague, of Dublin, formally petitioned his church not to increase his salary, "as I am plagued to death to get what is owing to me now," or to buy anything with it when he got it. The minister in Scarborough had to be paid £5,400 in paper money to make good his salary of £60 in gold which had been voted him.

"Living low" and "scrabbling along" seems to have been the normal and universal condition of the New England minister for some time after the War of Independence. He was obliged to go without his pay, or to take it in whatever shape it might chance to be tendered. Indeed, from the earliest colonial days it was true that of whatever they had, the church-members gave; meal, maize, beans, cider, lumber, merchantable pork, apples, "English grains," pumpkins,--all were paid to the parson. Part of the stipend of a minister on Cape Cod was two hundred fish yearly from each parishioner, with which to fertilize his sandy corn-land. In Plymouth, in 1662, the following method of increasing the minister's income was suggested: "The Court Proposeth it as a thing that they judge would be very commendable and beneficiall to the townes where God's providence shall cast any whales, if they should agree to set aparte some p'te of every such fish or oyle for the Incouragement of an able and godly minister among them." In Sandwich, also, the parson had a part of every whale that came ashore.

Various gifts, too, came to the preachers. In Newbury the first salmon caught each year in the weir was left by will to the parson. Judge Sewall records that he visited the minister and "carried him a Bushel of Turnips, cost me five shillings, and a Cabbage cost half a Crown." Such a high-priced cabbage!

That New England country institution--the "donation party" to the minister--was evolved at a later date. At these donation parties the unfortunate shepherd of the flock often received much that neither he nor the wily donors could use, while more valuable and useful gifts were lacking.

A very material plenishing of the minister's house was often furnished in the latter part of the eighteenth century by the annual "Spinning Bee." On a given day the women of the parish, each bearing her own spinning-wheel and flax, assembled at the minister's house and spun for his wife great "runs" of linen thread, which were afterward woven into linen for the use of the parson and his family. In Newbury, April 20,1768, "Young ladies met at the house of the Rev. Mr. Parsons, who preached to them a sermon from Proverbs 31-19. They spun and presented to Mrs. Parsons two hundred and seventy skeins of good yarn." They drank "liberty tea." This makeshift of a beverage was made of the four-leaved loosestrife. The herb was pulled up like flax, its stalks were stripped of the leaves and were boiled. The leaves were put in a kettle and basted with the liquor distilled from the stalks. After this the leaves were dried in an oven to use in the same manner as tea-leaves. Liberty tea sold readily for sixpence a pound. In 1787 these same Newbury women spun two hundred and thirty-six skeins of thread and yarn for the wife of the Rev. Mr. Murray. Some were busy spinning, some reeling and carding, and some combing the flax, while the minister preached to them on the text from Exodus xxxv. 25: "And all the women that were wise-hearted did spin with their hands." These spinning-bees were everywhere in vogue, and formed a source of much profit to the parson, and of pleasure to the spinners, in spite of the sermons.

Pieced patchwork bed-quilts for the minister's family were also given by the women of the congregation. Sometimes each woman furnished a neatly pieced square, and all met at the parsonage and joined and quilted the coverlet. At other times the minister's wife made the patchwork herself, but the women assembled and transformed it into quilts for her. The parson was helped also in his individual work. When the rye or wheat or grain on the minister's land was full grown and ready for reaping and mowing, the men in his parish gave him gladly a day's work in harvesting, and in turn he furnished them plenty of good rum to drink, else there were "great uneasyness." The New England men were not forced to drink liberty tea.

One universal contribution to the support of the minister all over New England was cord-wood; and the "minister's wood" is an institution up to the present day in the few thickly wooded districts that remain. A load of wood was usually given by each male church-member, and he was expected to deliver the gift at the door of the parsonage. Sixty loads a year were a fair allowance, but the number sometimes ran up to one hundred, as was furnished to Parson Chauncey, of Durham. Rev. Mr. Parsons, of East Hadley, was the greatest wood-consumer among the old ministers of whom I have chanced to read. Good, cheerful, roaring fires must the Parsons family have kept; for in 1774 he had eighty loads of wood supplied to him; in 1751 he was furnished with one hundred loads; in 1763 the amount had increased to one hundred and twenty loads, when the parish was glad to make a compromise with their extravagant shepherd and pay him instead £13 6s 8d annually in addition to his regular salary, and let him buy or cut his own wood. Firewood at that time in that town was worth only the expense of cutting and hauling to the house. A "load" of wood contained about three quarters of a cord, and until after the Revolutionary War was worth in the vicinity of Hadley only three shillings a load. The minister's loads were expected to be always of good "hard-wood." One thrifty parson, while watching a farmer unload his yearly contribution, remarked, "Isn't that pretty soft wood?" "And don't we sometimes have pretty soft preaching?" was the answer. It was well that the witty retort was not made a century earlier; for the speaker would have been punished by a fine, since they fined so sharply anything that savored of "speaking against the minister." In some towns a day was appointed which was called a "wood-spell," when it was ordered that all the wood be delivered at the parson's door; and thus the farmers formed a cheerful gathering, at which the minister furnished plentiful flip, or grog, to the wood-givers. Rev. Stephen Williams, of Longmeadow, never failed to make a note of the "wood-sleddings" in his diary. He wrote on Jan. 25, 1757,

"Neighbors sledded wood for me and shewed a Good Humour. I rejoice at it. The Lord bless them that are out of humour and brot no wood." In other towns the wood did not always come in when it was wanted or needed, and winter found the parsonage woodshed empty. Rev. Mr. French, of Andover, gave out this notice in his pulpit one Sunday in November: "I will write two discourses and deliver them in this meeting-house on Thanksgiving Day, *provided I can manage to write them without a fire*." We can be sure that Monday morning saw several loads of good hard wood deposited at the parson's door.

Other ministers did not hesitate to demand their cord-wood most openly, while still others became adepts in hinting and begging, not only for wood, but for other supplies. It is told of a Newbury parson that he rode from house to house one winter afternoon, saying in each that he "wished he had a slice of their good cheese, for his wife expected company." On his way home his sleigh, unfortunately, upset, and the gathering darkness could not conceal from the eyes of the astonished townspeople, who ran to "right the minister," the nine great cheeses that rolled out into the snow.

Another source of income to New England preachers was the sale of the gloves and rings which were given to them (and indeed to all persons of any importance) at weddings, funerals, and christenings. In reading Judge Sewall's diary one is amazed at the extraordinary number of gloves he thus received, and can but wonder what became of them all, since, had he had as many hands as Briareus, he could hardly have worn them. The manuscript account-book of the Rev. Mr. Elliot, who was ordained pastor of the New North Church of Boston in 1742, shows that he, having a frugal mind, sold both gloves and rings. He kept a full list of the gloves he received, the kid gloves, the lambswool gloves, and the long gloves,--which were for his wife. It seems incredible, but in thirty-two years he received two thousand and nine hundred and forty pairs of gloves. Of these, though dead men's gloves did not have a very good market, he sold through various salesmen and dealers about six hundred and forty dollars worth. One wonders that he did not "combine" with the undertaker or sexton who furnished the gloves to mourners, and thus do a very thrifty business.

The parson, especially in a low-salaried, rural district, had to practise a thousand petty and great economies to eke out his income. He and his family wore homespun and patched clothing, which his wife had spun and wove and cut and made. She knitted woollen mittens and stockings by the score. She unfortunately could not make shoes, and to keep the large family shod was a serious drain on the clerical purse, one minister declaring vehemently that he should have died a rich man if he and his family could have gone barefoot. The pastors of seaboard and riverside parishes set nets, like the

Apostles of old, and caught fish with which they fed their families until the over-phosphorized brains and stomachs rebelled. They set snares and traps and caught birds and squirrels and hare, to replenish their tables, and from the skins of the rabbits and woodchucks and squirrels, the parsons' wives made fur caps for the husbands and for the children.

The whole family gathered in large quantities from roadsides and pastures the oily bayberries, and from them the thrifty and capable wife made scores of candles for winter use, patiently filling and refilling her few moulds, or "dipping" the candles again and again until large enough to use. These pale-green bayberry tallow candles, when lighted in the early winter evening, sent forth a faint spicy fragrance--a true New England incense--that fairly perfumed and Orientalized the atmosphere of the parsonage kitchen. They were very saving, however, even of these home-made candles, blowing them out during the long family prayers.

Some parsons could not afford always to use candles. In the home of one well-known minister the wife always knitted, the children ciphered and studied, and the husband wrote his sermon by the flickering fire-light (for they always had wood in plenty), with his scraps of sermon paper placed on the side of the great leathern bellows as it lay in his lap; a pretty home scene that was more picturesque to behold than comfortable to take part in.

Country ministers could scarcely afford paper to write on, as it was taxed and was high priced. They bought their sermon paper by the pound; but they made the first drafts of their addresses, in a fine, closely written hand, on wrapping-paper, on the backs of letters, on the margins of their few newspapers, and copied them when finished in their sermon-books with a keen regard for economy of space and paper. The manuscript sermons of New England divines are models of careful penmanship, and may be examined with interest by a student of chirography. The letters are cramped and crabbed, like the lives of many of the writers, but the penmanship is methodical, clear, and distinct, without wavering lines or uncertain touch.

As every parsonage had some glebe land, the parson could raise at least a few vegetables to supply his table. One minister, prevented by illness from planting his garden, complained with bitterness that, save for a few rare gifts of vegetables from his parishioners, his family had no green thing all summer save "messes of dandelion greens" which he had dug by the roadside, and the summer's succession of wild berries and mushrooms. The children had gathered the berries and had sold them when they could, but of course no one would buy the mushrooms, hence they had been forced to eat them at the parsonage; and he spoke despitefully and disdainfully of the mean, unnourishing, and doubtfully healthful food.

In winter the parson's family fared worse; one minister declared that he had had nothing but mush and milk with occasional "cracker johnny-cakes" all winter, and that he had not once tasted meat in that space of time, save at a funeral or ordination-supper, where I doubt not he gorged with the composure and capacity of a Sioux brave at a war feast.

Often the low state of the parsonage larder was quite unknown to the unthinking members of the congregation, who were not very luxuriously fed themselves; and in the profession of preaching as in all other walks of life much depended on the way the parson's money was spent,--economy and good judgment in housekeeping worked wonders with the small salary. Dr. Dwight, in eulogizing Abijah Weld, pastor at Attleborough, declared that on a salary of two hundred and twenty dollars a year Mr. Weld brought up eleven children, kept a hospitable house, and gave liberally in charity to the poor. I fear if we were to ask some carnal-minded person, who knew not the probity of Dr. Dwight, how Mr. Weld could possibly manage to accomplish such wonderful results with so little money, that we should meet with scepticism as to the correctness of the facts alleged. Such cases were, however, too common to be doubted. My answer to the puzzling financial question would be this: examine and study the story of the home life, the work of *Mrs.* Weld, that unsalaried helper in clerical labor; therein the secret lies.

In many cases, in spite of the never failing and never ceasing economy, care, and assistance of the hard-working, thrifty wife, in spite of tributes, tithes and windfalls--in country parishes especially--the minister, unless he fortunately had some private wealth, felt it incumbent upon him to follow some money-making vocation on week-days. Many were farmers on week-days. Many took into their families young men who wished to be taught, or fitted for college. Rev. Mr. Halleck in the course of his useful and laborious life educated over three hundred young Puritans in his own household. It is not recorded how Mrs. Halleck enjoyed the never ending cooking for this regiment of hungry young men. Some parsons learned to draw up wills and other legal documents, and thus became on a small scale the lawyers of the town. Others studied the mystery of medicine, and bought a small stock of the nauseous drugs of the times, which they retailed with accompanying advice to their parishioners. Some were coopers, some carpenters, rope-makers, millers, or cobblers. One cobbler clergyman in Andover, Vermont, worked at his shoe-mending all the week with his Bible open on his bench before him, and he marked the page containing any text which bore on the subject of his coming sermon, with a marker of waxed shoe-thread. Often the Bible, in his pulpit on Sunday, had thirty or forty of these shoe-thread guides hanging down from it.

One minister, having been reproved for his worldliness in amassing a large enough fortune to buy a good farm, answered his complaining congregation thus: "I have obtained the money to buy this farm by neglecting to follow the maxim to 'mind my own business.' My business was to study the word of God and attend to my parish duties and preach good sermons. All this I acknowledge I have not done, for I have been meddling with your business. *That* was to support me and my family; that *you* have not done. But remember this: while I have performed your duties, you have not done mine, so I think you cannot complain."

Some of the early ministers, in addition to preaching in the meeting-house, did not disdain to take care of the edifice. Parson Everitt of Sandwich was paid three dollars a year for sweeping out the meeting-house in which he preached; and after he resigned this position of profit, the duties were performed by the town physician "as often as there shalbe ocation to keepe it deesent." The thrifty Mr. Everitt had a pleasing variety of occupations; he was also a successful farmer, a good fence-builder, and he ran a fulling-mill.

So, altogether, as they were wholly exempt from taxation, the New England parsons did not fare ill, though Mr. Cotton said that "ministers and milk were the only cheap things in New England," and he deemed various ills, such as attacks by fierce Indians, loss of cattle, earthquakes, and failure of crops, to be divine judgments for the small ministerial pay; while Cotton Mather, in one of his pompous and depressing jokes, called the minister's stipend "Synecdotical Pay." A search in a treatise on rhetoric or in a dictionary will discover the point of this witticism--if it be worth searching for.

XXII
The Plain-Speaking Puritan Pulpit

One thing which always interests and can but amuse every reader of the old Puritan sermons is the astonishingly familiar way in which these New England divines publicly shared their domestic joys and sorrows with the members of their congregations; and we are equally surprised at the ingenuity which they displayed in finding texts that were suitable for the various occasions and events. The Reverend Mr. Turell was specially ingenious. Of him Dr. Holmes wrote,--

> "You've heard, no doubt, of Parson Turell;
> Over at Medford he used to dwell,--
> Married one of the Mathers' folks."

His wife, Jane Coleman, was a handsome brunette. The bridegroom preached his first sermon after his wedding on this text, "I am black but comely, O ye daughters of Jerusalem." When he married a second time he chose as his text, "He is altogether lovely, this is my beloved, and this my friend, O daughters of Jerusalem!" It is possible that each of Parson Turell's brides may have chosen the text from which he preached her honeymoon sermon. It was the universal custom for many years thoughout New England to allow a bride the privilege of selecting for the parson who had solemnized her marriage, or at whose church she first appeared after the wedding, the text from which he should preach on the bridal Sabbath. Thus when John Physick and Mary Prescott were married in Portland, on July 4, 1770, the bride gave to Rev. Mr. Deane this text: "Mary hath chosen that good part;" and from it Parson Deane preached the "wedding sermon." When Abby Smith, daughter of Parson Smith, married 'Squire John Adams, whom her father disliked and would not invite home to dinner, she chose this text for her wedding sermon: "John came neither eating bread nor drinking wine, and ye say he hath a devil." The high-spirited bride had the honor of living to be the wife of one President of the United States, and mother of another.

Another ingenious clergyman gave out one morning as his text, "Unto us a son is born;" and thus notified the surprised congregation of an event which they had been awaiting for some weeks. Another preached on the text, "My servant lieth at home sick," which was literally true. Another, a bachelor, dared to announce this abbreviated text: "A wonder was seen in heaven--a woman." Dr. Mather Byles, of Boston, being disappointed through the non-appearance of a minister named Prince, who had been expected to deliver the sermon, preached himself upon the text, "Put not your trust in princes." But Dr. Byles was one who would always "court a grin when he should win a soul."

One minister felt it necessary to reprove a money-making parishioner who had stored and was holding in reserve (with the hope of higher prices) a large quantity of corn which was sadly needed for consumption in the town. The parson preached from this appropriate text, Proverbs xi. 26. "He that withholdeth his corn, the people shall curse him; but blessings shall be upon the head of him that selleth it." As the minister grew warmer in his explanation and application of the text, the money-seeking corn-storer defiantly and unregenerately sat up stiff and unmoved, until at last the preacher, provoked out of prudence and patience, roared out, "Colonel Ingraham, Colonel Ingraham! you know I mean you; why don't you hang down your head?" In a similar case another stern parson employed the text, "Ephraim is joined to his idols, let him alone;" though the personalities of the sermon made unnecessary the open reference in the text to the offender's name.

The ministers were such autocrats in the Puritan community that they never hesitated to show their authority in any manner in the pulpit. Judge Sewall records with much bitterness a libel which his pastor, Mr. Pemberton, launched at him in the meeting through the medium of the psalm which he gave out to be sung. They had differed over the adjustment of some church-matter and on the following Sunday the clergyman assigned to be sung the libellous and significant psalm. Such lines as these must have been hard indeed for Judge Sewall to endure:--

> "Speak, oh ye Judges of the Earth
> if just your Sentence be
> Or must not Innocence appeal
> to Heav'n from your decree

> "Your Wicked Hearts and Judgments are
> alike by Malice sway'd
> Your griping Hands by mighty Bribes
> to violence betrayed.

> "No Serpent of parch'd Afric's breed
> doth Ranker poison bear

The drowsy Adder will as soon
unlock his Sullen Ear

"Unmov'd by good Advice, and dead
As Adders they remain
From whom the skilful Charmer's voice
can no attention gain."

Small wonder that Judge Sewall writhed under the infliction of these lines as they were doubly thrust upon him by the deacon's "lining" and the singing of the congregation; and the words, "The drowsy Adder will as soon unlock his Sullen Ear" seemed to particularly irritate him; doubtless he felt sure that no one could doubt his integrity, but feared that some might think him stupid and obstinate.

Another arbitrary clergyman, having had an altercation with some unruly singers in the choir, gave out with much vehemence on the following Sunday the hymn beginning,--

"And are you wretches yet alive
And do you yet rebel?"

with a very significant glower towards the singers' gallery. In a similar situation another minister gave out to the rebellious choir the hymn commencing,--

"Let those refuse to sing
Who never knew our God."

A visiting clergyman, preaching in a small and shabby church built in a parish of barren and stony farm-land, very spitefully and sneeringly read out to be sung the hymn of Watts' beginning,--

"Lord, what a wretched land is this,
That yields us no supplies!"

But his malicious intent was frustrated and the tables were adroitly turned by the quick-witted choir-master, who bawled out in a loud voice as if in answer, "Northfield,"--the name of the minister's own home and parish,--while he was really giving out to the choir, as was his wont, the name of the tune to which the hymn was to be sung.

Nor did the parsons hesitate to be personal even in their prayers. Rev. Mr. Moody, who was ordained pastor at York in the year 1700, reproved in an extraordinary manner a young man who had called attention to some fine new clothing which he wore by coming in during prayer time and thus attracting the notice of the congregation. Mr. Moody, in an elevated tone of voice, at once exclaimed, "And O Lord! we pray Thee, cure Ned Ingraham of that ungodly strut," etc. Another time he prayed for a young lady in the congregation and ended his invocation thus, "She asked me not to pray for her in public, but I told her I would, and so I have, Amen."

Rev. Mr. Miles, while praying for rain, is said to have used this extraordinary phraseology: "O Lord, Thou knowest we do not want Thee to send us a rain which shall pour down in fury and swell our streams and carry away our hay-cocks, fences, and bridges; but, Lord, we want it to come drizzle-drozzle, drizzle-drozzle, for about a week, Amen."

They did not think it necessary always to give their congregations novel thoughts and ideas nor fresh sermons. One minister, after being newly ordained in his parish, preached the same sermon three Sundays in succession; and a deacon was sent to him mildly to suggest a change. "Why, no," he answered, "I can see no evidence yet that this one has produced any effect."

Rev. Mr. Daggett, of Yale College, had an entire system of sermons which took him four years to preach throughout. And for three successive years he delivered once a year a sermon on the text, "Is Thy servant a dog that he should do this thing?" And the fourth year he varied it with, "And the dog did it."

Dr. Coggswell, of Canterbury, Connecticut, had a sermon which he thrust upon his people every spring for many years as being suitable to the time when a young man's fancy turns to thoughts of love. In it he soberly reproved the young church attendants for gazing so much at each other in the meeting. This annual anti-amatory advice never failed to raise a smile on the face of each father and son in the congregation as he listened to the familiar and oft-repeated words.

The Puritan ministers gave advice in their sermons upon most personal and worldly matters. Roger Williams instructed the women of his parish to wear veils when they appeared in public; but John Cotton preached to them one Sunday morning and proved to them that veils were a sign of undue subjection to their husbands; and in the afternoon the fair Puritans appeared with bare faces and showed that women had even at that early day "rights."

How the varieties of headgear did torment the parsons! They denounced from many a pulpit the wearing of wigs. Mr. Noyes preached long and often against the fashion. Eliot, the noble preacher and missionary to the Indians, found time even in the midst of his arduous and incessant duties to deliver many a blast against "prolix locks,"--"with boiling zeal," as Cotton Mather said,--and he labelled them a "luxurious feminine protexity;" but lamented late in life that "the lust for wigs is become insuperable." He thought the horrors in King Philip's War were a direct punishment from God for wig-wearing. Increase Mather preached warmly against wigs, saying that "such Apparel is contrary to the light of Nature and to express Scripture," and that "Monstrous Perriwigs such as some of our church members indulge in make them resemble ye locusts that came out of ye Bottomless Pit." To learn how these "Horrid Bushes of Vanity" were despised by a real live Puritan wig-hater one needs only to read the many disparaging, regretful, and bitter references to wig-wearing and wig-wearers in Judge Sewall's diary, which reached a culmination when a widow whom he was courting suggested most warmly that he ought to wear, what his very soul abominated, a periwig.

Eliot had also a strong aversion to tobacco, and denounced its use in severe terms; but his opposition in this case was as ineffectual as it was against wigs. Allen said, "In contempt of all his admonitions the head would be adorned with curls of foreign growth, and the pipe would send up volumes of smoke."

Rev. Mr. Rogers preached against long natural hair,--the "disguisement of long ruffianly hair,"--as did also President Chauncey of Harvard College; while Mr. Wigglesworth's sermon on the subject has often been reprinted, and is full of logical arguments. This offence was named on the list of existing evils which was made by the General Court: that "the men wore long hair like women's hair," while the women were complained of for "cutting and curling and laying out of hair, especially among the younger sort." Still, the Puritan magistrates, omnipotent as they were, did not dare to force the be-curled citizens to cut their long love-locks, though they instructed and bribed them to do so. A Salem man was, in 1687, fined ten shillings for a misdemeanor, but "in case he shall cutt off his long har of his head into a sevill (civil?) frame in the mean time shall have abated five shillings of his fine." John Eliot hated long natural hair as well as false hair. Cotton Mather said of him, in a very unpleasant figure of speech, "The hair of them that professed religion grew too long for him to swallow." Other fashions and habits brought forth denunciations from the pulpit,--hooped petticoats, gold-laced coats (unless worn by gentlemen), pointed shoes, chaise-owning, health-drinking, tavern-visiting, gossiping, meddling, tale-bearing, and lying.

Political and business and even medical and sanitary subjects were popular in the early New England pulpit. Mr. Peters preached many a long sermon to urge the formation of a stock company for fishing, and canvassed all through the commonwealth for the same purpose. Cotton Mather said plainly that ministers ought to instruct themselves and their congregations in politics; and in Connecticut it was ordered by law that each minister should give sound and orthodox advice to his congregation at the time of civil elections.

Every natural phenomenon, every unusual event called forth a sermon, and the minister could find even in the common events of every-day life plain manifestations of Divine wrath and judgment. He preached with solemn delight upon comets, and earthquakes, and northern lights, and great storms and droughts, on deaths and diseases, and wonders and scandals (for there were scandals even in puritanical New England), on wars both at home and abroad, on shipwrecks, on safe voyages, on distinguished visitors, on noted criminals and crimes,--in fact, upon every subject that was of spiritual or temporal interest to his congregation or himself. And his people looked for his religious comment upon passing events just as now-a-days we read articles upon like subjects in the newspaper. Thus was the Puritan minister not only a preacher, but a teacher, adviser, and friend, and a pretty plain-spoken one too.

XXIII
The Early Congregations

On Sunday morning in New England in the olden time, the country church-members whose homes were near the meeting-house walked reverently and slowly across the green meadows or the snowy fields to meeting. Townspeople, at the sound of the bell or drum or horn, walked decorously and soberly along the irregular streets to the house of God. Farmers who lived at a greater distance were up betimes to leave their homes and ride across the fields and through the narrow bridle-paths, which were then the universal and almost the only country roads. These staid Puritan planters were mounted on sturdy farmhorses, and a pillion was strapped on behind each saddle, and on it was seated wife, daughter, or perhaps a young child--I should like to have seen the church-going dames perched up proudly in all their Sunday finery, masked in black velvet, a sober Puritan travesty of a gay carnival fashion. Riding-habits were hardly known until a century ago, and even after their introduction were never worn a-pillion-riding, so the Puritan women rode in their best attire. Sometimes, in unusually muddy or dusty weather, a very daintily dressed "nugiperous" dame would don a linen "weather skirt" to protect her fine silken petticoats.

The wealthier Puritans were mounted on fine pacing horses, "once so highly prized, now so odious deemed;" for trotting horses were not in much demand or repute in America until after the Revolutionary War. There were, until that date, professional horse-trainers, whose duties were to teach horses to pace; though by far the best saddle-horses were the natural-gaited "Narragansett Pacers," the first distinctively American race of horses. These remarkably easy-paced animals were in such demand in the West Indies for the use of the wives and daughters of the wealthy sugar-planters, and in Philadelphia and New York for rich Dutch and Quaker colonists, that comparatively few of them were allowed to remain in New England, and they were, indeed too high-priced for poor New England colonists. The natural and singular pace of these Narragansett horses, which did not incline the rider from side to side, nor jolt him up and down, and their remarkable sureness of foot and their great endurance, rendered them of much value in those days of travel in the saddle. They were also phenomenally broad-backed,--shaped by nature for saddle and pillion.

When trotting-horses became fashionable, the trainers placed logs of wood at regular intervals across the road, and by exercising the animals over this obstructed path forced them to raise their feet at the proper intervals, and thus learn to trot.

Long distances did many of the pre-revolutionary farmers of New England have to ride to reach their churches, and long indeed must have been the time occupied in these Sunday trips, for a horse was too well-burdened with saddle and pillion and two riders to travel fast. The worshippers must often have started at daybreak. When we see now an ancient pillion--a relic of olden times--brought out in jest or curiosity, and strapped behind a saddle on a horse's back, and when we see the poor steed mounted by two riders, it seems impossible for the over-burdened animal to endure a long journey, and certainly impossible for him to make a rapid one.

Horse-flesh, and human endurance also, was economized in early days by what was called the "ride and tie" system. A man and his wife would mount saddle and pillion, ride a couple of miles, dismount, tie the steed, and walk on. A second couple, who had walked the first two miles, soon mounted the rested horse, rode on past the riders for two or three miles, dismounted, and tied the animal again. In that way four persons could ride very comfortably and sociably half-way to meeting, though they must have had to make an early start to allow for the slow gait and long halts. At the church the disburdened horses were tied during the long services to palings and to trees near the meeting-house (except the favored animals that found shelter in the noon-houses) and the scene must have resembled the outskirts of a gypsy camp or an English horse-fair. Such obedience did the Puritans pay to the letter of the law that when the Newbury people were forbidden, in tying their horses outside the church paling, to leave them near enough to the footpath to be in the way of church pedestrians, it did not prevent the stupid or obstinate Newburyites from painstakingly bringing their steeds within the gates and tying them to the gate-posts where they were much more seriously and annoyingly in the way.

It is usual to describe and to think of the Puritan congregations as like assemblies of Quakers, solemn, staid, and uniform and dull of dress; but I can discover in historical records nothing to indicate simplicity, soberness, or even uniformity of apparel, except the uniformity of fashion, which was powerful then as now. The forbidding rules and regulations relating to the varied and elaborate forms of women's dress--and of men's attire as well--would never have been issued unless such prohibited apparel had been common and universally longed-for, and unless much diversity and elegance of dress had abounded.

Indeed the daughters of the Pilgrims were true "daughters of Zion, walking with stretched forth necks and wanton eyes, and mincing as they go." Save for the "nose jewels," the complaining and exhaustive list of the prophet Isaiah might serve as well for New England as for Judah and Jerusalem: "their cauls and their round tires like moons; the chains and the bracelets and the mufflers; the bonnets, and the ornaments of the legs, and the head bands, and the tablets, and the ear-rings; the rings and nose jewels; the changeable suits of apparel, and the mantles, and the wimples, and the crisping pins; the glasses, and the fine linen, and the hoods and the veils." Nor has the day yet come to pass in the nineteenth century when the bravery of the daughters has been taken away.

Pleasant it is to think of the church appearance of the Puritan goodmen and goodwives. Priscilla Alden in a Quakeress' drab gown would doubtless have been pleasant to behold, but Priscilla garbed in a "blew Mohere peticote," a "tabby bodeys with red livery cote," and an "immoderate great rayle" with "Slashes," with a laced neckcloth or cross cloth around her fair neck, and a scarlet "whittle" over all this motley finery; with a "outwork quoyf or ciffer" (New England French for coiffure) with "long wings" at the side, and a silk or tiffany hood on her drooping head,--Priscilla in this attire were pretty indeed.

Nor did sober John Alden and doughty Miles Standish lack for variety in their dress; besides their soldier's garb, their sentinel's armor, they had a vast variety of other attire to choose from; they could select their head-wear from "redd knitt capps" or "monmouth capps" or "black hats lyned at the browes with leather." They could have a "sute" of "dublett and hose of leather lyned with oyled-skin-leather," fastened with hooks and eyes instead of buttons; or one of "hampshire kerseys lyned." They could have "mandillions" (whatever they may have been) "lyned with cotton," and "wast-coats of greene cotton bound about with red tape," and breeches of oiled leather and leathern drawers (I do not know whether these leathern drawers were under-garments or leathern draw-strings at the knees of the breeches). They could wear "gloves of sheeps or calfs leather" or of kid, and fine gold belts, and "points" at the knees. In fact, the invoices of goods to the earliest settlers show that they had a choice of various materials for garments, including "gilford and gedleyman, holland and lockerum and buckerum, fustian, canvass, linsey-woolsey, red ppetuna, cursey, cambrick, calico-stuff, loom-work, Dutch serges, and English jeans"--enough for diversity, surely. Sad-colored mantles the goodmen wore, but their doublets were scarlet, and with their green waistcoats and red caps, surely the Puritan men were sufficiently gayly dressed to suit any fancy save that of a cavalier. Later in the history of the colony, when hooped petticoats and laced hoods and mantles, and long, embroidered gloves fastened with horsehair "glove tightens," and when velvet coats and satin breeches and embroidered waistcoats, gold lace, sparkling buckles, and cocked hats with full bottomed wigs were worn, the gray, sombre old meeting-house blossomed like a tropical forest, and vied with the worldly Church of England in gay-garbed church attendants.

Stern and severe of face were many of the members of these early New England congregations, else they had not been true Puritans in heart, and above all, they had not been Pilgrims. Long and thin of feature were they, rarely smiling, yet not devoid of humor. Some handsome countenances were seen,--austere, bigoted Cotton Mather being, strangely enough, the handsomest and most worldly looking of them all. What those brave, stern men and women were, as well as what they looked, is known to us all, and cannot be dwelt upon here, any more than can here be shown and explained the details of their religious faith and creed. Patient, frugal, God-fearing, and industrious, cruel and intolerant sometimes, but never cowardly, sternly obeying the word of God in the spirit and the letter, but erring sometimes in the interpretation thereof,--surely they had no traits to shame us, to keep us from thrilling with pride at the drop of their blood which runs in our backsliding veins. Nothing can more plainly show their distinguishing characteristics, nothing is so fully typical of the motive, the spirit of their lives, as their reverent observance of the Lord's day.